Mary Mackie is the author of nearly seventy books, published in varying editions and many languages. Earlier non-fiction titles include the best-selling *Cobwebs & Cream Teas* and its two sequels, telling tales of life behind the scenes with the National Trust at Felbrigg Hall, Norfolk; and *Sky Wards*, the history of the Princess Mary's Royal Air Force Nursing Service, 1918-2000.

Mary and her husband live in West Norfolk. They have two sons and four grandchildren.

By the same author

Non-fiction:
    Sky Wards
    Cobwebs and Cream Teas
    Dry Rot and Daffodils
    Frogspawn and Floor Polish
    Creative Editing

Fiction:
    Sandringham Rose
    A Child of Secrets
    The Clouded Land
    The People of the Horse

and many others.

www.eastanglianwriters.org.uk/profiles/MaryMackie

The Prince's Thorn

Edward VII and the Lady Farmer of Sandringham

Mary Mackie

The Prince's Thorn

Edward VII and the Lady Farmer of Sandringham

Pegasus

For my husband, Chris,
for being himself

ACKNOWLEDGEMENTS

This book could not have been written without help from many people who generously lent their time and expertise, allowed access to their properties, or opened their archives to assist in my researches. I am immensely grateful to them all. They include:

Her Majesty Queen Elizabeth II

Staff at:
> The Royal Archives, Windsor Castle
> The Parliamentary Archives, Palace of Westminster
> Sandringham Estate Office, Norfolk
> The National Archive, Kew
> The British Library, London
> Bedfordshire & Luton Record Office, Bedford
> Norfolk Record Office, Norwich
> East Yorks. Record Office, Hull
> Staffordshire Record Office, Stafford
> Cambridge University archives
> Oxford University archives
> Harrow School archives
> The Millennium Library, Norwich
> St Margaret's church office, Lynn
> Church and Town Guides, Lynn
> True's Yard Museum, Lynn
> Key-holders of remote churches in Norfolk, Bedfordshire and Hertfordshire

Members of the Cresswell family:
> Major William Archdale, West Winch, Norfolk
> Miss Pleasance Bett, Thornham, Norfolk
> William Cresswell Cooper and family, Texas
> the late Lady Wilhelmina Harrod (née Cresswell)
> Eric Cresswell Lavelle and family, Texas and Canada

Also:
    Colin and Nell Bailey, Old Bank House, King's Lynn
    David Burchell, Narborough History Group
    Kath Fryer, local historian, West Norfolk
    Ronald Greenslade, Suffolk FHS (Bury St Edmunds)
    Michael Groom, great-grandson of Farmer John Groom
    Michael le Strange Meakin, Hunstanton Hall
    M. J. O'Lone, agent for Sandringham Estate
    Ken Page, local historian, Biggleswade
    Mary Rhodes, local historian, West Norfolk
    Patricia Roberts at Stradsett Hall Estate Office
    Cyril Smith, Sandringham Estate
    Francis Wortley, for discovering a rare post-card picture of
        Appleton House
And all the unceasingly helpful staff and friends in:
    Lynn Borough Archive & Norfolk Record Office (with special thanks to the indefatigable Susan Maddock) *and* *Libraries of* Hunstanton St Edmund & King's Lynn.

Louise Cresswell's Texan family, mentioned above, have been of great help and support, particularly in letting me use the previously unknown portrait of their ancestress (on the cover and in the book); and more invaluable help from 'over the pond' came from Professor Fred Bailey, of the History Department at the University of Abilene, Texas, USA, and his wife Bonnie.

My thanks, too, to the editorial and production staff at Pegasus for having faith enough to bring this book to print.

Not least, my undying love and gratitude to my husband, Chris, my moral support, chauffeur, chief research assistant, companion and proof reader. It was Chris who first discovered the story of the Lady Farmer and who has shared the long quest.

Thank you all. If I have forgotten anyone, please forgive the unintentional omission and, if you spot any errors (there will be some, I don't doubt), they are entirely my own.

INTRODUCTION

In the twilight, with a cold October breeze rattling the shutters and empty rooms echoing the rap of her heels, Louise felt the ghosts begin to gather. Memories came crowding, of a baby's cries in the nursery, of a young husband's warmth and laughter, of servants squabbling in the kitchen, and many lonely evenings spent poring by lamplight over account books. Eighteen years...

All was ended now, the farm stock and equipment knocked down to the highest bidder. Most of the household furniture too. The few things she was keeping had gone to temporary storage in King's Lynn. Now it was time to say goodbye. Mindful of her status as a gentlewoman, she walked with conscious dignity down the familiar stairs – one last, painfully final, time.

In the hallway, her housekeeper Lucy Sparrow wept softly into a damp handkerchief, blotting at her eyes and her nose, murmuring, 'Oh, ma'am, it's so cruel. So unfair!' Louise made no reply. She needed no reminding of the villainy that had brought her to this pass.

Appleton House was filling with shadows. Beyond the open front door the carriage waited, its driver slumped in his seat behind a pair of tail-swishing horses. On that very spot the Princess Alexandra had sat at the reins of her dainty pony-carriage, sending word that she was so sorry, so very sorry to see her friend Mrs Cresswell leave the home she loved. That memory would provide one of the few bright moments in all this dreary desolation.

The door closed behind her, a dull thud accompanied by another sob from Lucy Sparrow. Louise moved away. Her own eyes stung, but she denied the tears. She felt like some clockwork toy, bereft of feeling, moving only at the whim of a remorseless master – an arrogant, uncaring, inhuman master. His Royal Highness, Albert Edward, Prince of Wales. How she hated him! And his willing agent, the detested Edmund Beck, notable only for his absence these last few weeks. Unable to bring himself to face her, coward that he was.

In the orchard some of the trees she had planted still bore their fruit, apples and pears waiting to be picked by the new tenant and his seven children – seven! Heaven help Appleton House when that tribe arrived. But for now all was silent. Horribly, eerily silent. No horses in the stables, no cattle in the stalls, no sheep in the fold, no ducks and geese on the pond, no chickens in the yard, no steam engine chuntering, no ploughs and harrows waiting... Even her farm labourers had absented themselves, as if they could not bear to witness the end of all her hopes and strivings. The very fields seemed to be mourning.

A skein of wild geese came winging across the sky in a ragged V, gossiping softly as they made for the marshes to roost. Somewhere in the nearby copses a pheasant cried its harsh warning, seeming to shriek a protest against the slaughter that would begin again when the Prince and his friends arrived for the first shoot of the season. As Louise glanced toward the gate a hare appeared there, pausing as if it sensed her eyes on it. It sat up, ears erect, taunting her: I'm still here and you're going away! Haha, haha!

Pulling her fur tippet closer round her throat, Louise straightened her spine, holding her head proud and defiant. She would not let them say she had scuttled away in defeat. She was not defeated. Far from it. Though the Prince and his lackeys had had the triumph, depriving her of her beloved home, driving her to penury and exile, she had a feeling they would not feel safe so long as she lived. Nor should they. Not while she had pen and ink available, and time in plenty to spare.

The book she planned to write would expose the full extent of their perfidy. And then, perhaps, they might regret having treated her so ill.

There seems no doubt that when Louise Cresswell left Appleton Farm in the autumn of 1880 she saw herself as the ill-used heroine of a tragic Romance.

A detached observer may, however, reach rather different conclusions.

* * *

Louisa Mary Cresswell (née Hogge) could truthfully claim to have been 'a girl who danced with the Prince of Wales'. As a tenant on royal Sandringham estate she was frequently a guest at the big house, for such events as balls, dinners or skating parties. But she was also the woman who dared openly to oppose His Royal Highness, charging into the fray *not*, as she sometimes longed to do, with a hunting whip (and happily not with the pistol she kept beside her when anarchists threatened), but with her tongue, her tears, and eventually with a pen and the help of a publisher. Her exposé, *Eighteen Years on Sandringham Estate*, was first published in 1887, seven years after she left Appleton Farm. Although it appeared under the pseudonym 'The Lady Farmer', Louise could not have hoped to remain anonymous; she was well-known in royal circles, far beyond West Norfolk, and no-one would have been in any doubt as to which particular 'Lady Farmer' had penned this diatribe.

Her memoir covers the years 1862-80, spotlighting her continuing battle with the hedonistic Prince and his conniving local agent. But in it she is vague about dates and time-scales, and she portrays herself as a woman very much alone after her young husband died, except for a farming mentor whom she dubs 'Mr Broome', and the kindly Sandringham rector, the Reverend W. Lake Onslow. Other friends and relatives, when mentioned at all, remain shadowy, distant figures, referred to in phrases such as 'the family dandy' or 'our worthy kinswoman', with occasional references to such people as 'Miss G— C—, a Scots kinswoman' and 'dear old F—'. Having discovered her story some twenty years ago, I became intrigued to know who these people might have been. And what of Louise herself? She and her husband did not spring fully-grown from nowhere, nor did they exist in a bubble.

Who exactly *was* Louisa Mary Cresswell? What influences affected her and made her behave as she did? What of her life *before* she became Mrs Gerard Cresswell? And what happened to her, and to her son, young 'G—', after she left Sandringham?

The more I studied her book, and the two pamphlets which she published, the more puzzles emerged.

And so I set out, with my husband's help, to search the original records and try to find a more rounded Louise. I won't say the 'real' Louise because no biographer can claim to have all of the truth. Even so, the woman who waited behind the lines of parish registers and near-illegible microfilm, in dusty papers and, most of all, in some startling and highly revealing letters hidden away in obscure corners of Bedfordshire and Luton Record Office, came as a surprise.

The final enlightenment waited at Windsor Castle, where I was privileged to be granted the Queen's permission to study a collection of documents relating to Louise Cresswell and her time at Appleton Farm, written by the people at the centre of her disputes with the Prince of Wales, written *to* Louise and *about* Louise, and – most tellingly of all – *by* Louise. During the two enthralling days which I spent trawling this unexpected treasure, a whole new aspect of the story emerged. Because, as the records reveal, in compiling her book Louise left out a great deal. And even the things she did write are… what shall we say? – told in the wrong order, given a make-over, twisted to suit her own purposes…?

It turns out that the Lady Farmer was a complex human being, with virtues and faults, loves and hates, prey to both soaring hope and bitter disillusionment. Members of her family, too, sprang into focus like characters from a historical saga, each one with a fascinating story to tell and all helping to shed new light on the extraordinary woman who, encouraged by a country neighbour to claim that she had been 'Rew-ined by Royalty!' did just that, in a book which Royalty tried hard to suppress.

Royalty chose to remain silent on the matter, as Royalty is wont to do. But here, at last, is the other side of this remarkable story.

Note: Remaining family members disagree as to whether their famous ancestor was known as Louisa or Louise. She was certainly baptized as Louisa with an 'a', but in her own book

when she quotes people addressing her familiarly by name, she
has them say 'Louise'. I have followed her lead.

All quotes from Louise Cresswell not otherwise referenced
are from the first edition of *Eighteen Years on Sandringham
Estate*, published in 1887 by The Temple Company, London.

Mary Mackie
Heacham, Norfolk

CHAPTER ONE

On Thursday, 24 April 1862, Louisa Mary Hogge left her father's elegant town house, tucked away in a corner of London's fashionable Rutland Gate, in Knightsbridge, a brief walk from Rotten Row, to travel to her wedding at the nearby church of Holy Trinity with All Saints. She would celebrate her thirty-second birthday on the last day of May that year. Her bridegroom, gentleman farmer Gerard Oswin Cresswell, of Sedgeford Hall, Norfolk, was twenty-five. The 'groom's uncle, Revd Oswald Cresswell, conducted the service and guests included many members of the couple's extended families.

The formal wedding notice in *London Society* informed its readers that the bridegroom was a son of the late Francis Cresswell, of King's Lynn, while the bride was the youngest daughter of William Hogge, Esquire, of Thornham, Norfolk, and of Biggleswade, Bedfordshire. And in West Norfolk, where the Hogge family and the Cresswell family were prominent citizens, the local paper, the *Lynn Advertiser*[1] for Saturday, 26 April 1862, had its own slant on the story:

Local News: WEDDING REJOICING – On Thursday last, the marriage of Gerard Cresswell, Esq, with Miss L Hogge, daughter of Wm Hogge, Esq, which took place in London, was celebrated by the exhibition of a profusion of flags in the streets of Lynn and from the shipping in the harbour; and by the joyous firing of guns and ringing of the church bells. The children of Mrs Cresswell's* school received a treat, and presents of clothing, and there were various other rejoicings of a private character.

*[*Mrs Rachel Cresswell, the bridegroom's mother]*

---

[1] The King's Lynn newspaper, founded in 1841, titled itself the *Lynn Advertiser, Wisbech Gazette and Norfolk and Cambridgeshire Herald.* In this book, for the sake of brevity, it is the *Lynn Advertiser*

Newly-weds at Sedgeford

Mr and Mrs Gerard Cresswell came home to Sedgeford Hall with high hopes, supported by a small income which came from their marriage settlement, plus Gerard's interest from his father's estate, and Louise's annuity from her grandfather Wells. She recalls the place as 'a small farm in the neighbourhood... The Hall and park went with it; it was in fact the dower-house of the family to whom it belonged, and was let with the Home-farm in the absence of the owner. It was a nice old place with comfortable low-ceilinged rooms and wainscot, and a Swiss dairy with painted windows and Dutch tiles opening into the garden. The farm yard was near enough for going in and out, and everything unsightly hidden by shrubs and trees...' A lovely spot to begin their life together.

They were young, and filled with optimism; the life that stretched before them seemed the most pleasant of existences. Hard work, yes, but they were not afraid of that. Indeed, they could hardly believe the bliss of being able to work together, out on their own farm, with the help of bailiff Tom Rumble and his hard-working if beady-eyed wife, Mary. Louise was to remember those early days as halcyon: 'when we had unpacked the cases and arranged the rooms it looked very liveable, and our life there is something to look back upon to the end of one's days, for I... believe that remembrance helps us to endure long after years of loneliness and waiting.'

In no way was she a typical farmer's wife, however. For one thing, she arrived complete with lady's maid, which she admits was a mistake: 'but it did not occur to me to break off old habits all at once and she [the lady's maid] behaved very well, considering the change it must have been to her and how greatly she must have missed the society of a housekeeper's room' (which says much about the households Louise herself was accustomed to). When the super-critical Mrs Rumble looked askance, apparently considering her new mistress to be a 'useless fine lady', Louise soon set her straight, 'my private allowance would more than make up for the invasion'.

The new Mrs Cresswell's main problem, though, was keeping within her budget; she had not been used to managing on such a small scale and neither, it turned out, had their cook – having previously worked as a kitchen-maid in a more affluent household, she rather resented being asked to economize. Louise says, in retrospect, that she would cheerfully have forgone her expensive trousseau, 'it takes up so much room and becomes old-fashioned before it is half worn-out,' if only she could have had the money instead. She found it trying to hear her precious wedding-present silver and china being banged about by the rough-handed country servants; she would not have minded doing the work herself, except that she much preferred to be out of doors with Gerard, riding, farming, and helping him break young horses. And he, for his part, liked having her company about the farm.

A source of irrepressible mischief was 'the boy' (the lad who did all the menial chores such as fetching coal and cleaning knives, in Norfolk commonly known as the 'backus boy' because he dwelt in regions at the back of the house); he became the bane of poor Mary Rumble's life. The bailiff's wife particularly objected when, sent by cook to the village to buy a leg of mutton for the servants' supper, instead of using Shanks's pony the boy elected to borrow her donkey, complete with an old spur to hasten it along. She fetched Louise to look at the results, and Louise duly set the house-servants straight, after which she and Mrs Rumble became better friends.

The farm being small, the Cresswells had leisure enough to enjoy visits to neighbours and family members, either on horseback or 'if we went with the brougham that had been given us, putting the man and the maid inside and driving on the box ourselves, rattling the cobs along, stopping to gossip with every description of acquaintance'. On such occasions Louise was able to give an airing to items from her fashionable trousseau.

'Sometimes,' she adds, 'we had "staying company," taking care to have people who did not mind our ways, or liked them for a change.' Some of her relatives were a bit sniffy about her reduced circumstances, but among the more tolerant visitors were her Cresswell brothers-in-law, who seem to have been a merry bunch of young men. They chaffed her and Gerard about their 'huge maternal pig', which, they declared, was the only thing that kept the farm going. However, the usually placid sow one day took exception to 'the family dandy [whose] airy and exceptionable get-up always reminded me of Rotten Row on a hot summer's day... no sooner did he appear in sight than [the pig] rushed between his legs, carried him off and upset him into the black and greasy oozings of a "muck heap"'. From that day on, the unfortunate chap 'ceased to take the slightest interest in our professional pursuits'. Hardly surprising when his family had found the whole incident hilarious.

Happy as that period was, in her book Louise omits to mention its brevity – they stayed at Sedgeford Hall for all of five months. Moreover, those months were shadowed by grief, for her father, William Hogge, died at his home in London a mere ten weeks after she and Gerard were married.

But she doesn't mention that, either.

A home fit for a Prince
Thoughts of matrimony preoccupied royal minds, too. Albert Edward, Prince of Wales, was twenty years old and already giving his parents a good deal of grief. Considering his knack of getting into trouble, especially with the opposite sex, Queen Victoria and her consort, Prince Albert, had decided that the sooner their oldest son married and settled down, the better for the monarchy. Accordingly, they set their courtiers the task of finding a country house that would be an appropriate home for Bertie and his future wife.

Of the several properties under consideration, Sandringham Hall seemed most suitable. This 'Estate of Magnitude and Importance, near Lynn, Norfolk' comprised a mansion placed on a lawn and surrounded by a deer park and pleasure grounds, the whole lying within a ring fence, and situated in 'one of the finest sporting districts where Hunting, Shooting and Fishing may be enjoyed'.[2]

---

[2] Description in official announcement of auction to take place in London on 12 July 1836, when the estate was bought by John Motteux, bachelor squire of Beechamwell

Bertie's father, Prince Albert, gave his approval of the purchase, but before matters could move further he fell ill. On 14 December 1861, the *Lynn Advertiser* reported that, for the past week, the Prince Consort had been unwell, with what his doctors described as a feverish cold, though 'no unfavourable symptoms' were apparent. Its next edition, just a week later, bordered every column on every page with broad black bands of mourning, for the Queen's beloved husband was dead. Not through a cold, but from typhoid.

Distraught with grief as she undoubtedly was, and remained so for ten years or more, the Queen determined to do everything as her beloved Albert had wished, including going ahead with the purchase of Sandringham for Bertie. True, her late husband had never actually seen the place, and the dictates of mourning prevented Victoria herself from travelling so far to view the property, even had she wished to do so; but loyal servants had looked it over and they knew well enough what was required.

Sandringham seemed the ideal choice: the estate lay deep in the countryside, with a good selection of respectable aristocratic neighbours to share weekend house parties, dinners and balls, plus amusements such as hunting and – Bertie's passion, though his mother disliked the sport – shooting. The rail terminal at Lynn had brought the capital within four or five hours' journey, and the rail link would be even more convenient when the Lynn to Hunstanton branch opened, with a royal halt at Wolferton, only two miles from Sandringham Hall (work on the branch line had begun after harvest 1861). Not least, the owner of the estate, the Hon. Charles Spencer Cowper (step-son to Lord Palmerston, the prime minister), ostensibly a 'diplomat' at the Swedish court, was also well-known as a playboy and gambler, constantly in debt and living mainly abroad with the notorious society beauty who had been his mistress but was now his wife. Such a man would surely be only too amenable to an offer. Thus the royal advisers reasoned and so Her grieving Majesty concurred. In this remote spot near the Norfolk coast, far away from his less desirable friends, away from the temptations of high society and the worldly pleasures of London, and with the right princess by his side, the Queen's sadly intractable son and heir might finally eschew his wild ways and metamorphose into the paragon she and her beloved Albert had earnestly willed him to be from his earliest days.

The Prince of Wales views his 'shooting box'

In proudly monarchist Lynn, the prospect of having the Prince of Wales as a regular neighbour provoked the *Lynn Advertiser*, for 8 February 1862, into deeply purple prose:

THE PRINCE OF WALES IN LYNN

On Monday last the loyal burgesses of this ancient borough were honoured by a flying visit from the heir apparent to the throne – an event, the like of which had not occurred since the visit of her *[sic]* Majesty, then the Princess Victoria, in the year 1835; and we are happy to state that the reception that the Prince of Wales met with, though not less cordial, was much more respectful, and must have been infinitely more agreeable to himself, than that which his royal mother received on the occasion referred to. *(See p40* et seq*)*

It had been for a few days previously darkly hinted that his *[sic]* Royal Highness was likely to come down for the purpose of inspecting the Sandringham Hall and estate, now the property of the Hon. Spencer Cowper, with a view to its purchase as a "shooting box"…

The Prince paid this first brief visit to his future home on Monday, 3 February 1862, accompanied by Sir Charles Phipps (Keeper of the Privy Purse), Major-General Bruce (the Prince's governor) and Lieutenant-Colonel Charles Grey (a royal equerry). They arrived in King's Lynn by train, to be welcomed by the mayor and a deputation which included one of the younger members of the Bagge family (one of Lynn's leading dynasties, merchants and brewers now transforming into politicians and country gentlemen). Thomas Edward Bagge, a friend of HRH from student days in Cambridge, had been invited to join the royal party for the tour of Sandringham.

Crowds of people had gathered, hoping for a glimpse of the young heir to the throne, but only a privileged few were allowed to join the welcoming party. No decorations or demonstrations of rejoicing had been planned, this visit being 'strictly incognito', and HRH and his suite arrived in 'an ordinary first-class carriage' wearing plain clothing, despite which 'they were all immediately recognised'. A carriage and horses had been ordered from the Globe Hotel, but the mayor 'had the honour of substituting his own'. So the Prince and his companions set off for Sandringham, using only two horses 'for the sake of greater privacy' instead of the four provided. Cambridge alumnus Thomas Edward Bagge went along too.

At Sandringham the Prince and his companions were met by the elderly land agent, John Beck[3], who conducted them around the house and the estate, which encompassed parts of seven different parishes. The Prince pronounced himself well pleased.

In fact, Sandringham Hall was at this time sorely in need of renovation. Largely rebuilt around 1771, it was a blockish, ugly house, slate-roofed and white-washed, with two main floors and an attic storey. An earlier owner, bachelor John Motteux, whose main home was Beechamwell Hall, had left the house unfurnished and prey to seeping damp, his main interest having been gardening; he planted many of the trees and shrubberies which helped to shape the gardens as they are today. On inheriting the place from Mr Motteux, the Hon. Charles Spencer Cowper had added tall Tudor chimneys (in an effort to cure the smoky fires), plus a gaudy conservatory and porch, in red brick and local ginger-coloured carrstone, which ill-suited the house and cured neither the damp nor the draughts, both of which were to plague Princess Alexandra in years to come.

Much of the estate surrounding the house was run down, too. Some of the tenant farmers – as a dismayed Louise and Gerard later discovered – had failed to keep the buildings, roads and hedges in good repair, or the land in good heart. However, it's doubtful that Albert Edward, Prince of Wales, even noticed these deficiencies. He was a hedonist, twenty years old and with the world hanging on his every whim. What appealed to him most was the prospect of a home of his own, away from the gimlet gaze of his royal mama, where he could entertain friends of his own choosing and indulge his passion for sport. Those

---

[3] John Beck retired in 1862, succeeded by Thomas Henry Burroughes and then in 1865 by his cousin's son, the better-known *Edmund* Beck

rolling acres of sandy heath positively swarmed with rabbits and hares; pheasants and partridges and woodcock called from coverts hidden in gently folding fields, and ducks and geese flew across wild sea marshes under wide, ever-changing skies. For a prince who enjoyed shooting, Sandringham was an ideal spot.

Seeing the estate as it is today, a handsome house set in beautiful gardens amid acres of woods, in whose summer shade purple rhododendron riot; with its visitor centre, welcoming tea room and shops; stunning scenic walks and drives; and the lovely old church with its silver altar and plaques commemorating so many generations of the Royal Family, it's hard to imagine how it was back in 1862, when Prince Albert Edward first saw it. Lady Palmerston, wife of the prime minister, thought it 'such a nice wild country with all its sandy drives and extent of heath and gorse and firs' (but then her son was the fortunate vendor so she was bound to praise the place). In the opinion of Lady Macclesfield (lady-of-the-bedchamber to Bertie's wife), Sandringham had 'numerous coverts but no fine woods, large unenclosed turnip fields, with an occasional haystack to break the line… The wind blows keen from the Wash and the spring is said to be unendurable'. A later visitor, Revd B. J. Armstrong, vicar of Dereham, felt that Sandringham was well-named, for the roads were 'all sand which blew about in clouds… the wildest and out of the way place imaginable, and the house but a cottage compared with some residences of Norfolk'. And to Louise Cresswell it appeared 'a most attractive place, a little bit of Scotland with heather and pines dropped down upon the Norfolk marshes and flats'.

The sale was publicly announced on 22 February 1862, to great rejoicing in West Norfolk. Astute observers, however, commented on the inflated price that His Royal Highness had apparently paid without question – £220,000 for an estate which then comprised roughly 7,000 acres. Compared with other estates of similar size, it was hardly a bargain.

Anomalies

Louise recalls that she and Gerard had always planned to take on a larger property, in due time, but 'before very long' a highly desirable opportunity presented itself in the shape of Appleton Farm on Sandringham Estate. 'It was extremely difficult to get a farm at that time, and a vacancy of rare occurrence, and it was very kind of the owner of Sandringham [Charles Spencer Cowper] to offer us one on his estate, when he was overwhelmed with applications for it… and had it still belonged to him when we migrated there, it might have altered our views as to the prudence of the undertaking; but, to our very great regret, it was suddenly sold to the Prince of Wales…'

Their dismay at the news was, she says, on account of the changing trends in shooting practices. The old-style of sporting shooting – two or three men striding the coverts with shot-guns over their arms and a few dogs padding along – made for an enjoyable day's outing; but Prince Albert, late Consort to the Queen, had introduced the Continental 'battue' system, with men acting as beaters to drive the game towards a battery of hidden guns. Gerard foresaw that this modern style of 'sport' might create havoc on a farm and, 'with the battue system creeping in, we would not have embarked upon a game farm on any account, however low the rent; and my husband told the London lawyer that he would give it up at once if such a thing were in contemplation. He was assured that we need be under no apprehension, and the rent was fixed with the agreement that no injury should be done by ground game [hares and rabbits]. The lawyer seemed very anxious to secure my husband for Appleton Farm'. She and Gerard were assured that they would be liberally treated by their illustrious landlord and, having shown their bank book to the lawyer, they were encouraged to invest their savings with 'all hope and confidence'.

Louise adds, however, that she privately harboured severe doubts – even forebodings – about the wisdom of such an early move from Sedgeford: 'we were happy and flourishing, and the idea of a change threw a shadow before it, and a presentiment that it would be better to remain as we were, and not risk a certainty for an uncertainty… It was a case of being over-ruled and over-persuaded, and it was especially urged upon me that if I influenced my husband in the matter, I should afterwards repent of having kept him in a narrow way of life, without enough to do, and no opportunity of developing his energies.' In the event, her presentiment of disaster was 'only too painfully realised…'.

That is what she tells us, but she is being disingenuous.

It is impossible to believe that during most of 1862, through their wedding and their first months at Sedgeford, she and Gerard remained ignorant of the fact that the Prince of Wales was to make his home at Sandringham. After all, His Royal Highness's possible move to Norfolk was being rumoured even before its official announcement in February of that year, and once the news broke *everybody* was talking about it. The Norfolk newspapers, especially, were ecstatic that the Prince had chosen their county as his home.

What is more, the move to Appleton was not, as Louise implies, a sudden decision taken when they had only just settled in at Sedgeford. In fact, Gerard had signed the lease agreement in April, *the week before he and Louise were married.*

Appleton Farm, one of several tenanted properties on Sandringham Estate, had been under lease to the Wetherell brothers for a term of eight years, this tenure being due to end on 11 October 1862, coincidentally the same date when the whole estate was to change hands. The Hon. Charles Spencer Cowper had certainly mooted the possibility of Gerard's taking Appleton when the lease fell vacant, but as to the rest…

Soon after the sale of Sandringham Estate was agreed, in February 1862, Charles Spencer Cowper wrote to the Prince's representatives requesting permission for his wife and himself to return to their former home for a month, in July or August, to remove their papers and settle their private affairs. He adds, 'I should be glad when you see Mr White [the royal solicitor] if you would call his attention to the fact that I have given (not a promise) but hopes that I would grant the lease of the farm now held by Wetherell at Appleton to Mr Gerard Cresswell when it became vacant. I mention this as I do not know whether the Prince or I grant the new leases in October… Mr Cresswell would be a most valuable tenant as you have probably heard from Mr Beck. He is a good practical farmer and *has considerable capital*[4]' [emphasis added].

Solicitor Edward White was senior partner in the firm of White, Broughton & White, which kept offices in West Hove, Brighton, and at 12 Great Marlborough Street (the other White in the partnership, his son Arnold, took over a few years later when his father died). As Crown solicitors they handled business for both the Queen and the Prince of Wales.

Edward White took up Spencer Cowper's suggestion, and Gerard Cresswell went to visit the solicitor's Great Marlborough Street office a few weeks later. Minutes of the meeting, dated 17 April 1862[5], confirm that on this date he was formally offered the tenancy of Appleton, the lease to extend for a period of twelve years, starting from Michaelmas 1862. The minutes add that Mr White has 'negatived Mr Cresswell's suggestions to build a new house and stipulated for his residing in present house on its being put into tenantable repair as for any other Tenant Farm'. (In the event, soon after the Cresswells moved in to Appleton, the Prince's representatives did agree to the building of a new house). However, the most relevant clause in these minutes stipulates unequivocally: 'reservation of all sporting rights to the landlord'. In her book, Louise insists, time and again, that an agreement was made whereby no damage should be done by ground game; but no documentary evidence remains to confirm this and it certainly did not find a place in the lease that was eventually drawn up.

Louise herself did not attend the meeting with the royal solicitor; women were usually excluded from such business dealings and, besides, she was not at this stage married to Gerard. However, he would not have had far to go to impart the joyous news that they had been accepted as tenants on the new royal estate; from Great Marlborough Street it was only a short hansom ride to Rutland Gate, where Louise was then living with her father, exactly a week before her wedding.

---

[4] Royal Archive LAW/SHM/31/1/7/1. The 'Mr Beck' mentioned is *John* Beck, the elderly and non-resident local agent, who retired in late 1862.
[5] Royal Archive LAW/SHM/12/10/2

Whatever she may have claimed in her book, she surely knew all along that she and Gerard would be moving from Sedgeford Hall to Appleton Farm by the end of the year, and that the Prince of Wales was to be their new landlord.

A bride for Bertie

The Queen's son and heir had been enjoying an energetic tour of Europe and the near East (Vienna, Venice, Cairo, Damascus...) He was also preparing, at his royal mother's insistence, to propose to the lovely young Princess Alexandra of Denmark.

His bride had been chosen for him in much the same way as his country house, being the most suitable of the available choices. Pity about her quick temper, her naivety, and her Danish blood (Denmark and Germany were engaged in a dispute over who had the better claim to Schleswig-Holstein, and since Queen Victoria had Hanoverian blood, and her beloved Albert had been born a German, naturally they sided with their own relatives), but everyone agreed that the Princess Alexandra of Schleswig-Holstein-Sonderburg-Glucksburg was lovely – 'outrageously beautiful' Queen Victoria wrote after seeing photographs of sixteen-year-old Alix. Bertie had met her once, in September 1861, and thought her 'charming and very pretty'. After his tour of foreign parts ended, plans for a Royal Wedding began to take shape.

Appleton

The natural cycle of the farming year ends and begins as the nights draw in and autumn scents the air with smoke and apples. Thus agricultural properties tend to change hands when harvest is over, the young animals have been sold, and before the winter sowing gets under way. In Victorian Norfolk, sales and leases dated from the day after Old Michaelmas, which fell on 10 October.[6]

---

[6] After the eleven-day adjustment for the Julian calendar in 1752, Michaelmas shifted to 29 September, but for a while Old Michaelmas continued to be observed on 10 October

This was the time when Louise and Gerard moved into their new home: their lease dates from 11 October 1862[7].

Appleton Farm (in the parish of Flitcham-cum-Appleton) lies on a long sloping hillside, with wonderful views over fields and woods and orchards which stretch for miles around. To this day it remains a most beautiful, tranquil spot. As Louise knew, Appleton had once been a stronghold of a famous Norfolk family – the Pastons – but their home had burned down a century before and a large, rambling house had arisen from the ruins. The sitting tenants, brothers John and William Wetherell, both in their sixties, were a pair of old reprobates who, under the less-than-watchful eye of their absentee landlord Charles Spencer-Cowper, had been happy to muddle through, doing as little as possible.

Louise claims that she and her husband had not yet seen their future home (though the archive documents reveal that Gerard's request for a new house to be built at Appleton had been rejected by the royal solicitor as early as February 1862). They had, however, heard tell that it was 'a mucky hole... a downfally place not fit to live in', but they were not prepared for 'the scene of dirt, ruin and desolation' that greeted them. They found the house 'tenanted by two queer old bachelors, who had made heaps of money in the days of low rents, cheap labour and war prices [the Napoleonic Wars], which was of no earthly use to them beyond the satisfaction of feeling that it was safely stowed away to increase and multiply... [However] they received us with every kindness and hospitality, met us at the door, got up some wine, and a woman was told off to show me round...'

The place was filthy, but on a later visit she was gratified to find that the old men had put 'every room through the unusual process of a soap and water scrubbing... on the score of gallantry to a lady, and general politeness to the newcomers...' Closer inspection revealed that 'room after room opened almost out of doors; I think there were nine separate entrances; nearly all the floors were of brick, and in one large, dreary den, a spring of water soaked up through the crevices; not a window or door fitted or shut properly, and the complimentary cleaning had not

---

[7] Royal Archive LAW/SHM/12/10/8

frightened off the bugs which swarmed in clusters, while the rats, after frisking about the house, swam round and round the dairy leads for a change'.

It was hardly the kind of place she had pictured as her future domain. The ground floor was damp, 'so suggestive of fever and rheumatism that we gave it up to the packing cases...' But bolstered by optimism and youthful enthusiasm, and by their belief that their bank balance was sufficient to see them through, they made the best of it. They turned the upper floor of the ramshackle house into their main living quarters and with fires blazing in the hearths it wasn't so bad. At least the upstairs rooms were spacious; if they were also ramshackle, well, it didn't matter much as neither she nor Gerard cared about appearances and they planned to be out of doors most of the time anyway. Not that the outdoors areas had much to recommend them: 'the old men had been model tenants in one respect, for they never asked for repairs and objected to anything that had tumbled down being built up again. The roads had not been mended for years and... as the rain set in [it left] a sea of mud and slush... and I could only get about by probing the ground with an alpenstock and jumping from one foot to another.'

Happily, Tom and Mary Rumble agreed to join the transfer to Sandringham: the bailiff and his wife had become staunch allies. The lady's maid, however, soon moved on, while the other indoor servants, especially the ambitious young cook, who felt she would be injuring her prospects by staying, took one look at the new place and gave notice, leaving Louise to employ other house staff, 'with the occasional assistance of an antediluvian from the village, and a boy from the farm'. The boy, having worked for the previous tenants, was relieved to learn that his new employers were less ready with the strap.

Settling in
The first few sets of visitors to the Cresswells' new abode had a trying time getting through, especially if they approached by what appeared to be the shorter and more navigable 'low road', where their carriages inevitably mired themselves in the mud. This made Gerard decide that the making of a better road must

be one of his priorities. Despite the teething problems, the Cresswells amused themselves in spare moments that first winter by sketching ideas for their dream house.

These dreams began to seem attainable after the royal steward from Osborne House (the Queen's retreat on the Isle of Wight) came to look over the Prince's new domain and decreed the old Appleton farmhouse an eyesore not fit to stand on a royal estate. After conferring with headquarters, he set plans in motion for the building of a new house, in line with the Cresswells' own designs. It was to be built on the rising ground north of the ruined church, on the site of the old Paston mansion. At the request of the last surviving member of the Paston family, they tried to preserve 'every relic that had escaped the desecration of the Wetherells, including the old nut walk and entrances to underground passages, the ruined church and ancestral vault, the sycamore trees by the Pilgrims' Well...'. (Appleton lies on one of the old routes leading to the shrine at Little Walsingham.)

Questions

Louise writes of those early days of her marriage with pleasure; her hope and happiness shine through. So where did it go wrong?

Part of the answer lies in her nature. She had, as we might say today, 'upwardly mobile' ambitions, and it seems clear that, on becoming Mrs Gerard Cresswell, she considered herself elevated to the status of 'a Lady'. Time and again she alludes to her husband's pedigree, introducing him as 'a younger member of one of those old historic families still to be found near the Scottish borders, who have possessed the same estates and called them after their own names from remote antiquity...' Undoubtedly the Cresswell name bore more cachet than her maiden name of Hogge; not to mention its being decidedly more euphonious.

The Cresswells traced their lineage back beyond the time of King John, while the original Hogg, a mariner of no fixed abode, had stepped off a ship in King's Lynn harbour a mere century before. And though Louise's father, William Hogge[8], was even more wealthy than her father-in-law Francis Cresswell, his fortune – and the fortunes of his forebears – had been made from what was despised by all well-bred folk as common 'trade'.

Can this be why, in her writing, while proudly mentioning her Cresswell connections, Louise makes not one single mention of any of her own family?

Although she made a conscious decision to omit them from her memoir, the Hogges were actually a strong influence in her life. Her mother had died a decade before and she lost her father soon after she married, but seven of her siblings remained, a particularly close companion and confidante being her older sister, Miss Fanny Hogge, who came to live in King's Lynn and who, though Louise never mentions her, was in fact a regular visitor at Appleton Farm, providing moral support for Louise through many of her troubles.

Family members all played their part in making Louise the woman – the *lady* – that she became. Perhaps we should bring them out of the shadows in which Louise hid them, and let them take their proper place in her story.

---

[8] The Hogg family added an 'e' to their name around 1830, the year Louisa was born

CHAPTER TWO

Although Louise's childhood home was in the busy market town of Biggleswade, Bedfordshire, through visits to her father's kinfolk she soon became very familiar with Norfolk, especially its north-western corner. There lay the Hogges' home-base, the ancient town of King's Lynn, and beyond it the winding, pot-holed road leading northward to wild and beautiful Thornham, on the coast, where Grandfather Hogg had built his country manor. Looking back in later life, Louise considered the county of Norfolk to be her real and much-missed home.

West Norfolk
West Norfolk is a beautiful, unspoiled part of eastern England, a land of gentle hills and woods, rolling farmland interspersed by fine country houses set in wide acres of deer-park, and with the occasional stretch of sea cliff or steeply sloping lane to surprise any visitor who may imagine the county to be nothing but flat fenland and watery broad. On the fringes of the great bay called the Wash, stony beaches are backed by swathes of wild sea-marshes where, as Louise observed, a haystack may look gigantic against the horizon, or a pollard bullock resemble an aurochs. But, viewed from the highest points, the landscape folds in curving vales and ridges, soil combed by the plough, coloured by sandstone or chalk, with crops green and gold – sugar beet, wheat and barley – or bright yellow with rapeseed flowers, purple with lavender, blue with linseed, lorded over by bright pheasants, and by the hares that became the bane of Louise's life. Here and there a fine church tower or tall spire rises from a bank of trees, amid red-roofed houses built of carrstone, or flint, or lumps of chalk called 'clunch', all under the canopy of wide, ever-changing skies where in winter thousands of geese fly in straggling, gaggling skeins.

The urban centre of this area is King's Lynn. Set at the southern corner of the Wash, between the North Sea and the broad river estuaries of the low-lying fens, Lynn has been a busy sea- and river-port for centuries. In this town of ancient houses and busy hostelries, with its famous chequered Town Hall and two imposing churches, markets were held every Tuesday and Saturday, and great fairs twice a year – the famous 'Mart' in February and the Cheese Fair in October. (The churches and many other historic buildings remain, hidden treasures in pockets of history, and though the Cheese Fair has long faded from memory the two weekly markets still bring shoppers flocking, while the Mart itself – the fun fair which signals the start of the travelling showmen's season – begins each year with a mayoral parade on Valentine's Day).

In earlier times a ruling council of aldermen encouraged modernization, which in the 1800s included paving the roads and introducing the new gas lighting to brighten the more fashionable districts. Gas lighting spread further with every year, though not as far as the crowded, disease-ridden yards and the damp tenements edging the sewer-like 'fleets' [inlets and streams] that poked watery fingers through the town. When the tide rose, the Great Ouse River filled the fleets with water. When the tide receded, the thick mud stank, slimy with offal and excrement that excited the gulls and attracted the rats. It was ever thus in a sea-port.

A visitor in the 1790s reckoned Lynn's river-side harbour to be capable of holding 250 ships: Louise's paternal grandfather, George Hogg, owned at least twenty-five of them. Whaling-ships and whelk-boats, merchantmen and luggers, they came to off-load their cargoes at the wharves. Many tons of those goods were transferred to horse-drawn barges for onward shipment up the Great Ouse River to the cathedral city of Ely, from there moving inland as far as Huntingdon and Bedford, and up the smaller River Ivel to Biggleswade and Shefford.

In Georgian times a handful of families dominated the council which governed the town, among them the Bagges, the Turners, the Allens, the Cases, and, not least, the Hoggs. They were merchant-adventurers, owning their own ships and trading in wholesale goods with Europe, Scandinavia and America. They made the rules by which the townsfolk lived; they formed partnerships in both business and marriage; they chose the freemen who conducted business in the town, and once a year they voted each other into the mayoralty. They also met on equal terms with county aristocracy and gentry such as the Cokes at Holkham, the Walpoles at Houghton, the Townshends at Raynham, and eventually with members of royal families from across Europe who came to West Norfolk as guests of the Prince of Wales at Sandringham.

The Hoggs of Lynn
The first recorded Hogg of Lynn – George Hogg, a mariner by profession – appeared in the town around 1720 *(for family details see Appendix A)*. His origins are obscure, but in his will he left money to the people of Paull, a coastal village near Hull, on the Humber, where Hogg is a familiar surname; so he may have been a Yorkshireman by birth. Soon granted the freedom to conduct business in King's Lynn, he married, took up the mercantile and shipping trade, and built up the largest merchant fleet the town had yet seen, most of the ships being built in local shipyards.

His only child, George the younger (or George Hogg [II], there being several generations of Georges Hogg still to come), increased the family holdings in and around Lynn. He also leased a large house on the south west corner of the Tuesday Market Place, premises that conveniently backed on to the Common Staithe and the river. When this house was destroyed by fire in 1768, Hogg (II) bought the freehold and built on the site a grand new mansion which became the family's main town house for future generations. (In Louise's day the premises served as a bank, which she had cause to know all too well as her farm drifted deeper into debt. The imposing building is currently occupied by a branch of Barclays Bank).

The third George Hogg – Louise's grandfather – became the most wealthy and successful of all. He was also the most fecund, which somewhat dissipated the family fortunes for the next generation, his *thirteen* surviving children. He married Dorothy Tayler *[sic],* daughter of local doctor, Joseph Tayler. Their first son, yet another George, arrived in July 1772 and was followed at regular intervals by eight brothers and five sisters, all of whom survived into adulthood. Among this huge brood, William (Louise's father), was the eleventh born and the seventh son. *(For details of these siblings, see Appendix B.)*

Thornham

Not only did Dorothy Hogg, née Tayler, bless her husband with fourteen healthy offspring, it was through her connections that he obtained his country estate, the ancient manor of Thornham, an idyllic spot which Louise, in her turn, came to know very well.

The quiet village of Thornham lies on the coast, some twenty miles north of King's Lynn and just four miles east of the colourful cliffs at Hunstanton, which brace like the prow of a ship against the sea-winds on the corner where the Wash meets the North Sea. Most of this north-west corner of the Smithdon Hundred belonged to the le Strange family, squires of Hunstanton, whose property shares its north-eastern border with the manor of Thornham. Along the coast, tidal creeks make good sailing for shallow-draught boats, twining among banks of tough grass and sea lavender to sheltered, secluded harbours. Smugglers once found the area ideal for the illicit trade in brandy and tobacco, aided by landlords of lonely village inns.

Thornham came into the keeping of George Hogg (III) when he bought it from his mother-in-law Ann Tayler in 1787. At that time the only half-suitable residence for a lord of the manor was a relatively modest dwelling called 'The Cottage'; so Hogg (III) sent for an architect and employed a firm of builders, who erected Thornham Hall. This fine house was topped by a turret room from which the new lord of the manor might observe the comings and goings of his ships, in and out of the Wash, with some vessels pausing to send boats in to the small harbour among the Thornham creeks. Hogg improved that harbour, adding jetties, two granaries and a solid storehouse – which chalk-and-carrstone building, standing amid butterfly-bright salt marshes (and still a picturesque subject for artists and photographers), is known as the 'coal' barn, though it was originally used to store stout that came all the way from London; inns usually brewed their own ale, but they had to import this stronger, darker beer. Lumbering wagons, drawn by heavy horses, came creaking, through winter mud and summer dust, down the track that wound along the creek banks, carrying farm produce, especially corn, from the fertile acres of the hinterland. Plodding back, they hauled imports such as oil cake, timber, coal, malt – and strong black stout.

Thornham made a pleasant summer retreat, but the Hoggs kept their main home in the elegant mansion on the Tuesday Market Place in Lynn. *(For more detail on Thornham and its land-holders, see Appendix C.)*

After George Hogg (III) died, on 23 July 1811, his wealth became the subject of much rumour and tittle-tattle. Landscape artist Joseph Farington noted in his diary for 17 November 1811: 'S Lane called. He spoke of the death of the late George Hogg of Lynn and said he died worth several hundred thousand pounds. He left 13 children – handsome fortunes to his sons and to each daughter £10,000.' This diary entry has been quoted by many historians, but in fact 'S Lane' was passing on speculation and gossip: the third George Hogg was a very wealthy man, but not quite *that* wealthy. He provided handsomely for Dorothy his wife, leaving her £5,000 immediately, with an annuity of £500 a year, plus the mansion on the Tuesday Market Place with 'all appurtenances, plate, furniture, horses, carriages', etc. To his twelve surviving younger children he left money: £3,000 each to eight sons, £2,000 each to four daughters. In time his oldest four sons would also share in a trust left by their grandfather,[9] which would double their initial inheritance. Louise's father, William, the seventh son, had to content himself with his original legacy.

William Hogg

William Hogg was twenty-four years old when he married in 1809. His bride Elizabeth Wells, two years his junior, was the younger daughter of Samuel Wells, a wealthy brewer based in Biggleswade, Bedfordshire. Wells and his partner Denis Herbert

---

[9] George Hogg (II) had married his second wife, Mary Sharpin, in 1769. He made his will the following year, providing for his children by first wife Ann, now deceased, and for Mary and any children she might bear. (See Appendix A)

had shared business dealings with the Hoggs of Lynn for some years, so the marriage cemented this alliance and brought greater financial security for William. The young couple began their married life in King's Lynn, where William engaged in the family mercantile business, and it was in Lynn that their first child, Eliza, was born on 21 March 1811.

That summer, as we have seen, William's father died, leaving him £3,000 – not quite a fortune, but still a fair sum. With his pregnant wife and baby daughter, the ambitious young man moved away from Lynn and settled in Elizabeth's home town of Biggleswade. There he proceeded to establish himself as one of the up-and-coming businessmen of the area. He was in partnership with his oldest brother George, who had inherited the property and businesses in Lynn; also with his younger brother Frederick, who besides being a general merchant made bricks and burnt lime at Girtford, near Sandy, a few miles north of Biggleswade; and a third business alliance William formed with his father-in-law Samuel Wells, under the company name of Wells & Co, later Wells, Hogge & Lindsell.

William and Elizabeth's second child, a son and heir named William Samuel, arrived in March 1812, one year after his sister Eliza. Another nine siblings came along at regular intervals over the next twenty years.

Around 1830, most members of the Hogg family added an 'e' to their name, making it Hogge. The exception was Louise's youngest uncle, Frederick, who had set up in business in the delightfully named Sandy, Beds. In all family documents he determinedly remains a plain old Hogg

The Hogges of Biggleswade

Louisa Mary, tenth child of William and Elizabeth Hogge, was born in Biggleswade on Monday, 31 May 1830. Two earlier siblings (one of them also named Louisa) had died untimely, but three brothers and four sisters remained, the oldest, Eliza, being a young woman of nineteen by the time Louisa Mary arrived. Two years later, little Charles completed the family. Nine survivors out of eleven. Not a bad tally for the times.

Family of William and Elizabeth Hogge

Eliza, born 21 March 1811 in King's Lynn – all others in Biggleswade
William Samuel, born 1 March 1812
Frances (Fanny), baptized 28 April 1814
Louisa, infant, buried 14 March 1815 aged 9 weeks
George, born 27 Sept 1817
Henry, baptized 29 June 1819, buried 7 June 1823, aged almost 4
Harriet, baptized 1 May 1821
Anna Allen, born 5 May 1825
Frederick, born 2 Oct 1827
Louisa Mary, born 31 May 1830
Charles Wells, born 12 July 1832

Less fortunate children lived in city slums or country hovels, worked long hours in factories or picked stones in muddy fields, and might be lulled to sleep by gin or laudanum (a derivative of opium). They were lucky if they survived beyond the age of five. Some faced the world badly scarred by small-pox. Many more died in the 1831 cholera epidemic.

Compared with these poorer souls, the young Hogges enjoyed an idyllic childhood. A butler and footman attended the family; cook and kitchen-maids prepared the best of foods fresh from the surrounding farms and market gardens; and housemaids kept the place spotless, lighting fires every morning in winter and opening the windows to let fresh air billow clean muslin curtains in summer. Oldest sister Eliza looked forward to marriage; older brothers William and George were away completing their education, followed in turn by Fanny, Harriet, and Anna. For the three youngest Hogges, Frederick, Louisa, and Charles, nurse-maids and nannies attended all needs from dawn to midnight.

The centre of Louise's young world was an imposing town house named Ivel Bury. This grand Georgian mansion fronted onto Shortmead Street, one of the main thoroughfares of Biggleswade and part of the Great North Road, along which carts and wagons and herds of cattle lumbered through winter mud and summer dust, linking the town with the fertile countryside surrounding it. Thundering stage-coaches, pulled by six sweating horses and with post-horns blaring, brought a whiff of the metropolis some fifty miles south, or came plunging in bearing travellers from the wilder uplands far to the north.

A more leisurely link to the outside world lay behind the house, where, along busy riverside wharves on the narrow river Ivel, horse-drawn barges, or 'lighters', offloaded cargoes of coal, iron and timber and took on corn and barley, peas and beans from the farms and market gardens of Bedfordshire. Before the coming of the railways, the waterways provided the main means of inland trade. A horse towing a string of three or four water-borne barges could carry twenty-five times as much as a horse pulling a wagon, except when a very dry summer or an ice-bound winter stopped the water from flowing.

A noisy, odorous maze of warehouses and wharves, lying between Ivel Bury's coach yard and the river, rang with the trundling of barrels, the creaking of timber and the shouts of sweating bargees and warehousemen. To the younger Hogges the wharves were fascinating, forbidden territory, as were the vast cool cellars beneath the big house, filled with wine and spirits awaiting distribution via Papa's various mercantile outlets.

William Hogge was, by this time, a successful businessman – banker, brewer, maltster and merchant, with shops and other business premises in Biggleswade, in the small town of Shefford a few miles away, and in Baldock, another busy market town lying to the south along the Great North Road. These businesses made good use of the canalized river Ivel, trading in timber from the shores of the Baltic and coals from Newcastle, grain from British farms, iron and steel, sherry from Spain and vodka from Russia. And at the far end of the river route, where the Great Ouse ran out into the Wash and thence to the North Sea and the oceans beyond, other members of the Hogge dynasty had labourers waiting to offload the cargoes for onward shipping, and to re-stock the barges with goods bound back up the rivers to supply the English midlands.

Samuel Wells's legacy

Louise's maternal grandfather, Samuel Wells (1755-1831), was already an old man when she came on the scene and he died just fourteen months later, aged seventy-six. Although she did not remember knowing him, his legacy was to affect her life for decades to come.

Sam Wells had made his fortune from making and selling beer. In 1817, when Biggleswade boasted five main coaching inns, Wells owned three of them. He also owned several taverns in the town centre and others in nearby villages. He was a major dealer in malt and associated with other brewers, notably the famous Samuel Whitbread. From 1807 he also set up as a banker and, thanks to the Ivel Navigation Company which opened up the waterway, he traded, via the Ivel and the Great Ouse, with the sea-going merchants of King's Lynn in Norfolk.

When Sam Wells died, on 24 July 1831, he left £10,000 to each of his legitimate daughters, Mrs Elizabeth Hogge and Mrs Frances Lindsell. He also provided for an illegitimate daughter, Hannah, and for her mother; but he bequeathed only £200 a year to his wife Frances with instructions that she was to accept this as her full entitlement. All real estate and stock in trade was to be sold and turned into cash, though he specifically stipulated that his sons-in-law, whom he appointed executors and trustees, should have a right to purchase the property and businesses. This is what happened, in the end – Hogge and Lindsell bought the businesses: they did not, as some historians suggest, inherit them.

In the original will, made in 1816, the 'residue and remainder', mainly the cash accruing from the sale of real estate, was to be divided between Sam's two grown sons, who had moved away along with their mother (was there a rift because of the bastard child Hannah?). However, when older son Samuel William predeceased his father, unmarried and without issue, Wells Snr made a codicil leaving this half of his fortune to be shared among the grandchildren, as and when they came of age. In due time, thirteen grandchildren (all off-spring of Sam's daughters Frances and Elizabeth) each received £5,000, a goodly sum in those days.

Louise would gain legal title to her share when she came of age in 1851; meantime the moneys were invested in the family businesses, with Papa and Uncle Robert Lindsell acting as trustees. Documents in the Bedford Record Office reveal that

Louise received some of her money in 1862, on her marriage. However, she and the other grandchildren were still arguing over their various inheritances in the late 1870s and, as we shall see, the row dragged on until near the end of the century.

But at least Louise did benefit in adult life from a regular income accruing from this legacy. Her youngest brother Charles Wells Hogge/Archdale wasn't so lucky. As one of his grandsons, Major William Archdale, recalled with wry amusement, Charles was 'always sore' about being born too late to share in the bounty from grandfather Wells's estate.

Uncle George, Gentleman – and royalist extraordinaire
King's Lynn has been linked with royalty for a thousand years, since William the Conqueror sent his bureaucrats to make notes of all his new assets for his *Domesday Book*. Later, as *Pigot's Norfolk Directory, 1830,* records: 'during the civil wars between King John and the Barons, Lynn was eminently distinguished by its unshaken fidelity to the monarch.' Indeed, it was after a visit to Lynn that King John (allegedly) lost his famous treasure while crossing the Wash. In 1643, during the other Civil War (Cavaliers v Roundheads), the citizens of Lynn initially declared for Cromwell but changed their minds and took the King's side, making a loyal and heroic, if hopeless, stand against overwhelming Parliamentarian forces.

Down the years the town and its leading citizens remained royalists at heart. None more so than George Hogge (IV), Louise's uncle. In September 1835, he had just been elected to his fourth term as mayor of the borough when he discovered that the future Queen, the sixteen-year-old Princess Alexandrina Victoria, and her noble mother the Duchess of Kent were due to pass through his town on their way to visit the Earl of Leicester at Holkham Hall. Galvanized by the prospect of having Their Royal Highnesses in Lynn, however briefly, he and other members of the corporation undertook a hundred-mile round trip to Burghley House, near Stamford in Lincolnshire, where the royal ladies were staying with Lord Burghley.

Sad to say, Mayor Hogge didn't manage to meet the ladies, but he respectfully requested of an equerry that the town of Lynn should be allowed to mark the auspicious moment by a show of loyal respect and welcome. The Duchess replied with a message informing him that it was her 'invariable rule… not to receive any addresses from Public Bodies, on her merely passing through a Town', as the notice put out later by the town clerk phrased it. The notice added, however, that the mayor hoped that Lynn's citizens would 'individually shew *[sic]* every demonstration of loyalty and attachment to their Royal Highnesses, on the occasion of this their very first visit to the town…'

The resulting 'loyal demonstration' is wonderfully described by J.D. Thew, editor of the local paper: '…they organised a procession, with party flags, favours and music, to meet the royal party at the South Gates and conduct them through the town. The roughest of 'long-shore men, coal porters, and others, joined in the display and with undisciplined warmth some of them not only insisted on shaking hands with the alarmed young Princess, but, despite all remonstrances, unyoked the horses, and dragged the carriage pell-mell through the streets, and very nearly succeeded in upsetting it and throwing its terrified occupants into the road. I have heard that they took refuge for a time in a house on Buckingham Terrace, but were at length persuaded to rëenter *[sic]* the carriage and then went through the ordeal with the best grace and courage they could muster.' How relieved the grand ladies must have been to be reunited with their team of horses and allowed to go on their way to recover their dignity amid the peaceful surroundings of beautiful Holkham, home of agricultural pioneer Thomas Coke, Earl of Leicester.

Mr Thew imagined how the old folk would later reminisce about the day, 'shake their knowing heads and add with many a sigh, "Ah, ower congratulations quite overcame the young mawther; you may b'lieve me, but her nerves wor so scattered, that she upped and sayed, ses she, 'There, I oan't never come to that there horrid place agin!' " '

Nor did the royal lady revisit Lynn, until nearly forty years later when she was Queen Victoria and the critical illness of her oldest son compelled her presence in West Norfolk.

The new Queen

The death of King William IV, in June 1837, brought the young princess to the throne. After years of being led by absurd old duffers, mad, bad, or merely incompetent, the country rejoiced in the bright new age promised by the arrival of this fresh young queen. She was eighteen years old, just under five feet in height, and as plump as a ripe peach. She was also self-possessed, determined, and had a strong sense of duty. When her ministers debated how their new monarch was to be known (some felt that 'Alexandrina' was too unusual; it sounded – heaven forfend! – vaguely foreign), she herself chose to use her second name, Victoria. Her coronation in June 1838 sent waves of patriotic celebration across Britain.

Eighteen months later, the bunting and floral decorations came out again when, on 10 February 1840, the young Queen married her German cousin, the handsome Prince Albert of Saxe-Coburg-Gotha. It was a love match, everyone knew.

In common with so many women of her time, for the tiny Queen (God bless her!) marriage meant conceiving at regular intervals. The first child – Victoria, the Princess Royal – arrived promptly nine months after the wedding, proving the fecundity of the union. Less than a year later, on 9 November 1841, a second royal child was born, this time a son, Albert Edward, who when barely a month old was created Prince of Wales. At last, after eighty long years, a reigning monarch had produced a male heir. How the church bells rang! What parades were held, what dinners given! Gallons of champagne and ale flowed to greet the arrival of such a lusty lad.

Over the next decade and a half Victoria bore a further seven healthy children, three princes and four princesses, the last being Beatrice, born in 1857.

Across the kingdom, loyal subjects such as the extended Hogge family enjoyed the official sports events and parties that took place in the early reign of the new Queen. In Biggleswade the raising of many loyal toasts, to celebrate the royal wedding and the safe births of the Queen's first babies, helped to swell the profits of the Wells & Co (Hogge & Lindsell) brewery.

Louise's family circle widens

The four fine sons of William Hogge of Biggleswade were confidently expected either to take their place in the family businesses or to go off to earn their own living, as soldiers or priests – this was how society worked. Daughters were another matter, to be married off to suitable husbands as soon as possible. Unhappily for Louise, she found herself the youngest of five – five, count them! – sisters, all inevitably maturing toward marriageable age.

Louise was eight years old when, on 30 September 1838, her oldest sister Eliza (26), became Mrs Henry Williams Beauford. The twenty-four-year-old bridegroom was the son of a clergyman and he and Eliza began married life as tenants on a farm at nearby Holme, a property owned by one of the Lindsell relatives. In time the Beaufords had at least five children. The first, a daughter named Mary, arrived in 1839, making Louise an aunt for the first time when she herself was only nine. The Beaufords' first son, Henry Walter, was born in 1841, the same year as the new Prince of Wales.

By this time Louise's brother Frederick (14) was under tuition at Mr Gardener's select school in Beaminster, Dorset, while Louise and her sister Anna spent much of the year in company with twenty-or-so other girls aged from seven to fifteen at the Academy for Young Ladies on Marine Square, in fashionable Brighton. When the Brighton to London railway opened in 1841 it made the journey from Sussex back to Biggleswade far more convenient.

What fun they had during holidays, visiting Eliza and her babies on a real farm, with horses and cows, chickens and piglets. What a lovely life, with a nurse to look after the children and servants to cook food and run the house (evidence suggests that this seemingly idyllic existence had a profound effect on Louise). Sadly, Eliza's husband turned out to be not quite the ideal match. He began borrowing money, incurring debts which his father-in-law, William Hogge, either wrote off or stood surety for in his will twenty years later. However, in even later years Henry Williams Beauford became a magistrate and landowner, so his fortunes evidently improved as he grew older.

Second sister Frances (Fanny to her intimates) had signed the register as a witness to Eliza's marriage. Fanny was then twenty-four and probably hoping for a wedding of her own before long, but the next marriage festivities, in June 1842, marked the union of second brother George (25) to a girl from Devon named Mary Harness. Only two months later, the church in Biggleswade provided the setting for the marriage of third sister Harriet. Aged twenty-one, she married lawyer John Lindsell, another clergyman's son, nephew to Uncle Robert Lindsell with whom Papa was in business. She and John set up home in London.

So two of the Hogges' five daughters and one of their sons were safely settled. The Lindsell cousins were pairing off, too, and producing babies. Weddings and christenings dotted the families' appointments calendar.

Uncle George Hogge's legacy

In Norfolk, Uncle George Hogge grew older, increasingly aware of his own mortality and his lack of an heir. As the oldest of the thirteen siblings he had inherited all the properties and businesses in and around Lynn (and down the river, with premises at various pausing places such as Mepal, near Ely), plus several properties centred on Thornham; and 'all the Rest and Residue'. Back in 1811, when his father died, George had been thirty-nine, still a single man and living with his mother in their grand town house on the corner of the Tuesday Market Place. He eventually married on 10 May 1818, when he was nearly forty-seven. His bride, Margaret Ainslie (28), was an heiress from the north west of England, her family's main fortune stemming from the manufacture of iron and gunpowder.

One old citizen of Lynn (J.H. Pratt) remembered that this Mr and Mrs George Hogge lived in great style. Their town house on the Tuesday Market Place boasted a circular entrance hall with a double staircase shaped like a horse-shoe, and rooms with very fine mantelpieces. Legend told that, on one occasion, Alderman Hogge emerged from his mansion to find a 'half-witted man called Billy' outside. Thinking to have some fun with him, Hogge offered the man a shilling if he could make a verse on his name, whereupon Billy extemporised: 'Here stands an old hog, There lives his old sow, He's got plenty of money And nobody knows how!' Mr Hogge beat a hasty retreat, says Mr Pratt, adding, 'In the next generation the family changed their name to Archdale.' Cause and effect? Maybe.

As they grew older (he with an eighteen-year head start) the George Hogges enjoyed summer days spent in the tranquil splendour of their country house at Thornham, with its high turret room overlooking the marshes and the sea, where Hogge-owned ships plied to and fro. A full staff of servants attended their every need. Frequent visitors were George's two spinster sisters, Anna and Mary, both of independent means thanks to their father's legacy.

George had remained in reasonably amicable contact with the rest of his large family. 'Reasonably' because the will that he began making in 1821 was tweaked over the years with seven codicils. These reveal a few problems with his brothers: Revd Martin Hogge of West Acre borrowed money and didn't repay it (though when Martin died before him, in 1846, George forgave the debt and left money for Martin's six children); brother Henry seems to have been a spendthrift, an early lump sum left to him is altered to an annuity hedged about with conditions, but this too became void when Henry died and in his place his son inherited cash; and Revd Edward appears to have been in and out of favour, first given money, and then cut out, only to be written back in…

Sadly, despite all his assets and affluence, Uncle George had no child of his own. His chosen heir was, therefore, the younger brother who had proved himself the most adroit businessman – William Hogge (brewer, banker and merchant of Biggleswade). And so, in 1842, when Uncle George reached the age of seventy, he summoned his nephew, newly-wed George, William's second son, to come to West Norfolk and assist with the running of the businesses in Lynn.

When George Hogge (IV) died, on 3 January 1847, he left monetary legacies to his surviving siblings: spinsters Anna and Mary each received £2,000 to top up what they had had from their father, which ensured their comfort for their remaining years; their remaining brothers gained £5,000. The widow, Margaret Hogge, received £1,000 immediately, with a generous annuity, plus the use, during her lifetime, of the properties in King Street and Tuesday Market Place and all contents, with carriages, carriage horses, harness, wines, liquors and linen… Interestingly, Aunt Margaret also inherited 'three pews in St Margaret's Church and two pews in the North Gallery at St Nicholas Chapel in Lynn'. After her, the main properties were assigned to her husband's brothers (Fountaine to have the house on Tuesday Market Place, William all the rest). As it happened, both Fountaine and his only son died before the widow Margaret did, so the properties eventually devolved in entirety to William.

When all was settled, Louise's father, William Hogge, held title to most of the family businesses, land and properties in West Norfolk. These included the Setch brewery partnership, the teeming Hampton Court properties (today a listed historic building) on the corner of Nelson Street and the wonderfully-named St Margaret's Muckhill Lane, along with various other buildings in Lynn and all the holdings around the coast, centred on the manor of Thornham. This last bequest had strings attached: William benefited from rents and revenues but had to pay his sister-in-law's annuity from the proceeds. She, for her part, had right of tenure of Thornham Hall for her lifetime and, since George had left her all the furniture and contents, without condition, could eventually assign those to her own chosen heirs. Margaret Hogge was only fifty-seven when her husband died. She was to remain a sitting tenant at Thornham for many a year.

These legacies added immensely to William Hogge's already considerable assets. He himself was no longer a young man (he was sixty-two when his brother George died), but he did have four sons to follow him. The younger two, Frederick and Charles, were still at school; but second son George was married and established as manager of the Lynn businesses; and son and heir William Samuel, currently enjoying a successful military career, would soon resign his commission, come home and take a wife, and settle down to succeed his father in the Bedfordshire enterprises. At least… that was the way everyone expected the future to turn out.

Major William Samuel Hogge, Louise's oldest brother

In the wider world, troubles of many kinds continued to flare. In England the Chartists fomented riots and strikes, and in Ireland a terrible potato blight meant starvation for many. Overseas, with the Empire still expanding, Britain's army and navy stood guard in several areas of the world – in Afghanistan, India and China, and in the expanding Cape colony in southern Africa, where trouble between white settlers and native tribes had been erupting since the 1770s.

Originally, the British Government's only interest in the area had been the security of Cape Town, which provided a convenient port of call for ships bound for the Far East or the Antipodes. However, as time went on and troubles escalated, the Foreign Office found itself obliged to send ever more British troops to impose order. Among the different factions on the Cape, sporadic skirmishes and cattle rustling, accompanied by the occasional murder, kept breaking out into more general mayhem, graced by the generic title 'The Kaffir Wars'[10]. This conflict was to give Louise's oldest brother a place in the history books.

Louise did not know William Samuel well. Eighteen years her senior, he had been a student at Oxford when she was born and straight after university he joined the army, which kept him often away from Ivel Bury. However, as his career progressed he became a figure of increasing wonder and heroism to his younger siblings. Louise was fifteen when he and his regiment took ship for the Cape colony in Southern Africa. There, even in relatively peaceful interludes, the scarlet-coated, sabre-wielding, brilliant horseman Captain William Samuel Hogge of the 7th Regiment of Dragoon Guards (the Princess Royal's Own), covered himself

---

[10] The term 'kaffir' meant, historically, a member of the Xhosa-speaking peoples of South Africa and/or their language. In the mid 20th Century the word became grossly offensive when used as a generic term to describe any black person; hence the 'Kaffir Wars' are now referred to as the 'Frontier Wars', or, in modern South Africa, the 'Wars of Dispossession'

with glory and was twice mentioned in dispatches – an honour in which any soldier, and his family, took immense pride.

In June 1848, William Samuel returned home a hero. He had been promoted – he was *Major* Hogge now, thirty-six years old and ready to settle down. With cuts in the armed forces being ordered, he retired from the army and assumed the mantle of a country gentleman, taking over as Master of Fox Hounds (MFH) with the Oakley Hunt in Bedfordshire. In her book, Louise comments that she was 'raised to sport… the cry of hounds was music to my ears'; in adolescence and early womanhood she often rode out with the hunt, through colourful autumn woods and snowy winters, and she helped her oldest brother and the huntsmen to manage the fox hounds and rear orphaned foxcubs – a skill which was to prove useful in later years.

The highly eligible bachelor, Major William Samuel Hogge, also paid court to the oldest daughter of a wealthy and colourful character named Hollingworth Magniac, former MFH of the Oakley Hunt and squire of Colworth Park.

Magniac had made a fortune from trading in the Far East, one of his company's main cargoes being opium. They had worked from a base in Canton, China, and his two oldest children had both been born in Macao. On his return to Britain, in the early 1830s, his vast wealth enabled him to buy the Colworth estate, north of Bedford, and to build up a fabulous art collection. He also fathered six more children – three boys and three girls all born at Colworth and baptized at the pretty church in nearby Sharnbrook village. *(For more on Hollingworth Magniac, see Appendix D.)*

In that church, on 9 May 1849, Squire Magniac's oldest daughter, Helen Julia, married Major William Samuel Hogge, with both families and a crowd of friends to wish them well. The bride was twenty-four, her groom a rather more experienced thirty-seven. The *Bedford Times* recorded it as a joyous occasion 'despite the unseasonably grey weather'. The bridegroom's uncle, Revd Edward Hogge of Fornham, Suffolk (one of Papa's eight brothers), performed the ceremony and many members of the extended Hogge family gathered to share this 'interesting nuptial event'.

Louise was by this time a young woman, her nineteenth birthday only three weeks away. She was quite tall at five feet eight inches, fair skinned, with light brown hair and brown eyes[11]. However, in an age that expected girls to be docile and amenable, pale and pliable as wilting lilies, Louise was a decidedly thorny rose. Early in life, as the youngest girl in a large family, she had learned to stand up for herself. She was assertive, even prickly and opinionated, and ready to throw tantrums to get her own way. She also knew that a few judicious tears, complaints of headaches, stomach pains, or the occasional fit of the vapours, might work to soften opposition when outbursts of temper failed. She was not a great beauty, but on that overcast spring day, dressed in her best clothes and on her best behaviour, she had sufficient youth, health and vigour to attract her share of attention from the young men attending her oldest brother's glamorous wedding. Her own turn to walk down the aisle would come soon, would it not?

Less than a year after this happy occasion, however, sorrow returned for Louise and her family – her mother, Elizabeth Hogge, died on 12 March 1850, aged sixty-two. But six months later there was joy again at the birth of William Samuel and Helen's first child, another niece for Louise, who was already aunt to five children produced by her sisters. Naming the new baby Edith Eliza, the proud parents settled down to dwell in the spacious, gracious Riverside House in Sharnbrook, with a small army of servants in attendance.

Lord Grey appoints commissioners to South Africa
The year 1850 ended with more bloodshed around the Cape of Good Hope, which ignited the Eighth Kaffir War, the most violent of them all. At the same time, disputes with Boer settlers reached a crisis when they demanded autonomy beyond the Orange river. The British Government, and the British people, grew weary of the never-ending trouble and expense of trying to establish order among all the ungrateful, warring factions in southern Africa. All they had ever wanted was enough land to

---

[11] Physical description taken from a ship's manifest of 1909

protect their naval base on the Cape. Protests began to mount, speeches in the House, letters to the papers, editorials...

In response to all this pressure, in May 1851 (just as the Great Exhibition was getting under way in London) the *Globe* newspaper reported that Colonial Secretary Lord Grey had appointed two commissioners 'to proceed to the Cape for the purpose of enquiring into the recent disturbances in Caffraria *[sic]*'. One of the selected diplomats was Charles Mostyn Owen, a specialist in the Xhosa language spoken on the Cape; the other was a certain Major William Samuel Hogge, whose 'intimate acquaintance with the affairs of the colony... will no doubt conduce much to render the inquiry advantageous', as the *Globe* had it. What an honour for William Samuel! How proud his family must have been.

On their voyage to the Cape, six or seven weeks at sea, the entourage accompanying the two commissioners included a nursemaid to take care of nine-month-old Edith Eliza Hogge.

Baby Edith, along with her mother Helen and the others of the party, arrived on the Cape in early summer 1851. The ladies remained in the relative comfort and safety of Cape Town (under the protection of Lady Smith), while William Samuel and his co-commissioner sailed on up the coast to King William's Town, there to meet and confer with Colonial Governor Sir Harry Smith. Governor Smith, however, had other priorities, being deeply embroiled in the war on the eastern frontier; so he sent the two commissioners on up to Bloemfontein, capital of the Orange River Sovereignty, with instructions to settle the dispute with the disaffected Boers as best they could.

In January 1852, Hogge and Owen, accompanied by their military escort, servants and bearers, finally met with Andries Pretorius, the main Boer spokesman, at a makeshift camp on the banks of the Sand river, near the borders of what would one day be Southern Rhodesia. Within a few days they had reached an agreement which effectively gave Boer settlers beyond the river Vaal their independence in return for a guarantee that, among other things, they would not sell arms to African natives and they would end their policy of slavery. The Sand River Convention, as it came to be known, was signed on 17 January 1852 and cleared the way for the establishment of the Orange Free State and, a little later, the Transvaal.

In southern Africa, news from up-country could take many days to reach Cape Town, from where ships departed every month or so bearing the latest intelligence which, seven or eight weeks stale, would be eagerly disseminated across Britain. So it was late March before the good news of William Samuel's success at the Sand river reached his family in England. How proud they were, and with what joy they anticipated his return.

The next couple of ships brought only news of continuing strife down there beyond the equator; then in May the family heard that William Samuel had sailed back to Cape Town to be reunited with Helen and little Edith. Just three months later, on Monday, 9 August 1852, the SS *Propontis*, coming from the Cape, docked at Plymouth. Among her passengers was Helen, Mrs W. S. Hogge, and her nineteen-month-old daughter.

Helen Hogge wore deep mourning; she had been a widow for two months.

The *Bedford Times* for Saturday, 14 August, tells the story succinctly:

> Major Hogge, one of Her Majesty's Assistant Commissioners for settling affairs on the frontier, died at Bloem Fontein *[sic]*, Orange River Sovereignty, on the 9th of June. He left England 13 months previously, and lost his life through fever, caught by exposure in the rain at a meeting of chiefs in Moshesh's *[sic]* country. The intelligence conveyed to this neighbourhood by a short telegraphic message, as given in The Times of Tuesday, created a great sensation, especially as we believe the family of the lamented officer had not then received any intimation of the melancholy event…

What desolating news for Louise and her family.

In South Africa the struggle went on. Sir Harry Smith was replaced as Governor by General Cathcart. Charles Mostyn Owen, the other special commissioner, returned to England and later became Chief Constable of Oxfordshire. But Major William Samuel Hogge, Louise's oldest brother, lay interred in the cemetery at Bloemfontein, his story ended at the age of forty.

If he had lived, would William Samuel have contented himself with engaging in the family businesses after all his adventures? Other young men in his position spent only a few years in uniform, but he had chosen to continue his military career into his late thirties. Perhaps his talents and inclinations did not include brewing, trading and banking. Anyway, his death in 1852 made the question moot.

With second brother George (35) away in West Norfolk overseeing the family businesses there, it was third brother, Frederick (who turned 25 that year), who became Papa's trusty lieutenant in the Biggleswade, Shefford, and Baldock concerns.

Louise's siblings at the end of 1852

Eliza (41), married to Henry Williams Beauford (43); with Mary (13), Henry (11), William (10), Caroline (9), John (5), and Louisa (2)

William Samuel, died 9 June 1852, aged 40; widow Helen (27), daughter Edith Eliza (2)

Frances (Fanny) (38), still single, living at home in Biggleswade

George (35), married to Mary, living in West Norfolk, employed in family businesses there. No children

Harriet (31), married to lawyer John Lindsell; with Elizabeth (3) and Frederick (16 mths); living in London

Anna Allen (27), recently married to Revd Charles George Douton, Vicar of Biggleswade

Frederick (25), working in family businesses in Beds. and Herts., still single

Louisa Mary (22), still single

Charles Wells (20), still single, an Ensign in the 85th Light Infantry

The youngest member of the family, Charles Wells Hogge, had followed his oldest brother's example and, after completing his education (which included a resident course with Thomas Hunt, a 'corrector of stammering', at his residence on Golden Square in Westminster, London), had taken a commission in the army. The remaining unmarried siblings, Fanny, Louise, and Frederick, still lived in the family home at Ivel Bury with their father. They employed a resident staff of seven – housekeeper, cook, footman, housemaid, kitchen-maid, and a lady's maid each for Louise and dear old Fanny, who was nearing forty and settling inevitably into spinsterhood.

Louise still had her dreams of a more fulfilling future. She was not the type to sit on fine cushions while sewing fine seams; she liked to be out and about, riding and hunting, working with animals, enjoying the delights of the outdoor life. She played the piano, she loved to read and study, and she liked to express her opinions and thoughts in writing. She was twenty-two years old. Life and all its heady promise lay waiting for her.

CHAPTER THREE

When visiting their relatives in Lynn and Thornham, the Hogges of Biggleswade mixed socially with other worthies of the area, prominent among these being the 'blue-blooded' Cresswells of Lynn, closely allied with their cousins and in-laws the Gurneys, a large and well-to-do family of businessmen and bankers whose roots lay at Earlham Hall, near Norwich. Though in after days Louise proudly proclaimed her ties with her husband's Cresswell ancestors, she refused to acknowledge any relationship with the wealthy Quaker Gurneys. It was, after all, a Gurney who most bitterly betrayed her, in the end.

Gurneys' Bank, Lynn

During the eighteenth century, the wealthiest of Lynn's citizens, such as the merchant-mariner Hoggs, eased the flow of money in and around the town by extending credit and mortgage loans to less-wealthy businessmen and customers. The rich merchants themselves, in times of need, drew on the reserves of banks in London – a state of affairs which proved ever more cumbersome as business practices expanded.

In Norwich, in 1775, the Gurney family of Earlham Hall opened their own bank; seven years later they added a branch office in King's Lynn. Members of the Gurney family ran the branch with various partners until in 1809 young Daniel Gurney, aged eighteen, was sent to join his older brother John at the Lynn office, working with local partner Henry Birkbeck.

<table>
<tr><td>

Daniel Gurney (1791-1880)

Daniel was the youngest of eleven surviving children of John and Catherine Gurney of Earlham Hall, Norwich. One of his older sisters, Elizabeth (1780-1845), married Joseph Fry and became famous for her work in improving prison conditions for women and children.

Daniel Gurney was a mainstay of the King's Lynn branch of the family bank for many years. His brother John, with whom he had lived

</td></tr>
</table>

in Lynn, died in 1814 and sister Rachel Gurney came to keep house for her youngest brother. In 1816 they moved to North Runcton Hall, four miles south of Lynn, and in 1822 Daniel married Lady Harriet Hay, daughter of the Earl of Errol. Four sons and four daughters were raised by Daniel alone after their mother died in 1837.

Runcton Hall was always a lively place, teeming with family members and children. For a time, Daniel's nieces Katherine and Rachel Fry, daughters of his older sister Mrs Elizabeth Fry, lived with him. Later, at the age of 72, he took in his seven Troubridge grandchildren after their parents died[12]. However, after he lost his fortune in the collapse of the Overend, Gurney & Co Bank in 1865, he and his grand-children were able to stay on at Runcton only with financial help from other members of the family.

In his near-ninety years Daniel Gurney wrote a lengthy family history tracing his origins back to Norman times, and he is remembered as a charismatic character, a great benefactor and philanthropist. He was succeeded at the Lynn bank and at Runcton Hall by his youngest son, Somerville Arthur Gurney (a significant figure in Louise's story).

A new partner for the Lynn bank took his post in the 1820s. He had married Daniel Gurney's niece, Rachel, second daughter of Elizabeth Fry, and, as Thomas Southwell[13], an old employee of the bank, recalled, 'to this I believe he owed his introduction to the banking firm.'

The new man's name was Francis Cresswell.

Francis Cresswell

The Cresswell family, based in Northumberland, owned a long pedigree, but second son Francis Cresswell chose the sea as his livelihood. In those days, ships' officers began their careers as young boys, often before puberty: Nelson joined his first ship at the age of twelve, and Francis Cresswell's third son would be fourteen when his turn came, as would Queen Victoria's second son, Alfred. Francis Cresswell, too, worked his way up through

---

[12] Life at Runcton Hall is described in *Life Amongst the Troubridges: Journals of a Young Victorian 1873-1884*, by Laura Troubridge (found in various versions)

[13] Thomas Southwell joined the staff of the Lynn bank in 1846 and worked there for many years. His reminiscences are recorded in *Annals of an East Anglian Bank*, by W H Bidwell (1900)

the junior ranks until promoted to fourth mate, then third, second and, eventually, first mate.

At the advanced age of twenty-six, he leaps from the records into vivid, swash-buckling life as commander of the mighty East Indiaman *Astell*, a three-decked, heavily-armed merchant ship sailing under the red and white striped ensign of the Honourable East India Company. Three times he took the *Astell* on dangerous, year-and-a-half voyages out to the Far East, trading in spices, silk and opium, and by the time he strode down the gangplank after his final voyage on 30 May 1821, aged thirty-one, he was independently wealthy, enough to settle down, marry and embark on a second career in business. *(For more detail on Francis Cresswell, his Northumberland roots and his early career, see Appendix E.)*

The contrast between his adventurous seafaring life and his subsequent role as a banker in King's Lynn seems extraordinary, though no doubt he was able to empathize with the ship-owners and captains who did business with the bank. Did he find it easy to settle down? Or was the lively young Rachel Fry, who became his wife, sufficient excitement for a not-so-very-old sea-dog?

Daughter of a legend
Rachel Elizabeth Fry, born in London on 25 March 1803, was the second of eleven children of Joseph and Elizabeth Fry (née Gurney). Her mother is well-known to history as a tireless reformer of prison conditions; indeed, in mid-career Elizabeth Fry was one of the most famous women in the country, admired and fêted by all. But her good works meant that she tended to neglect her health, as well as her family. Some of her children – and her husband – bitterly resented her constant absences.

Elizabeth Fry and her daughter, Rachel

The Frys and their Gurney relatives were members of the Society of Friends. Some were extremely devout, others more sceptical, and a few grew up to be openly antagonistic to the strict rules of Quaker life. Elizabeth Fry, 'Betsy' to her family, had rebelled in her youth but as an adult she became immensely pious and truly believed she had been called to do God's work. She may have hoped that her rebellious second

---

daughter, Rachel Elizabeth, might follow her example; but the girl proved a sad disappointment.

Rachel turned out to be a tomboy, wayward and inclined to mock the 'peculiarities' of her family's chosen religion. When she was thirteen her parents fell on hard times and, having just acquired a tenth baby and lost a daughter aged only five, feeling overwhelmed by it all they sent Rachel and her older sister Katherine to live for a few years with Uncle Daniel Gurney at North Runcton.

Daniel was a sceptic about religion and especially hated Betsy's habit of breaking into spontaneous preaching at every opportunity; however, they remained fond of each other. He was then only twenty-five, living at North Runcton with older sister Rachel Gurney acting as housekeeper. Another sister was the wife of the local vicar.

All these non-Quaker influences had their effect on young Rachel Fry, confirming her own doubts, though her sister Katherine was less affected (she became her mother's close companion and biographer in later years, while many of her siblings, including Rachel, broke entirely away from the Society of Friends).

The journals left by Elizabeth Fry reveal her distress at the news that her daughter Rachel had fallen in love with the dashing Captain Francis Cresswell and had accepted his proposal of marriage. The family, both Frys and Gurneys, liked and approved of the young man – after all, he came of an excellent family and had made a considerable fortune by his own efforts – but Betsy Fry deplored his not being a 'Friend'. The Society's rules meant that Rachel would be disowned by them if she married a non-Quaker, in an Anglican church, in front of a 'hireling priest', and Betsy herself would not be allowed to attend the ceremony.

However, the pair were duly married, in North Runcton church, on 23 August 1821. No parental consent is noted in the register, though Rachel was only eighteen. Her bridegroom was almost thirty-two. Their main witness was her uncle, Daniel Gurney. The bride's mother, though desolated, obeyed the Society's rules and absented herself from the church ceremony; for Betsy Fry this was a dark, dark day – the first of her children to be wed, and she not there to see it. Against the date in her journal she scored a great black cross.

Francis and Rachel Cresswell spent the first year or two of their married lives on the outskirts of London, south of the Thames, in a house on Dartmouth Row, Blackheath, near to Francis's birthplace at Charlton, Kent. Their first son, Francis Joseph (generally known as Frank, though he was Joe to the family) was born there on 1 November 1822, the same day his grandmother Elizabeth Fry bore her eleventh and last child; so uncle and nephew shared the same birthday. Frank's brother Addison, two years younger, was born at the Frys' home in Pleshet, Essex. However, it was not long before the Francis Cresswells moved to King's Lynn, to what was to be their permanent home, occupied on lease – the small but dignified Bank House, adjoining Gurneys' bank on King's Staithe Square, near the noisome Purfleet and only a few yards from the historic Customs' House.

Francis Cresswell became a partner in the Lynn bank around 1825. The business, then Gurney, Birkbeck & Cresswell, was run jointly by the older and non-resident Henry Birkbeck and his two recently-wed partners, Daniel Gurney and Francis Cresswell. Over ensuing years the two younger men founded the Lynn and West Norfolk Hospital, worked on various committees and supported many other local charities. Between them, they also sired fifteen children: at North Runcton the Gurneys raised four sons and four daughters, while the Bank House welcomed the arrival of four brothers for Frank and Addie, and, finally, a sister to complete the family.

Children of Francis and Rachel Cresswell

Francis Joseph (Frank), born 1 Nov 1822
Addison John (Addie), born 18 Oct 1824
Samuel Gurney (Gurney), born 25 Sept 1827
William Edward (Bill), born 27 May 1835
Gerard Oswin (Gerard), born 4 April 1837
Oswald (Ossie), born 20 Oct 1839
Harriet Frances Elizabeth, born 22 Aug 1842

As the above list shows, almost eight years separate the births of Gurney and Bill. Did Rachel suffer a miscarriage or two? She was so ill in the autumn of 1833 that her mother, away on a working visit to the Channel Islands, rushed back to nurse her back to health. But Elizabeth Fry had a habit of rushing to any sickroom or death bed, as if she were the only one who could possibly be of help. When her brother Daniel's wife died in 1837, leaving him to cope with eight children under twelve, Betsy hastened to North Runcton to offer cheer and comfort. Daniel appreciated the kindness, but forbade her to preach or give readings of scripture while she stayed with him. He was by then forty-six, a successful banker and member of the county elite; he heartily disapproved of women preachers.

In Lynn, Rachel and Francis Cresswell felt the same. Rachel was due to give birth again and, though Betsy was anxious to be with her, she proved more nervous than the mother-to-be, all agitated and tearful while Rachel waited calmly in between pangs that produced Gerard, on 4 April 1837.

While staying at the Bank House with her daughter and son-in-law, Betsy Fry preached to public meetings at a large Methodist hall in Lynn, where huge crowds gathered to gape at this worldwide celebrity. Betsy lapped up the adulation, as usual, while the Cresswells, along with Daniel Gurney, found it all so embarrassing that Rachel berated her mother, recalling all her pent-up resentment of maternal neglect during her childhood. In her journal of that time, Betsy commented on how little support she had had from her family in her religious calling.

Returning again to Lynn in October 1839, when Rachel was gravid with sixth son Ossie, Elizabeth Fry noted with horror and dismay that her oldest grandson, Frank (then seventeen) was contemplating a totally 'unChristian way of life' – young Frank wanted to join the army. His grandmother set wheels in motion to stop him and, by the end of the year, Frank was a junior clerk in the bank of his Uncle Samuel Gurney, in Lombard Street, London. However, he soon rebelled against his place at the 'back desk' and in September 1842 signed on as an ensign with the 26th Cameronians.

The regiment was then fighting around Ningpo, in China, but returned to Hong Kong where, in October, the latest assignment of recruits, just off the boat, were sadly afflicted by fever. Two years later, stationed in Edinburgh in May 1844, the

26th received new colours. The old, tattered and war-torn flag was proudly paraded by two junior officers – Ensign Mountain and Ensign F. J. Cresswell. Frank, however, was not destined to be a soldier for long. After being promoted Lieutenant he resigned his commission, on 19 March 1847, and, much to his grandmama's relief, took a post with Gurney, Birkbeck & Cresswell, at their banking offices on King's Staithe Square, King's Lynn.

Elizabeth Fry spent her declining years in sojourns with various members of her family. She required full-time care, for her hard work and journeyings, her need to 'be there' when her family needed her, and, not least, her reliance on 'porter' and, latterly, opium, had ruined her health. She died on 13 October 1845.

In August of that same year, 1845, Francis Cresswell was elected mayor of Lynn. He was in his fifty-sixth year, a well-respected member of his community, having for some time been a member of the council, an alderman, Justice of the Peace, chairman of the Paving Commission, a charity trustee, a director of the hospital, treasurer of the District Visiting Society (of which his wife was also a stalwart), and supporter of many other charitable enterprises. Bank employee Thomas Southwell considered that his boss was a fine man: 'he had commanded an East Indiaman, a post of some consideration in those days, and he brought with him the manners and bearing of the quarter deck. His appearance was somewhat rough and austere, but his business capacity was great...' Mr Southwell remarks that the financial affairs of the borough had been 'in confusion' when Francis Cresswell took them on, but he left them 'in a state of prosperity'.

Francis Cresswell had also raised six fine sons. To his and Rachel's great sorrow, the youngest of their family, their only daughter, Harriet Frances Elizabeth, died in 1849, a month past her seventh birthday.

The Cresswells' oldest son, Frank, while still a young bachelor, began to emulate his father in charitable works:–

Founding of 'the poor man's church', St John's, in Lynn

As testified by the will of George Hogge (IV), church pews in St Margaret's and St Nicholas' were owned by well-to-do families and could be passed on to their heirs. This practice kept the poorer members of the congregation at the rear and on their feet – or sent them to more welcoming non-conformist chapels and meeting houses.

The story goes that Mr John Motteux, wealthy owner of Sandringham and Beechamwell estates, occasionally stayed in Lynn and, while doing so, liked to attend church. On one occasion he went in to St Nicholas' Chapel and took an empty seat, only to be politely moved on by a churchwarden, who explained that the pew belonged to a gentleman of the town. Mr Motteux chose another pew, whereupon the churchwarden politely informed him that it too was owned by someone. Taking the hint, Mr Motteux decided not to sit but to walk up and down the aisle, only to be told that this, too, was prohibited.

As a result, the wealthy land-owner opened a subscription for the building of a new church, where all pews would be freely available to everyone. He himself donated the first £1,000.

The church was built on the edge of the open park known as the Walks, and consecrated, in the name of St John the Evangelist, on 24 September 1846, by the Lord Bishop of Norwich. Mayor Francis Cresswell was among the dignitaries attending. His oldest son, Frank J. Cresswell, evidently approved of this innovation. He was twenty-four when he subscribed £100 to the fund and he remained, throughout his life, a great supporter of 'the poor man's church'. After he died, a subscription raised funds to erect in his memory an impressive stone pulpit and reading desk, still to be seen in the church.

The Cresswell sons

Frank Cresswell, having married the Hon. Charlotte Frances Georgiana Gough, daughter of Lord Calthorpe, in August 1850, soon founded a family of his own. They lived in Lynn, their address being 3 King Street, only two minutes' walk from the senior Cresswells' home at Bank House.

Younger brother Addison enjoyed a successful career as a confidential clerk with Messrs Gurney & Co., on Bank Plain in Norwich. Bank clerk Thomas Southwell clearly remembered how Addie and his friend Henry Birkbeck (son of the third bank partner) arrived at the door of the Lynn bank one morning in 'a handsomely-appointed gig with a pair driven tandem... How it got there I never could quite understand, for the only approach to the Bank was by a lane as crooked as a dog's hind leg and generally encumbered by farmers' waggons *[sic]* delivering corn at the merchants' granaries... From this gig alighted two splendid young fellows in all the glories of Melton driving coats and buttons as big as tea saucers. [They were] Mr Addison Cresswell and... Mr Henry Birkbeck, who had driven through from Norwich, as was their custom, changing horses at Swaffham...' What a pair of fine young swells!

Meanwhile the third Cresswell son, Samuel Gurney ('Gurney' to the family), had joined the Royal Navy as a 'volunteer apprentice' in early 1842, at the tender age of fourteen. His unique career is fully documented elsewhere[14], though Thomas Southwell's reminiscences tell the gist: 'In 1850, Mr Cresswell's son, Gurney, then a lieutenant in the navy, sailed in the Investigator, under Captain McClure, in search of – and as it proved, to discover – the North West Passage [a navigable waterway which would allow ships to pass between the northern Atlantic and Pacific oceans], and had it not been for the foresight of his father, the ship and crew might – and probably would – have shared the fate of their predecessor, Franklin, but a communication from Mr Cresswell to the Admiralty of that day, advising the direction in which search should be made, providentially influenced their instructions to the relief expedition, and in the words of Sherard Osborn, the historian of the voyage, "it was fortunate for England's naval history and for humanity that a parent's solicitude for a son absent on this expedition was more clear sighted [than that of the committee advising the Admiralty]"...'

The safe return from the Arctic of Lieutenant (later Captain) Samuel Gurney Cresswell, RN, caused intense rejoicing, especially in his home town. Lynn held a grand Civic Reception on 26 October 1853 to welcome him home.

---

[14] For the full story of Captain Samuel Gurney Cresswell's naval career, see *War, Ice and Piracy,* edited by Dominic Harrod (Chatham Publishing, 2000)

The three youngest of the Cresswell brothers – Bill, Gerard and Ossie – were following the usual pattern of younger sons, one aiming for the church, one for the army, and the other with dreams of a rural idyll. But for none of them did the future turn out as expected.

Waiting for Mr Right

'Oh! The hearts that have been broken for younger sons! Why should the British matron hold them in such terror? No true sensible love match ever came to grief yet.' So wrote Louise in 1875[15], looking back with pride and passion. Her own husband had, of course, been one of those less-favoured younger sons.

The records don't reveal exactly when and how she met Gerard Cresswell, but the combined Cresswell/Gurney clan moved in the same social circles as did the Hogges, with ample opportunities for the younger generation to meet and dally, perhaps during theatrical productions and musical concerts at the Athenaeum in Lynn; or at charitable sales and on committees; at tea parties, river regattas, fox hunts and pheasant shoots, church services and Sunday walks, private dinners and county balls...

A great setting for parties was the large town house of Louise's aunt, Mrs Fanny Allen, located on St Ann's Street, Lynn[16], its hall famously adorned by leather hangings painted with bright birds and flowers. There, a resident staff of seven servants attended the widowed Mrs Allen's every need. The great grey hulk of St Nicholas' Chapel (before the spire was added) brooded in its broad churchyard across the road and, in the quiet garden behind the house, Aunt Fanny's late husband, Thomas Allen, had caused a deep well to be sunk, of geological importance because it demonstrated the immense thickness of the clay and the impossibility of finding spring water by boring. This topic might help to crack the ice of shyness, failing which the

---

[15] Cresswell: from her pamphlet, *Norfolk and the Squires, Clergy, Farmers and Labourers, etc,* published 1875 by Simpkin, Marshall & Co, London, and by Thew and Son, King's Lynn

[16] Descriptions of places in this section come from memoirs of Lynn citizens J.H. Pratt and J.D. Thew

younger set might discuss the ghost that haunted the billiard room, while trying to ignore the smell of hops from the brewery next door, which at least disguised the worst stink from the river, the sewer-like Fisher Fleet and the crowded yards and tenements where the fisher-folk dwelt half out of doors, their houses being so small and their families so large.

Aunt Margaret Hogge's equally elegant house occupied a corner of the Tuesday Market Place, a spacious mansion where she employed eight servants. Working men staggering out of the Globe Hotel or the Maiden's Head paused to smear the windows with their noses as they gaped at the bright glitter inside those magnificent rooms. Alternating residences between here and Thornham Hall, Uncle George's widow lived in great style and enjoyed entertaining visitors, many of them from the Ainslie side of her family. She wrapped her diminutive figure in sable for concerts at the Athenaeum, or performances at the theatre, and local urchins watched with glee for her carriage and pair, a great sight to behold, with her fat coachman seated up on the box flanked by a pair of spoiled Skye terriers.

Did Louise ever dream of appearing at the head of Aunt Margaret's elegant, curving double staircase, to find her ideal man standing in the circular hall below, handing his hat and gloves to the butler and looking up with wonder as she drifted down like one of the heroines from a Bronte romance? Perhaps not. Louise was a realist. She certainly had no pretensions to great beauty, though in her book she admits to being 'by no means insensible to the attractions of Elise gowns with a sprinkling of diamonds'. However, she adds with her usual practical briskness, above all she favours 'a thoroughbred in the stable and a prize heifer in the stall'.

In May 1860, Louise reached the depressing age of thirty, still unwed. She must have been viewing the future with increasing anxiety. With the exception of dear old Fanny, now a hopeless old maid of forty-six, her sisters were all long married, and older brothers George and Frederick each had a suitable wife.

Frederick, as it happened, had been married twice by this date. His first wife, Alice Georgiana Dew, died a short while after their wedding in 1854. Then he met the young daughter of the rector of Great Ringstead, near Thornham. Reverend Frederick Thomas William Coke Fitzroy was a grandson of the first Lord Southampton and married to Emilia, elder sister of Henry Styleman le Strange, squire of Hunstanton; so their daughter was an excellent catch. Her name had been Emily Katherine le Strange Harriet Eliza Fitzroy, but was now, since 1859, Mrs Frederick Hogge. She presented her husband with his first son in June 1860. They lived for a while on England's south coast, in Bournemouth, a house named Ringstead Lodge after Emily's home village, but were soon to move to Biggleswade, where Frederick had assumed command of his father's businesses. William Hogge, nearing his seventies, had retired and migrated to a fine residence in London.

Louise's youngest brother, Charles, now twenty-eight, had been in the army for seven years and remained a bachelor – sensible chap since an officer's pay was hardly sufficient to support a wife. Promoted Lieutenant in 1853, he had spent two years in Mauritius, and since January 1859 had been soldiering on the Cape of Good Hope (did he, one wonders, visit brother William Samuel's grave in Bloemfontein?). Charles was making his own way in the world.

How much more difficult it was for a woman! Louise grew anxious about her own future. Was she to remain an old maid like Fanny? Or settle for a churchman, as had Anna, now established in the rectory in Biggleswade with three small children? Such a life would not have been to Louise's taste. Though she had uncles, brothers-in-law and friends who happened to be clerics, she herself was no devout churchgoer: 'many a dreary Sunday morning have I sat with frozen feet and hands through the drawled-out and gabbled prayers, the ill-sung hymns, and the tedious lifeless sermon, and how I have admired the old women in long cloaks who really seemed to find some comfort in it all.' Nor did she have much respect for the general run of clergy, many of whom were 'parish busybodies, or ritualistic vagaries, or [members of] the so-called evangelical school, making religion incompatible with all the enjoyments of life'. (Was this a dig at the Quaker Gurneys?) No, Louise would not have made a suitable wife for a vicar.

For her, a far more congenial future was one such as her oldest sister Eliza had chosen – to live on a farm, to grow crops and raise animals, and perhaps a brood of rosy children. Louise loved the country life. She had been raised to sport: she loved to ride to hounds, or to walk out in the fresh air with dogs running about her. That was what drew her to her future husband – a mutual interest in all things rural.

The prospective bridegroom
The three oldest of the six Cresswell sons were out in the world – Frank well-married and settled at the bank in Lynn; Addie established at the main family bank in Norwich; and Samuel Gurney a successful naval officer. To Rachel Cresswell's great grief, her fourth-born son, Bill (William Edward), away at St John's College, Cambridge, studying to be a clergyman, had caught a fever, lain ill for three weeks, and suddenly died on 3 December 1857 – he was just twenty-two years old that dark winter day. The family felt his loss keenly. Youngest brother Ossie (Oswald) had been admitted to Trinity College earlier that same year, aged eighteen, but after Bill died he quit Cambridge and the following April obtained a commission in the 26th Regiment, the Cameronians (his brother Frank's old regiment), being posted to Ireland in October 1859. Which left only the future of Rachel's second youngest son, Gerard Oswin Cresswell, to be settled.

His destiny appeared in the shape of Louisa Mary Hogge.

Gerard Cresswell may not have been quite the ideal husband Louise had hoped for. He was seven years her junior and not especially bright or well-educated; he had been briefly at Harrow School, from September 1851 to Christmas 1852 (when he was fifteen and a half), but did not attend university. (Hints in family letters suggest that he may have suffered from undiagnosed depression.) On the surface he and the intelligent, well-read Louise had little in common.

However, being a younger son with few prospects, he had need of a wife with means of her own and, if Louise was no tender young blossom, at least she would bring a fair marriage portion with her, namely her annuity from her grandfather Wells's estate and a marriage settlement which would bring extra capital when her father died. For her, on the plus side, Gerard was a fine young man, fit and healthy, even athletic. More, they enjoyed the same things – the countryside and its sporting pursuits, an active outdoor lifestyle among horses and dogs. This deep mutual interest could provide a better basis for marriage than many couples enjoyed. And so, with the blessing of both families, they became engaged.

As Louise explains, they had to decide what sort of future they would choose; either they tried to manage on an 'inconveniently small income', forever the poor relations relying on the charity of richer relatives, or they found an appropriate way of earning a living. Given their shared passion for the country and its ways, they agreed that the only acceptable future for them lay in agriculture.

Gerard had for some time been 'learning farming', as Louise puts it, with a mentor named 'Mr Broome' – another pseudonym, as it turns out, though changing a couple of letters in his name would not have fooled anyone who knew her, or him. In reality this great friend and sturdy supporter was John Groom, a substantial farmer who, at the start of their acquaintance, lived at Congham, in West Norfolk, farming 1700 acres and managing a huge labour force of fifty men and sixteen boys. Groom was ten years older than Louise, about forty when she first knew him.

John Groom, yeoman farmer (1820-1908)

John Groom was born in Walsingham, a place of pilgrimage, but in his early married life he and wife Celia lived at nearby Hindringham, where their first three children (John Edmund, Celia and Edmund) were born. Around 1852 they moved the twenty miles or so to take over from his parents at the family farm at Congham, where the next three children, Arthur John, Horace and Frederick came along. There too came young Gerard Cresswell to lodge and learn as a farming apprentice.

Later, Groom continued to cast a kindly eye over his pupil's agricultural affairs, first at Sedgeford and then at Appleton, which was only a four-mile ride away from Congham, down winding country lanes. The journey became slightly longer after Groom acquired Ashwicken

Hall and another 500 acres of farmland, in the late 1860s, leaving his oldest son to run Congham and care for the grandparents, who both lived into their nineties.

They were a long-lived, caring family. Louise's friend 'Farmer Broome' was eighty-seven when he died in 1908. He and his wife Celia were remembered by their family with great love and affection, demonstrated by the fond inscription on two stained glass windows dedicated to them in the church at Ashwicken.

When Gerard's intention to take up farming became known, well-meaning friends and family warned him that agriculture was not a proper profession for a gentleman. All very well to be squire of an estate, however small, or a yeoman tilling broad acres which had belonged to your family for generations; but to become a tenant on someone else's land was 'not quite the ticket'. Your social set found the notion somewhat bewildering; other farmers doubted your abilities and sneered at your grand connections; and the local country wits stood around waiting for you to make a fool of yourself. However, though many before them had failed in similar ambitions, Gerard and Louise determined to be the exceptions to the rule.

Unfortunately for them, the country way of life which had obtained in Britain for centuries was already under threat. The agricultural recession of the early nineteenth century had sent many country folk to seek work in expanding industrial towns and, as the century progressed, industrial innovation was to alter the entire face of the countryside. Meanwhile, in Europe, political conflicts loomed.

Gerard joins up

In 1859, the year in which Darwin's *Origin of Species* first saw print, warlike stirrings from abroad motivated the British government to muster a force of volunteers who would defend the homeland in time of invasion (a sort of early Dad's Army, except that these Victorian volunteers were mostly young and agile men). The people of Lynn responded by holding a meeting to inaugurate their branch of this new corps and among the town worthies who attended were Alderman Francis Cresswell and his three sons – banker Frank (36), naval officer Gurney (31) and apprentice agriculturalist Gerard (22).

Alderman Cresswell had been in poor health for some time, his wife Rachel blaming his decline on the long and terrible suspense of their son Gurney's absence in the *Investigator,* lost amid the Arctic wastes. As reported by the *Lynn Advertiser,* on being asked to speak and propose the first resolution, Francis Cresswell said he 'felt himself not to have voice' to address the meeting except to formally propose the motion: 'That a Rifle Corps be formed in this borough, and that a list be opened for the enrolment of names.' Seconding, Mr Armes (another leading citizen) acknowledged that some fellow townsmen objected to civilians taking up arms, but he reasoned that Britain could no longer rely entirely on 'the wooden walls of old England' (i.e. the ships of the Royal Navy). He knew that 'rifles and bayonets no more taught peace than Chubb's patent locks taught honesty, but all were equally useful while rogues were abroad'. The resolution being carried unanimously, the three Cresswell brothers stepped up among the first to sign on: Frank became Lieutenant of the Corps but took over as Captain eighteen months later and ran the troop with great discipline and efficiency for seven years; Gurney and Gerard were among his first troopers.

Gurney (Captain Samuel G. Cresswell, RN), plagued by a recurring illness which kept him at home on half pay, was unhappily idling his time away between Lynn, London, and his cousins' place in Northumberland, waiting and hoping to be assigned a new ship. He must have been more than happy with a chance to get back to active service, however amateur, with the rifle corps. Within three months, seventy volunteers had signed on, forty of them providing their own equipment. The uniform was not as glamorous as some – grey with black braid – but it gave them a purposeful air. And the ladies like a chap in uniform, don't they?

That meeting was the last official appearance for Francis Cresswell, who turned seventy that year and who was clearly suffering from 'the infirmities of advancing age' (as the newspaper put it). After it, he withdrew from public life and, in

December 1860, became so ill that he was not expected to recover. However, when he rallied enough to be able to walk out in the fresh air, in hopes of further building up his strength his wife took him on a visit to the countryside, to stay with their bachelor son, Gerard, in his recently-acquired new home.

At the age of twenty-three, Gerard had begun on the dream he shared with Louise: he had taken the tenancy of Sedgeford Hall and planned to live there, gaining experience by managing the small home farm, until Louise could join him as his wife.

Sedgeford

South of Hunstanton and two miles inland from Heacham, the village of Sedgeford lies along a hillside above the valley where the Heacham River, fed by clear chalk-filtered springs, winds its narrow way through a landscape of cool woods and gently sloping fields. Sedgeford is an ancient place, with a history of settlement going back at least as far as the Iron Age.

In 1859, Charles Neville-Rolfe, squire of Heacham and Sedgeford, found himself obliged to raise a mortgage of £3,400 in order to renew the lease on a part of the Sedgeford estate which was owned by the Dean and Chapter of Norwich (as was part of William Hogge's property in nearby Thornham). The Neville-Rolfes packed up and went to live in Italy, renting out both Heacham Hall and the smaller Sedgeford Hall. The tenant selected for Sedgeford was Gerard Oswin Cresswell.

When the chance came to rent the neat Queen Anne house and its accompanying farm – a small place, only 140 acres, employing three men and three lads – Gerard seized it with eager hands and with a £2,000 loan from his father. His tenure began at Michaelmas 1859. The farm had a well-experienced farm bailiff in Tom Rumble, and a dairywoman and chicken keeper in Tom's wife Mary. The couple, now in their fifties, had been working as a team for years; they inhabited a cottage just beyond the gates of the Hall grounds, on the lane to Fring. Moreover, Gerard's farming mentor, John Groom, wasn't so very far away; so Gerard moved, with a small household staff, into Sedgeford Hall. He planned to progress to bigger things, with an estate of his own his eventual goal, after he and Louise were married.

To this pleasant spot, in the early weeks of 1861, came the ailing Francis Cresswell, with his wife and personal servants, to stay with his son and, they hoped, to recover his strength. It was not to be. The intrepid sea-captain turned banker died on Friday, 22 March 1861, aged seventy-one. His body was taken back to the Bank House in King's Lynn and, from there, on the following Thursday, his funeral cortège departed promptly at 1.30 p.m., with the bell of St Margaret's tolling in regret. Townsfolk turned out in hundreds to pay their respects as the hearse passed by, while shops, and the windows of private houses, remained closed and curtained for two hours.

The funeral took place at North Runcton, the church where Francis and Rachel had been married forty years before, and there he was buried in the family vault in the churchyard, beside his young daughter, Harriet, and his student son, William. In accordance with custom, his widow and the other ladies did not attend all the mourners were male. Riding in carriages behind the hearse came the five remaining Cresswell sons (Frank, Addison, Gurney, Gerard and Oswald); the Right Hon. Sir Cresswell Cresswell (Francis's brother, judge of the divorce court); his nephew Harry Baker Cresswell, MP, from Northumberland; several gentlemen of the Fry family; Norfolk gentry including some Rolfes from Heacham and a couple of ffolkes *[sic]* from Hillington; lawyer and brewer Mr Seppings; various clergymen and sundry other worthies. At Runcton they were joined by some of the Gurneys, among them Daniel and his four grown sons, second cousins to the Cresswell brothers. 'The church and churchyard were filled by a very large number of the most respectable inhabitants of Lynn and of the neighbourhood...' added the *Lynn Advertiser*.

No Hogge is named in the long and respectful obituary, but Louise's brother George may have been represented by his partner from the Setch brewery, William Seppings. George had by this time acquired a house in Hyde Park Gate, Kensington, London, as well as his residence in West Norfolk, and was describing himself as a 'gentleman'. He had not much taste for commerce, preferring a literary life of books, magazines and theatre-going, of which there was more to be had among the artistic set in London.

The bereaved Cresswell family gathered back at Sedgeford Hall with Gerard. Some of them were still there on the night of 7 April, when the census for 1861 was taken. It names Gerard (24), as head of the household, and his mother, Rachel (58), a widow of 'independent means'. Also resident that evening were Gerard's brothers, Captain S. Gurney Cresswell, RN, and Lieutenant Oswald Cresswell, along with oldest brother Frank's two daughters, Charlotte (9) and Edith (6)[17]. Heading the staff was housekeeper Harriet Lancaster (34), who had been nanny to the Cresswells' lost daughter, Harriet, and who remained in Rachel Cresswell's service for the rest of Rachel's long life. Other staff were a cook, two housemaids, a coachman, a footman, and a nursemaid to look after the girls.

Frank Cresswell's oldest son, George (8), was at home in Lynn with household servants, while Frank himself, along with his wife Charlotte and youngest child (a four-year-old boy who bore the impressive name Cresswell Augustus Cresswell), was staying in Norwich with brother Addison. Addie had matured from the young fop who had impressed the bank staff by arriving in a two-horse gig with large buttons on his coat; now thirty-six, he recorded himself as 'magistrate, alderman and banker'. Indeed, later that year he would be elected Sheriff of the City of Norwich. That April, however, just ten days after they had buried their father, as his chosen trustees and executors the brothers were no doubt preoccupied with legal matters.

Francis Cresswell's estate was calculated as 'not exceeding £60,000': the bulk of it went to widow Rachel for her lifetime. That November each of the brothers received £4,000, as their

---

[17] The 1861 census cites Frank Cresswell's daughters as being at Sedgeford Hall, but also shows Frank's older son, George Frederick Addison Cresswell, 8, at home in King Street, Lynn, with sisters Frederica, 9, and Edith, 6. There is obviously an error – Frank had only two daughters: Charlotte Rachel Frederica and Edith Frances Louisa cannot have been in both Sedgeford and in Lynn on the same night

father had willed, with interest to come at regular intervals from the capital held in their mother's name.

Gerard immediately used half of his legacy to pay back the loan he had had from his father when he took the lease on Sedgeford. Happily, with the promise of regular top-ups to his bank balance and considerably more capital to come in due time (when his mother died), he was now in a position to marry Louise, though, out of respect for his father, a year's mourning would be observed before the wedding took place.

Mrs Gerard Cresswell

By this time, Louise was resident in London. Her brother Frederick and his family had taken over at Ivel Bury, the family home in Biggleswade, and father William had moved to his elegant town house at 43 Rutland Gate, Knightsbridge, near Hyde Park. On the night of the 1861 census, when the Cresswells gathered with Gerard at Sedgeford, William Hogge had both of his unmarried daughters staying with him – Louise and her sister Fanny (47), each with her own lady's maid; plus a domestic staff of five – a housekeeper, a housemaid, a kitchen maid, a butler and a young footman. In the porter's lodge lived a gardener and his wife. Considering this brigade of servants, it is hardly surprising that Louise found her transition to less affluent country living something of a culture shock.

Gerard continued to farm at Sedgeford while he and Louise waited for the twelve months of mourning to pass, she gathering her trousseau while her future husband contemplated a move to Sandringham Estate and, just a week before their wedding in April 1862, Gerard signed the lease which would take him and his bride on to Appleton Farm six months later.

So they were wed, and came to spend six months at Sedgeford Hall. As we have seen, in her book Louise recalled that period with delight, describing it as idyllic, full of amusing incidents and happy times. She chose not to mention that she lost her father, quite suddenly, that same summer.

Death of William Hogge

William Hogge died at his London home on 7 July 1862. Had he lived another month he would have been seventy-seven. His estate was calculated as 'not exceeding £70,000', so he was even more wealthy than Francis Cresswell.

Of his generation of Hogges there remained now only Uncle Fred, the black sheep, still proud to be an 'e'-less Hogg, and still going strong at seventy-three back there in Sandy, Beds. (Fred Hogg had never married, but at the age of fifty-two he had sired an illegitimate son, Fred Safford, whom he acknowledged and who took over the brick works and lime burning concerns in Sandy. In years to come both Uncle Fred Hogg and Cousin Fred Safford left useful legacies to Louise.)

William Hogge's will is particularly fascinating for what it reveals about members of the family. In gist, it leaves all properties and businesses in West Norfolk to oldest surviving son George; all properties and businesses in Bedfordshire to second son Frederick; and cash inheritances for all the other children – £8,000 for soldier son Charles and £4,000 each for five daughters (the married ones had already had part of their share as marriage settlements). William also continued to provide for his sister-in-law Margaret Hogge, under the terms of the will left by her husband.

However, the original document, drawn up in 1858, is amended by five codicils which gradually withdraw responsibilities from son George and transfer them to son Frederick. Evidence suggests that George had no head for, or no interest in, commerce, though he was still to inherit the properties in Lynn, including the mansion on the corner of Tuesday Market Place (after Aunt Margaret passes on), plus all ships and vessels, and also the partnership in Setch brewery. Frederick's share was equally valuable – all mercantile outlets, all shares in the banks in Biggleswade and Baldock, and a half share in the Wells & Co. brewery, which by this time owned seventy-five public houses in Bedfordshire. Other amendments in William's will concern son-in-law Henry Beauford (Eliza's husband), releasing him from the £3,000 debt incurred twenty years before (no part of it has been repaid nor is it likely to be, says the testator), and making provision to cover an additional debt owed by Henry to his father Revd H. Walter Beauford.

The monetary legacies left to his children were not paid out in lump sums but put into funds managed by trustees, who in this case were William's most businesslike son, Frederick; his nephew Charles Lindsell; his lawyer friend William Seppings (partner in the Setch brewery, near Lynn) and confidential clerk George Newbury. In practice, the capital remained invested in the businesses, interest being paid on a regular basis to the legatees.

Nearly half of William's lengthy will is, however, taken up in legal complexities concerning Thornham, his copyhold manor on the coast near Hunstanton. Thirteen years before, he had signed the income from the estate over to his oldest son, William Samuel, as a marriage portion. When Major William Samuel Hogge died prematurely, at Bloemfontein in South Africa, predeceasing his father and leaving no will, legal tenure of Thornham had reverted to William, who now willed that the manor and its income was to be held in trust by his widowed daughter-in-law Helen, for the benefit of her daughter Edith, aged twelve.

For Louise and Gerard, one suspects, the most galling aspect of her father's will was his specifying that they were not to be entitled to receive the £4,000 due from their marriage settlement for at least ten years, providing that interest at four per cent was regularly paid. This, too, was to be at her brother Frederick's discretion. Since their marriage settlement had agreed that the money should be paid *six months* after her father's death, they may have been a little irritated that the capital was out of immediate reach. Or perhaps a regular income of four per cent was sufficient, for the time being. However, making Frederick the main trustee over his siblings' finances would prove to have been an error. It was to cause bitter contention in the family later on.

CHAPTER FOUR

New Hunstanton

As Louise and Gerard were in the process of moving from Sedgeford to Appleton, the new fifteen-mile railway between Lynn and Hunstanton opened, on 3 October 1862. The track snaked out from the station at Lynn, turning north along the low-lying sea marshes on the eastern edge of the Wash, through North Wootton and across the Babingley River to Wolferton (which, lying only two and a quarter miles from Sandringham Hall, was to be the royal halt). From there it continued via Dersingham, Snettisham ('pronounced *SNETS*'m, as if you're sneezing', as poet John Betjeman remarked) and Heacham, to end at the new town, the still-under-construction seaside resort, of Hunstanton St Edmund.

The new craze for sea bathing, partaking of ozone, and an innovation called 'holidays', had inspired squire Henry Styleman le Strange of Hunstanton Hall to dream of creating a town that would supply what was being demanded. His own ancient village of Hunstanton seemed inappropriate for his purposes (besides which he liked his privacy), but west of it a wide open sheep-run lay above spectacular layered cliffs of ginger carrstone and red and white chalk (one of the few spots in England where one may stand on the east coast and watch the sun go down over the sea).

In 1846, le Strange had built his New Inn, of brick and carrstone, at a spot from where the land sloped down towards a sandy shore. The only other building in sight was the lighthouse, half a mile away on the point and already a tourist attraction. Carriage customers flocked to the new hotel, while a horse-drawn coach service brought day-trippers to admire the sea views and the magnificent sunsets; so the enterprising squire organized a company to build a railway to bring the people in. The promise of this new line saw the town mushroom with hotels and guest houses, shops and banks, soon to be joined by schools and beach entertainments. This settlement, named Hunstanton St Edmund, became known as New Hunstanton (or simply Huns'ton, since in Norfolk they have a habit of missing out the middle syllables of names), while the much older, more sedate settlement nearby would be 'Old Huns'ton'. Sadly, Henry le Strange did not live to see the first train chug over the new track; on 27 July 1862, just ten weeks before that momentous occasion, at the age of forty-seven, he died of a heart attack, leaving his twenty-one-year-old son Hamon to continue his work.

The first inn, soon renamed the Golden Lion, was rapidly joined by other hotels, including the grand Railway [later Sandringham] Hotel – adjacent to the station, where the branch line ended less than a hundred yards from the beach – and the Buckingham Palace Hotel, a little higher up the slope on St Edmund Terrace. Both of these latter hotels were leased to the Setch-based brewing firm of Hogge & Seppings. (The lease for the Railway Hotel, dated 1863, was for ninety-nine years, signed by Louise's brother George and his partner).

In the handsome new town, built entirely of the local honey-red carrstone from the quarry at Snettisham, leases were rapidly taken up. The best locations ranged in an arc looking down across the amphitheatre-like bowl of the Green, which Henry le Strange had decreed must never be built on and which still remains (largely and contentiously) open ground. On one of the most desirable locations rose a pair of large adjoining houses – Mintlyn House, property of (Sir) Richard Baggeof Gaywood, and the appropriately-named Cliff End House, built as a seaside home by Louise's brother, Frederick Hogge. His lease for Cliff End was, in fact, the first to be purchased in the new town.

The Hogge family's links in West Norfolk had increased with the years: Frederick's second wife, Emily, was first cousin to Hunstanton's new squire Hamon le Strange, and other Hogge relatives had country homes at Thornham, only a few miles away, Aunt Margaret retaining the tenancy of the Hall while the manor itself belonged to young Edith Eliza, under guardianship of her widowed mother, Helen. And, of course, Louise and her new husband were themselves not far away at Appleton. Hardly surprising, then, that Frederick and Emily should take the opportunity to build a residence in the new town and bring their children – William Frederick (2) and Alice Georgiana (fourteen months) – to benefit from the sea air, while Emily waited out the last weeks of her third pregnancy with her mother and her cousins close by.

Cliff End House was a holiday home, let out to other people when the Frederick Hogges didn't need it. They kept another house on the south coast, in Bournemouth, but maintained their regular base at the old family home, Ivel Bury, in Biggleswade. (Having businesses in both Biggleswade and Baldock, roughly six miles apart, Frederick rode between the two places so frequently that his horse wore a pathway, popularly known as 'Hogge's track'.)

Only days after celebrations to mark the arrival of the first train in the resort, Frederick and Emily's second daughter, Louisa Emilia, emerged into the world at Cliff End House. The chosen godfather, young squire Hamon le Strange, observed of his tiny second cousin, 'I think it is the first native of the place'. Since the new town had no church as yet (that came three years later), the baby was baptized, on 19 October 1862, in the parish church at Old Hunstanton, not far from the Hall where the le Stranges resided.

While joining in the celebrations, Aunt Louisa and Uncle Gerard Cresswell may have confided that they, too, were expecting a happy event in the spring. Their first child was due at the end of March.

Early the following year (February 1863), the Prince of Wales returned to Norfolk, enjoying the hospitality of several of his new neighbours and riding out with local packs of hounds. As ever, his presence in the county excited great curiosity and crowds of sightseers flocked to watch his every public outing, however 'incognito' he might try to be. The Prince had begun to resent these intrusions into his private life. After one incident he wrote to Mrs Bruce, the wife of his governor: 'Fancy on Saturday last a reporter from Lynn actually joined the beaters while we were shooting, but as I very nearly shot him in the legs as a rabbit was passing, he very soon gave me a wide berth. Gen.

Knollys [comptroller at Sandringham] then informed him that his presence was not required, and he "skidaddled," as the Yankees call it. The next day he wrote an apology for his infamous conduct, and I don't think he will trouble us any more.'[18]

His Royal Highness also paid a visit to the Cresswells in their damp and rambling farmhouse, where Louise was now large with child. The young Prince raced about the ramshackle old house, hugely amused over such 'queer quarters' and generally charming everyone in sight; Louise comments on his power of putting everyone at ease.

The Prince was not a particularly handsome young man, having inherited too many of his mother's Hanoverian features – pudgy, chinless face, protuberant eyes and full under-lip – and, like his mother, he was not very tall, only five feet seven inches (an inch shorter than Louise), though he compensated for that by having elevated heels fitted to his size eight boots. However, at the age of twenty-one, with blue eyes and fair curly hair streaked to gold by the sun that gave his skin a healthy outdoor glow, he was a personable enough chap, with a cheery, boyish manner. Most of those who actually met him were, like Louise and Gerard, charmed by his good humour, his frank, friendly manner, and his way of remembering names and faces with flattering accuracy.

After his visit to Appleton, Bertie returned to London in time to greet his bride, who disembarked from the *Victoria and Albert* at Gravesend on Saturday, 7 March 1863, to find her Prince striding up the gangway to meet her. That same day in King's Lynn, artillerymen at St Ann's Fort on the shores of the Great Ouse River marked the moment of the Princess's arrival on British soil by firing the Sebastopol gun, brought from its usual station outside the Athenaeum to boom out a royal welcome.

When the gun sounded again, three days later, proclaiming the joining in matrimony of the heir to the throne and his lovely young wife, Lynn went wild in celebration, people cheering and church bells ringing; leafy green boughs, floral tributes,

---

[18] Lee, Sir Sidney: *King Edward VII, a Biography, Vol I* (Macmillan, 1925), p144

triumphal arches and ribbons decked streets and shops and houses; excited schoolchildren gathered for special dinners; military men in dress uniform, and dignitaries in wigs and robes, paraded through the streets and made speeches. And everyone cheered. And cheered again. Later, when they all gathered on the cobbled expanse of the Tuesday Market Place, the Rifle Corps raised their rifles and fired volleys into the air. J.H. Pratt, then a small child, recalled being terrified by the noise.[19]

Spectators crowded at windows overlooking the square. Among them Louise, very near her time of confinement, probably observed the jollifications from the safety of the family mansion on the corner next to the Corn Exchange, the home of Aunt Margaret Hogge, now a dowager of seventy-two. Other ladies of the family may have joined them, including Mrs Rachel Cresswell, with her other daughter-in-law, the Hon. Charlotte (Mrs Frank Cresswell), and Louise's sister Fanny. Fanny Hogge (48) had taken a ten-year lease on The Cottage at Thornham, but also had a home at 2 King Street in Lynn, opposite the Frank Cresswells and not far from Mrs Rachel Cresswell's home at the Bank House. None of these residences, however, had windows with a clear view of that day's main ceremonies on the Tuesday Market Place, where three of the Cresswell brothers played their part: naval officer Samuel Gurney Cresswell, mounted on a fine horse, helped the police to control the crowds; Frank Cresswell captained the grey-uniformed Rifle Volunteers; and amongst their ranks Gerard Cresswell stood to attention, forming an honour guard with his fellow militiamen outside the house where the mayor and corporation gathered.

Having these special guard duties to attend, the Rifle Corps did not join in the main processions through the town. They had held their own parade earlier, at the cricket ground off Austin Street, and later sat down to a slap-up lunch, drinking many a loyal toast in wine liberally supplied by the mayor.

Despite grey skies that threatened rain, the cricket field also provided the venue for an afternoon of Rustic Sports, including a

---

[19] Pratt, J H: *Recollections*. Unpublished reminiscences (King's Lynn Library collection)

donkey race (the mayor's steed was named Don Quixote) and foot and hurdle races. Gerard Cresswell distinguished himself, demonstrating his health and fitness by winning first the 400-yard foot race for members of the Volunteer Rifle Corps (in an excellent time of 59 seconds), and then the 600-yard foot and hurdle race, with three flights of hurdles, which was 'open to all England'. Among the other runners was his best friend and second cousin, Somerville Arthur Gurney (28), youngest son of Daniel Gurney of Runcton, who now lived at Middleton with his wife and family and worked alongside Frank Cresswell at the Gurney & Co. bank. Gerard won this race by putting on a last-minute spurt and overtaking the struggling front man, who fell over. Gerard took a tumble, too, but only after breasting the tape to be declared the winner.

Louise's young husband must have been a fine athlete.

That evening, the Rifle Corps, chaired by Captain Frank Cresswell and with his brother Gurney as local-hero guest, dined at the Albion Hall on Broad Street. Their brother Gerard attended the even more splendid dinner taking place at the Globe Hotel (close by the Hogge mansion), where twenty-four clergymen and chief tenants from Sandringham sat down to a hearty meal as guests of their landlord, His Royal Highness the Prince of Wales.

Nor was that an end to the rejoicing. The people of West Norfolk spent the rest of the month preparing for their greatest moment yet, the day when their Royal Highnesses would come home to Sandringham. By that time, very close to her confinement, Louise remained within doors at the Bank House; but, though she took no active part in the celebrations, she and her mother-in-law, Rachel, heard all about the excitement from Gerard and his brother Frank, both of whom were very actively involved.

Royal newly-weds come home to Sandringham
Having spent a blissful week honeymooning at Osborne House, on the Isle of Wight, Bertie and Alix returned to London. Ten days later, on Saturday, 28 March 1863, accompanied by their usual entourage, they set off again for the rail journey to their country home in Norfolk, travelling from London's Shoreditch

station behind an engine and tender painted cream and garlanded with flowers. With bands and cheering people greeting them at even the briefest of halts, they arrived, four long and wearying hours later, at a similarly crowd-infested Lynn, alighting at around 4.10 p.m. to a rapturous welcome.

Only the weather proved unkind. 'Very fresh' westerly winds had flags snapping, skirts and hats flying, cheeks glowing and floral decorations battered to pieces; some of the more delicate gauze banners and silken flags were not used, said the newspaper, and 'the statues of Peace and Plenty had to be barricaded in their niches in a way that raised a smile...' The Lynn (5th Norfolk) Rifle Corps (without Gerard Cresswell, who was awaiting the train at Wolferton), turned out on parade under the command of Captain Frank Cresswell, who was thanked by the Prince's comptroller General Knollys. The mayor made a loyal address of welcome. As the *Lynn Advertiser* commented: 'Everyone was charmed beyond measure by the ingenuous and truly English countenance of the Prince, by the exceeding grace and loveliness of the Princess, and by the cordiality (condescension is too harsh a term) and the untiring good humour with which they again and again returned the joyous greetings of the people around them.'

Lynn station was, and still is, a terminus, so to avoid delay the flower-decked engine and tender were left behind and, with another engine attached at the rear, the train drew out again. The royal party had 'been detained at Lynn not more than five minutes', the newspaper assures us. (The town had spent weeks preparing for that five minutes.) Along the Hunstanton branch line every building in sight fluttered with flags, ribbons, banners bearing loyal mottoes, wind-swept evergreens, flowers, anything that came to hand; every window provided a balcony for a happy band of well-wishers, and yet more crowds waved and cheered from either side of the track. The newspaper estimated that 20,000 people lined the route between Lynn and Wolferton, having journeyed by train, in carriages, on horseback or on foot from all points around.

How pleased Bertie and Alix must have been to realize that they had only a few more miles to go before they reached the royal halt and the end – almost – of their lengthy journey.

The royal halt at Wolferton

The hamlet of Wolferton, part of Sandringham estate, lies on the edge of a broad stretch of coastal creeks and salt-marshes some six miles north of Lynn. When the railway company applied to HRH for permission to use his land, he extracted a promise that some additional 'mod cons' would be added to the station at Wolferton, including having the platform covered as a refuge from the elements, and a comfortable waiting room provided for the convenience of Her Majesty his mother. Considering that Queen Victoria didn't much care for the place and visited it only three times (twice when the Prince was seriously ill in 1871, and again in 1889 for the lying-in of her grand-daughter Princess Louise), it seems more likely, and more in character, that the Prince required the extra comforts for his own and his wife's sake, and also to facilitate the droves of illustrious guests who would soon be arriving to enjoy the sport and the hospitality he could offer at his own private country home.

On that homecoming day, Wolferton station was decorated out of all recognition, clamorous with officials, clergy, soldiers, carriages, horses, and numerous members of the *hoi polloi*, all come to cheer their future King and his bride. Amid swirling dust thrown up by the brisk wind, the local company of the Rifle Corps mounted guard alongside the Norfolk Light Horse; this contingent of regular soldiers, with their horses, had travelled from Norwich by train earlier in the day, disembarked at Lynn, paraded through the town to the Tuesday Market Place, paused for lunch and then ridden on to Wolferton.

Waiting with them, also on horseback, were the tenant farmers of the royal estate, a dozen or so gentlemen all wearing white favours as a distinguishing badge. Among them were Gerard Cresswell of Appleton, and George Brereton, who lived on Sandringham Heights, the highest spot for miles around, popularly renamed Balaclava Heights since the Crimean War. Brereton was a local 'character', a lovable eccentric whose house boasted an observatory turret from which that day a large flag flared, while over his door an inscription welcomed the Danish Princess Alexandra to Sandringham – in her own language.

When the royal train arrived, at 4.25 p.m., the royal pair walked across the red carpet to their carriage. Their most senior courtiers entered a second carriage, officials cleared a way through the throng and the procession set off, led by the mayor of Lynn (changed out of his mayoral finery and now mounted on horseback). The gentlemen tenants rode behind, leading the two royal carriages, flanked on either side by the mounted troops. Hundreds of flags and leafy boughs lined the way, with banners and waving, cheering people, the crowds growing ever more dense as the procession neared the Lynn Lodges at the western entrance to Sandringham Park.

Part of the road from the station had been damped down by a water cart sent from Lynn, but further up there was nothing to stop the dust from rising, stirred up by hooves and wheels to be further swirled about by the brisk breeze. As the *Lynn Advertiser* wryly observed: 'the day's pleasure was diminished by the clouds of sand and dust which flew along the roads and lodged upon the persons and clothing of the public (especially pedestrians), giving them all a uniform yellowish tinge derived from the pulverised car stone *[sic]*. Painters might have admired the "warmth of tone" thus imparted to the appearance of everything and everybody; but, as a matter of personal experience, the subjects of it found it decidedly disagreeable – especially as the gritty matter so profusely distributed effected a firm lodgement in the hair, the eyes and the nostrils, and between the teeth of the public generally.' The reporter loyally adds, however, that the spectators would have endured far worse to catch a glimpse of the Prince and his Princess, and indeed few of them even noticed the dust until after the parade had passed.

How many people in that enthusiastic crowd managed to catch more than a glimpse of Their Royal Highnesses beyond the press of mounted soldiers, waving handkerchiefs and veils of scouring dust? And what kind of impression remained with the eighteen-year-old Princess of her first arrival at her new home?

At the Lynn Lodges more congratulatory addresses, printed on vellum, were presented. Beyond, two hundred schoolchildren lined the way into the park, sprinkling the way with wild flowers. Another mile or more across the heathy upland the carriages trundled, past the rectory and the church, and on around the lake, until finally they reached the big house, where the military contingent paraded again and presented arms, the clergy made speeches, the Princess received a bouquet… and the officers were invited in to partake of refreshment. Later, the vicar, Revd Moxon, treated the children to tea in his school room, after which, at about 7 p.m., the royal couple came out again onto their terrace, to hear the children sing a special version of the National Anthem, paeoning the Prince and his bride (complete with three new doggerel verses all quoted in full in the newspaper). By that time the crowds were drifting away, many of them making for the station, where extra trains had to be run, crammed to twice their expected capacity. The last of the trains did not return to Lynn until 10 p.m.

Illuminations in the town that evening were ruined, thanks to high winds which also caused the planned balloon ascent to be deferred(!), though the firework display in the Tuesday Market Place was much enjoyed by all. Meanwhile, up on Sandringham (Balaclava) Heights, a display of rockets and a huge bonfire were put into the shade by a less official blaze which had been started on the heath nearby and which 'continued burning vigorously over a large surface for several hours'.

An over-heated end to a memorable day.

A daughter for Louise and Gerard
As the excitement over the royal wedding faded into history, the heavily-pregnant Louise remained with her mother-in-law at the Bank House in Lynn, where her baby daughter arrived on Friday, 10 April 1863, less than a year after she and Gerard had been married. At last, after so many boys – except for Gerard's little sister, Harriet, who had died at the age of seven – there was a Cresswell girl to coo over.

However, bearing a child was relatively easy; raising it to maturity could be more problematical, subject to God's inscrutable will. Evidence suggests that the new baby may have been sickly from birth; there being no record of her being baptized, the ceremony may have been private, performed at home at the Bank House. They named her Frances Dorothea: Frances was a familiar name among the Hogges (Louise's aunt and sister both bore it), but allied with Dorothea it was pure Cresswell, echoing the names of Gerard's paternal grandmother, the last of the direct Cresswell line in Northumberland.

Sunlight and shadow

If little Frances Dorothea Cresswell ever came home to the old farmhouse at Appleton, her stay must have been brief. That spring, builders swiftly set to work to demolish the ramshackle dwelling, along with all the old outbuildings, walls, barns, sheds – everything – with orders to build a fine new farmhouse, in line with plans the new tenants had themselves sketched out. Across the whole estate, building and improvements continued over many years, fitting Sandringham for its new status as the country home of the future King; local builders Messrs Goggs & Co., of Swaffham, benefited greatly from the amount of work involved.

Louise says nothing of this period, but it seems likely that she, with her child, remained at the Bank House for the duration of the building work. The arrival of their daughter evidently prompted the Gerard Cresswells to look more closely at their future security; they had, after all, managed to persuade their royal landlord to build them a new house and so, since they were obviously favoured tenants, why not ask for further concessions?

One can imagine the ambitious, assertive Louise urging her young husband to write to the Prince's solicitor, Mr White. Obediently Gerard did so. But his suggestion that his twelve-year lease might be extended to twenty-one years received a politely negative reply – it would set a bad precedent on the estate: 'but... if you carry on the Farm, as I'm sure you will,' Mr White wrote on Thursday, 2 July 1863, 'I am sure you will have a renewal upon equitable terms.'[20] He adds that the Prince has agreed to pay almost £3,000 for the rebuilding of Appleton, but because this is more costly than he had anticipated (their 'ideal home' being rather more grand than was normal for a farm-

---

[20] Royal Archive LAW/SHM/12/10/4

house), they were asked to pay five per cent interest on two-thirds of the price [£1,935], from Michaelmas that year. Mr White did, however, agree to recommend extending the lease to fourteen years instead of twelve, because the first two years were being disrupted by the rebuilding.

Replying the following day, Gerard reasons[21] that, as he won't see the benefit of the new building until Michaelmas 1864, its due date for completion, he should not be expected to pay the interest until that date; after all, he will be obliged to hire another house for the winter, plus moving furniture, upheaval, inconvenience... (Had he been listening to Louise again?)

Mr White admits to finding some validity in this argument and, 'as I know it to be your Illustrious Landlord's wish that you should be liberally dealt with'[22], he agrees the five per cent interest should not start until Michaelmas 1864.

The Norwich Gates
The good people of Norfolk had been invited to contribute to the purchase of a wedding gift for the Prince and Princess of Wales – a pair of magnificent wrought-iron gates, designed by architect Thomas Jekell and manufactured by the firm of Barnard, Bishop & Barnard, based in the city of Norwich; hence the name – the Norwich Gates. Their fine workmanship had fascinated visitors to London's International Exhibition of 1862.

The gates stand twenty-four feet high and forty wide, their design incorporating acorns and leaves of various trees; four griffins holding coloured shields of arms rear high on pillars; and over all stand the Royal Arms surmounted by a crown, among roses and sprays of holly (decoration sadly vandalised now thanks to memento-hunters). The gates originally stood about a hundred yards closer to the house than they are now.

A deputation of mayors and sheriffs from across the county, led by the High Sheriff and Lord Lieutenant, made the formal presentation to Their Royal Highnesses at Sandringham on Tuesday, 7 April 1863. Later a book was printed, containing the

---

[21] Royal Archive LAW/SHM/12/10/5
[22] Royal Archive LAW/SHM/12/10/4

loyal address given by the High Sheriff that day, with the Prince's reply and a list of over eight hundred names of subscribers to the gift. Among the more interesting names (for our purposes) are:

Mrs Thomas Allen of Shouldham (Louise's Aunt Fanny)
John Beck, the recently retired royal land agent
3 Bagges (businessmen, brewers and leading citizens of Lynn)
2 Fitzroys (related to Louise's sister-in-law, Frederick's wife, Emily)
John Groom, Jnr, of Congham (Gerard's mentor)
10 Gurneys, inc. Daniel of North Runcton and his son Somerville Arthur
    of Middleton
W.M.R. (Rider) Haggard of Braddenham Hall (the author)
Mrs George Hogge of Lynn (Aunt Margaret)
5 Keppels (a name later to be inextricably linked with the Prince's)
The Earl and Countess of Leicester, Holkham Hall
Revd G. B. Moxon, vicar of Sandringham
Revd W. Lake Onslow, RN, of HMS *Racoon* (who will become rector
    of Sandringham and figure largely in Louise's story)
Mrs Onslow and Miss Agnes Onslow of Blofield
William Seppings (Hogge & Seppings brewery, Setch)
The Marquis and Marchioness Townshend, of Raynham Hall
The Walpoles of London and Rainthorpe Hall
Lord and Lady Walsingham of Merton Hall,
and not least –
Mrs (Rachel) Cresswell
F. J. [Frank] Cresswell
Captain S. G. Cresswell, RN
and G. O.Cresswell of Appleton.

The most elevated of these personages would soon be playing host to their royal neighbours during their regular winter sojourns in Norfolk.

In September 1863, Gerard's older brother, Captain Samuel Gurney Cresswell, missed the chance of his first command, as captain of HMS *Scylla*. Because he was staying with his cousins in Northumberland at the time, he received the letter after a few days' delay and, anxious not to be late with his acceptance, he rushed to Sheerness in person, only to collapse with one of the bilious attacks which had so often debilitated him since his return from China five years before. Obviously he was not well enough to undertake a voyage to the Far East.

Bitterly disappointed, Gurney returned to King's Lynn, his promising career in the Royal Navy curtailed by ill health.

'The Lord gave and…'
The Prince and Princess of Wales spent Bertie's twenty-second birthday, 9 November 1863, at Sandringham, a habit they were to continue in years to come. With Alix's birthday being only three weeks later (born on 1 December 1844, she was three years younger than her husband), they usually celebrated by spending most of November and at least part of December in Norfolk, holding balls and house parties. With nice synchronicity, this period coincided with the opening of the shooting and hunting seasons, when being in Norfolk suited Bertie perfectly.

Christmas they normally spent wherever Queen Victoria happened to be, with the extended family gathering for the festive occasion, but the Waleses more often than not returned to Norfolk for the New Year and the period immediately following, entertaining at Sandringham or visiting neighbours such as the Earl of Leicester, Lord Coke, at Holkham; Lord Townshend at Raynham; or Lord Walsingham at Merton, so that hunting and shooting could continue unabated, through January and into February. Princess Alix was not so keen on shooting, though she enjoyed riding to hounds, looking beautiful and elegant in her riding habit and jaunty hat.

That year, Christmas with the Queen at Frogmore proved more trying than usual, for Alix's father, having succeeded to the Danish throne as King Christian IX, found himself at war with Prussia, in an old dispute over who owned Schleswig-Holstein. Naturally, Queen Victoria sympathized with her German relatives, while Alix could see only the threat to her father. Much to the Queen's annoyance, Bertie sided with his wife.

Queen Victoria often behaved like a self-obsessed monster, picky and demanding, apparently determined to undermine her oldest son's confidence. She was a product of her upbringing, spoilt and totally convinced of her own 'God-given' authority.

Desolated by the loss of her adored husband, rather than bearing up stoically she went into retreat, wallowing in self-pity and constantly trying to ensure that everyone, especially her hag-ridden children, saw things her way and did only as she wanted. When they failed to obey she was offended and indulged in monumental sulks. She probably expected to bully the young Princess of Wales into becoming another compliant daughter, but Alix had her own kind of stubborn independence, besides which at Christmas 1863 she was heavily pregnant, emotional, and concerned for her family in Denmark. Nevertheless, constantly referring to her mother-in-law's relatives as 'bestial Germans' was less than diplomatic. (Family Christmases can be a trial!)

That winter was unusually cold and ice remained thick on the ponds into the new year, making for marvellous skating. Bertie and Alix were still at Frogmore when her labour pains started – two months prematurely. Her firstborn, Prince Albert Victor Christian Edward (known to his family as 'Eddy'), arrived on 6 January 1864, a tiny child weighing only three and three quarter pounds. But to everyone's relief he lived, and thrived.

When the news reached King's Lynn, St Margaret's church bells rang joyfully, flags flew during the day and at night the houses of the mayor, town clerk and other inhabitants were brightly illuminated. So said the *Lynn Advertiser* on 16 January.

By a sad irony, that same edition of the paper reveals that while the royal family were rejoicing in a new heir, tragedy had struck for Louise and Gerard. The obituary column has the entry:

> On the 15th inst., at the Bank House, King's Lynn, the residence of her grandmother, Frances Dorothea, the only child of Gerard Oswin Cresswell, Esq., of Appleton, and Louisa Mary, his wife, aged nine months.

The death certificate reveals that she died of convulsions caused by 'cerebral effusion', or fluid on the brain.

They buried the baby in North Runcton churchyard, not far from her paternal grandfather, Francis Cresswell. The place is marked by a plain granite slab with the inscription: 'In memory of Frances Dorothea, only child of Gerard Oswin Cresswell and Louisa Mary his wife, born April 10 1863, died Jan 15 1864. The Lord gave and the Lord hath taken away. Blessed be the name of the Lord.' The parish register reveals that Revd William Hay Gurney, one of Daniel Gurney's sons, performed the service, and the child's residence is given as 'King's Lynn'.

In the writings she left, Louise Cresswell mentions her lost daughter only once, a brief afterthought amid other griefs.

Saddened though Louise and Gerard must have been to lose their daughter, few families in those days escaped without losing at least one child; examples were all around. But, as the spring came, Louise knew she was pregnant again, this new child due in late autumn. She could hold her head up high and smile when she heard that sister-in-law Emily had presented Frederick with another son. Once again the nursery suite at Ivel Bury, in Biggleswade, was filling with youngsters and nursemaids.

Country wedding
That year, 1864, the youngest of the Biggleswade Hogges was also settling down. Captain Charles W. Hogge, of the 85th Light Infantry, had fallen in love with Emilia Jane Bagge, daughter of William Bagge, JP (later Sir William, MP). This branch of the Bagge family resided at Stradsett Hall, deep in the beautiful Norfolk countryside, a few miles south of Lynn.

Charles and his Emilia were married by special licence on Thursday, 16 June 1864, four days after the bride's twenty-eighth birthday. The bridegroom was four years older and still a serving officer, based at Shorncliffe in Kent. As the *Lynn Advertiser* reported the following Saturday, it was: 'an event of the greatest interest to the locality and to the wide circle of friends of the allied families; and we are happy to record that the arrangements passed off with the greatest *éclat*. The bridal party walked from the Hall to the church, passing through the park, which was handsomely decorated with flags. The churchyard was similarly ornamented, and flags floated from the summits of the Hall and the church. There were also two triumphal arches *en route*. The pathway from the churchyard gate was lined with the village children, who strewed flowers in the path of the bride and bridegroom. The church was crowded...'

The newspaper's list of guests includes, naturally enough, many Bagges – they were a prolific family; but the bridegroom's siblings had gathered in force, too: Frederick and Emily came from Biggleswade; Fanny (Miss Hogge) from Lynn; Louise and Gerard from Appleton; and George from nearby Wormegay.

Four witnesses signed the register, the first being 'Louisa Mary Cresswell', the fourth 'George Hogge'. Louise's forward-slanting, spiky, assertive hand typifies the woman who penned it, while her brother's tiny, hurried, self-effacing writing seems suited to the retiring, book-loving man suggested by sources.

George and Mary Hogge now had a residence at Hyde Park Gate, in London, but they also kept a home at The Grange, in the village of Wormegay, convenient for the Setch brewery, which was thriving; by this time Hogge & Seppings owned many public houses in the area, including the two new hotels in Hunstanton St Edmund. But the other Norfolk businesses were in decline; in the shipping line, for instance, everything was changing, steam rapidly succeeding sail. Louise's brother George had already disposed of most of his Lynn holdings.

Never much enamoured with the mercantile side of business, George had decided to consolidate his finances and live well on the proceeds, for with every passing year the chances of his producing an heir grew more remote (he was now forty-seven, his wife forty-two, and they had been married for twenty-two years). However, he still owned the mansion on Tuesday Market Place (where Aunt Margaret remained in residence, having reached the advanced age of seventy-five) and he maintained his partnership in the brewery at Setch.

Just a few days after the family wedding at Stradsett, Gerard Cresswell felt confident enough to enter horses in two classes for Norfolk Cart Stallions at the Agricultural Show in King's Lynn. He won no prizes but at least he made a show and let the farming world know that he was on his way.

For Louise, her youngest brother's marriage had been a hopeful, happy occasion, with her siblings in attendance, her young husband by her side, the new child quickening in her womb, the second year's crops growing in Appleton's fields, and her new home nearing completion.

The new Appleton House

'We moved into the new house as soon as the building was sufficiently advanced,' she writes. 'The rooms on one side were all brightness and sunshine, looking over the Sandringham heath, and woods of cathedral-like pines through which a blaze of glory penetrated when the sun set into the sea beyond, and on the other over the farm premises which promised to be worthy of a Royal estate and our animals to be as well housed as ourselves.'

Their new home was a splendid place, set on a broad piece of level ground on a long sloping hillside. In after years, when all the work had been completed, visitors would arrive via the neat carrstone lodge on the rise and pass down the carriage drive, admiring the wide views of fields and deep woods rolling off to their right. In the distance the vale fell away, verdant meadows hatched with blackthorn and hawthorn that blossomed white in spring. And from the highest point they might catch a glimpse of the 'German Ocean' [the North Sea] before their conveyance dipped down the slope and reached the sweeping left-hand turn, passing gardens laid to ornamental trees, shrubberies, and lawns. The ruined church across the lane added a picturesque touch.

The house itself was spacious, light and airy. On the ground floor it boasted a morning room, a drawing room, and an office, all with marble chimney pieces; a dining room with an oak chimney piece; plus a front kitchen and a back kitchen, complete with pantry and larder; a housemaid's closet; a store room; a man servant's sleeping room, and a cool dairy. Up the broad staircase lay, firstly, the master bedroom, whose marble chimney piece had cupboards either side; then two more large bedrooms; a day nursery and a night nursery for the expected child, and two smaller rooms for a nurse and, in time, a governess. Beneath the house lay a useful range of brick cellars.[23] A photograph taken later shows a conservatory added, too. Compared with other

---

[23] Royal Archive LAW/SHM/12/10/9

farmhouses in the area, this was a very fine dwelling. The Cresswells, with their dreams of becoming landed gentry, delighted in their new home.

Their joy was slightly marred by the loss of the busy and energetic Mary Rumble, who died that year aged fifty-three. She had asked Louise to make sure that a suitable 'steady, respectable person' was chosen to take her place and care for her dear old Tom. Louise complied, but the replacement wife, who had 'outlived the age of romance, if it ever existed', never quite fitted in as Mary had, being interested only in the domestic side of her life, not in working with the hens or the dairying. (How Tom Rumble felt about being organized in this manner Louise doesn't say, except that 'it might have been too much for the old man'!)

Before long, other worries intruded, beginning with the arrival of a sinister new type of under-gamekeeper – stern, scowling men, who swiftly acquired the nickname of 'Velveteens' because of their green velvet, heavily-braided German-style uniforms, and caps decked with jaunty feathers. The sole purpose of these gamekeepers was to rear as many pheasants, partridges and hares as the land would stand, and woe betide anyone who stood in their way! One of their first tasks was to plant new strips of hedges, forming grids across the farmers' fields to provide shelter for nesting birds and cover for the guns. Until the hedges were established, the farmers were forbidden to allow hoeing in among the young hazel and hawthorn, with the result that weeds grew wild and shed their seeds in among the crops.

Under the Game Laws of the time, the landlord had a perfect right to raise as much game as he pleased, in whatever way suited him best. The land and the wild life on it belonged to him, and if the pursuance of his sport interfered with the tenant farmers' work then… hey ho, that was the way of the world. The Velveteens had been hired to protect the Prince's interests and they took pride in serving His Royal Highness. They prowled about the fields day and night, on the lookout for poachers, spying on the tenants, and reporting back to their masters on any action of the farmers that didn't suit them.

It was an ominous hint of things to come.

To Gerard and Louise, a son

Autumn was turning to winter, the shooting season well under way and the fox-hunting season beginning, when Louise again went to stay at her mother-in-law's home, the Bank House in King's Lynn, for her second lying-in. This time, to everyone's joy and delight, on Sunday, 9 October 1864, she produced a healthy son and heir. At the delayed christening, held at St Margaret's church in Lynn a month later, 13 November, they named him Gerard Francis Oswald, all good Cresswell names.

The year so sadly begun with the death of her infant daughter now ended with hope and promise. Before Christmas, Louise and her husband even attended a small private party with the Prince and Princess at Sandringham Hall, an event she always looked back on with great delight. She was on her way, socially accepted by royalty, with a fine house and a promising future, as wife to a gentleman farmer and mother to his son and heir – a Cresswell heir, bearing the blue blood of his ancestors. What satisfaction for the daughter of a Biggleswade tradesman!

The new land agent

Early in 1865, a new face came on the scene when the Prince of Wales appointed a new agent for Sandringham. John Beck, the elderly man who had held the post under Charles Spencer Cowper, had been replaced by Thomas Henry Burroughes soon after the Prince took possession of the estate, in late 1862, but Burroughes held the post for only two years. He departed in January 1865, replaced by one Edmund Beck, whose father William was a first cousin of the former agent. (The name Beck was a familiar one in Norfolk, members of the extended family being employed in various places as agents, auctioneers and/or farmers). The keen and eager-to-please Edmund Beck was the same age as Louise, thirty-five, and sire of a growing family.

Edmund Beck (1830-91)

The new Sandringham agent was born at Mileham, in mid-Norfolk. In 1854 he married local girl Anna Maria, of Snoring, and they settled down on a 500-acre farm in the parish of Oxwick-cum-Pattisley, just south of Fakenham. On this farm, Edmund Beck employed nineteen men, nine

---

women and eight boys, and further augmented his income by working as an auctioneer.

By April 1861 he had fathered five children – Edward William (6), Marian (5), Anna Maria (3), Ernest Claud (2) and Alice (1). Wife Anna Maria, helped in the house by a cook, a housemaid and two nursemaids, was heavily pregnant yet again with her third son, who was born that June and christened Reginald Frank*. Arthur Clement followed four years later, and Sophia and Margery rounded off the family. The Becks moved to West Newton, the nearest village to Sandringham Hall, in 1865, when Edmund became land agent to the Prince of Wales. But he also retained his farm at Oxwick – some of his letters are written from there.

*In the register of baptisms at Oxwick, the third Beck son is named as Reginald Frank, baptized on 9 June 1861. Ten years later, at school at Downham Market, he is recorded as 'Frank R'. Evidently he preferred to be known as Frank and that is how history remembers him. *(See Chapter Fifteen.)*

Louise soon found reason to despise Edmund Beck, whom she describes as 'a sharp country auctioneer who had been employed in selling wood in the plantations'. To her mind he was, as Norfolk people might have said, 'a botty little man', a jumped-up nobody, self-important and high-handed, to whom this royal appointment promised to bring all the advantages he could ever have hoped for.

Elsewhere...

Even in sleepy Norfolk, people kept in touch with the wider world. Under the heading 'American News, By Electric And International Telegraph', the *Lynn Advertiser* had reported in detail on the horrors of the Civil War raging on the other side of the Atlantic. In April 1865, the same column told of the ending of that war and, only a few days later, came news that President Abraham Lincoln, the man who had inspired the fight to end slavery, lay dead, shot by an assassin.

English people denounced the crime with appropriate horror, but it soon faded into history. One Norfolk matron, Mrs Windham of Felbrigg Hall, Norfolk, casually noted in her journal: 'The Times gave the news that President Lincoln was assassinated. Sent to know how the dog was and heard it was quite well.[24]' Life went on.

In May that year, in Biggleswade, Frederick Hogge and his wife Emily welcomed their fifth new member, Amy Katherine, another sister for William Frederick, Alice Georgiana, Louisa Emilia and George Fitzroy. The fecund pair had been married for just six years.

The following month, a second son for the Prince and Princess of Wales was born at their London home. His names, the cause of much argument between Marlborough House and Windsor Castle, were eventually settled as George Frederick Ernest Albert (the last insisted upon by his grandmother, still ostentatiously mourning her late husband). The new Prince (Georgie to his family) would one day be King George V.

The rose window in St Margaret's
As the days lengthened towards midsummer, the Cresswell family and their friends gathered once more in King's Lynn, to attend a service in St Margaret's (more properly the Church of St Margaret, St Mary Magdalene and All the Virgin Saints). The occasion marked the dedication of new stained glass, specially made to replace the old plain glass in the huge rose window at the eastern end of the church. The glass depicts the figure of Christ, flanked by St Margaret and St Mary Magdalene, these three surrounded by a score of the aforesaid 'Virgin Saints', with blue floral patterns in the smaller lights which fill out the circle.

The glorious and finely-worked pictorial glass was the gift of the ailing Captain Samuel Gurney Cresswell, RN. As a boy, attending services with his family and seated in the family pew, Gurney had often gazed at the clear glass window and wished it could be filled with colour. Now, forced by illness into early retirement, he had brought his boyhood dream to fruition. As a small brass plaque, in the wall below the window, confirms, he dedicated the gift in thanksgiving for his safe delivery from the frozen wastes of Arctic Canada twelve years before, and in

---

[24] Mrs Windham's unpublished diaries are kept at Felbrigg Hall, near Cromer in North Norfolk

gratitude for the reception the town had given him on his return. Recording the occasion, the *Lynn Advertiser* adds that Captain Cresswell also wished the window to be a memorial to his late father, Alderman Francis Cresswell.

Politics

During that hot summer of 1865, at a meeting to confirm the parliamentary candidates for West Norfolk, Gerard Cresswell turned out to lend his support to the Conservatives in the shape of the Hon. Thomas de Grey (son and heir of Marquis Townshend of Raynham) and William Bagge, Esq. (now related to the Hogges by marriage, being father to Charles's new wife). During the electioneering, Louise's sister-in-law, George's wife, Mary, made a deep impression on local news editor J.D. Thew, who remembered her as 'a very attractive lady'. With George still in business locally at the Setch brewery, and expecting any day to gain full possession of the mansion on Tuesday Market Place, he and his wife retained their strong links with Lynn.

Women were, of course, not allowed to vote until the twentieth century but, long before the Suffragettes began their outright protests, many ladies took an active interest in politics, by encouraging their menfolk to stand up and be counted, and by supporting causes that seemed just. Louise Cresswell was that kind of woman, holding strong opinions and not afraid to express them, especially when it came to conditions in the countryside, which affected her own life and experience. She was particularly attracted by the views of politician and farmer Clare Sewell Read, a strong spokesman for the agricultural community.

Clare Sewell Read, MP, JP (1826-1905)

C. S. Read was a Norfolk man born and bred. A watercolour caricature, painted by Carlo Pellegrini and printed in the magazine *Vanity Fair* in 1875, shows the MP as a tall thin figure in top hat and tails, with enormous apish side-whiskers.

By the time he was thirty-four he had a 600-acre farm at Little Plumstead and was employing nearly sixty labourers. The household included an agricultural pupil aged twenty, who was learning the farming business from Farmer Read much as Gerard Cresswell had learned from Farmer Groom. In September 1862, Read's farm hosted a trial and demonstration of a new reaper built by McCormick of Norfolk. Later he moved to a larger farm at Honingham with his wife and two daughters, born 1861 and 1879.

In July 1865, Clare Sewell Read was elected to parliament as member for East Norfolk. He remained a member of the House of Commons for many years, his main area of interest being the agricultural cause: he made many speeches on the subject in the House and frequently chaired meetings of the Agricultural Association in Norwich. In the late 1870s, as the agricultural depression threatened bankruptcy for many, Read and a colleague made an exhausting fact-finding trip across America, hoping to bring back new ideas to help the struggling British farmer. His essay on *'The Farmer's Year'*, published by Jarrold & Sons c1900, gives a succinct and illuminating glimpse of life on a Victorian Norfolk farm.

As prospective candidate for East Norfolk, C. S. Read appeared on the West Norfolk hustings, in Lynn, to speak on behalf of fellow Tories Bagge and De Grey. From that time on, Louise followed his career with interest and, when she needed help from someone who wielded real influence, it would be Mr Read to whom she appealed (with disastrous consequences, as it turned out).

Long hot summer

In Dover, that year of 1865, Captain Charles Wells Hogge and his new wife Emilia celebrated the arrival of their first child, a boy whom they named George Francis (sometimes confused with his cousin George Fitzroy of Biggleswade, both of them being 'George F. Hogge, later Archdale,'). Meanwhile at the newly-built Appleton House another 'G. F.', young Gerard Francis Oswald Cresswell, flourished as babies will, beginning to sit up, then pulling himself to his feet and trying to communicate – not that his mama tells us anything about his development; she notes only, in passing, that she occasionally sat with 'the child' and his nurse in the shade of the Pastons' old nut walk, whose peace provided a welcome haven, especially that hot, dry summer when trouble stalked the countryside.

The cattle disease 'Russian murrain', or 'rinderpest', was spreading across England, creeping ever closer to Sandringham.

In Norwich, the Agricultural Association, presided over by Clare Sewell Read, MP, discussed ways of combating the plague, eventually closing the cattle market in the city and abandoning plans for the next agricultural show. The Norwich cattle market remained closed for around eighteen months.

Happily, the herds from Appleton, grazing on the rich sea marshes around Babingley and Wolferton, remained free of the disease, but still Gerard came home after riding around his fields increasingly worried by the condition of his farm. Little rain had fallen, so that roads and fields alike were turning to dust. Norfolk soils tend to be light, which makes them easy to work – you could plough there with a brace of rabbits and a clasp knife, so said the country folk – but the topsoil tends to erode into fine dust clouds, dispersing on the lightest breeze when the weather is dry. Worse, hares abounded that year. The weather suited them and they bred prolifically, bringing their young to nibble at the plumpest ears of ripening wheat and barley, or to chomp on the lushest green tops of the mangolds. It was frustrating, Louise recalls, hundreds of buck-teethed, long-eared predators feasting off your precious crops – eating away your profits! – and you with no right to harm the little beasts. If you didn't take inordinate pains to keep them out, they'd be in your kitchen garden, too, dining off every tender lettuce shoot, carrot top and flower bud. Kangaroos, the villagers called them – 'blasted furry kangaroos…'

The Game Question
Everywhere people gathered, they hotly debated the rights and wrongs of the 'Game Question': newspapers published all sides of the argument; agricultural associations raised angry protests about the unfairness of the status quo; and in parliament Clare Sewell Read strongly reiterated the farmers' point of view. Reporting on a meeting of the Midland Farmers' Club, whose members had deprecated the excessive preservation of game in certain localities, *The Times* opined that, surely, the tenant farmer took on the land knowing perfectly well what conditions attached. Generally the landlord may indeed reserve the shooting for his own use, but the tenant is free to make deductions for

damages from the rent he pays – a simple matter of regular calculation and voluntary contract; after all, if the landlord is unwilling to play fair then the tenant need not take the farm in the first place... The writer makes it sound so easy – just like that! – but then he was evidently an ignorant 'townie' who knew little about farming.

At Appleton, Gerard Cresswell determined to put in an official complaint about the marauding game, but, Louise says, she persuaded him to wait until he could appeal to the Prince in person; she had no faith in His Royal Highness's arrogant minions but felt sure that the Prince himself would set matters right. However, when he did come down to Sandringham she recalls that 'all hope of relief vanished; he was infatuated with the shooting; it became a perfect passion with him, and nothing made him more angry than the slightest opposition to it...'.

The Cresswells' innate optimism began to droop as problems increased and their outgoings escalated. Much as Louise loved the new house, its luxury came at a price – they were spending far too much on everything, trying to improve the land with manure and expensive guano products, buying the best seeds and stock animals, acquiring the latest machines... Their savings were dwindling alarmingly fast. Then, to her and Gerard's dismay, new cottages erected at either end of the farm were allotted, not to their own farm labourers as they had expected, but to some of the officious Velveteens, the under-keepers posted in to act as guardians of the game. Meanwhile the hares went on nibbling away at the choicest crops. And the agent began muttering about the rubble remaining on the farm making the place unsightly – builders' rubble, which should have been cleared at their landlord's cost, Louise felt.

She fretted over the effect the accumulating problems were having on Gerard. Her usually energetic young husband seemed low in health as well as in spirits. 'He, who had been all that was cheerful and strong, one of those people who make the dullest room seem brighter when they enter it, would now come in wearied... harassed at the destruction going on out of doors, until at last it positively haunted him...'

Lighter intervals offered brief respite: the summer round of fêtes and shows was under way and, this being England, there was cricket. In a junior friendly match in early August, a team from North Runcton (home to Daniel Gurney and his Troubridge grandchildren) played a team from Middleton (home to Daniel's son Somerville and family). For this occasion, bank executives and second cousins Frank Cresswell and Somerville Gurney put aside their accustomed *gravitas* to act as umpires, while Frank's two sons, George and Cressie (aged twelve and eight), played for Middleton. Later in the month, the Lynn Rifle Corps enjoyed an afternoon of sports and games at Reffley Spring, led by Captain Frank Cresswell and Lieutenant Somerville Gurney – an inseparable team both at work and at play, it seems, though Frank was the elder by thirteen years, being forty-three in 1865 while S. A. Gurney turned thirty.

On 28 September, the Thornham Horticultural Society, newly-formed, held its very first show in a barn festooned with flags and boughs of evergreen, with fairy-like baskets of flowers suspended from the roof, dahlias of all colours formed into star-shaped displays, and the band of the Rifle Volunteer Corps engaged to play selections of music. The newspaper declared it a great social success, attended by 'all the principal families within ten or twelve miles'. Gerard Cresswell, Esq., of Appleton, acted as one of the judges, while his wife's niece, Miss Edith Hogge (daughter of the late Major William Samuel and heiress to the Thornham estates, soon to reach her fifteenth birthday), gave out the prizes.

'I minded this more than all...'
Only days after judging the entries in the horticultural show at Thornham, Gerard Cresswell fell ill, with what appeared to be bronchitis; but his condition rapidly deteriorated and the family decided he ought to be at his mother's house, closer to the doctors in town. Farmer Groom agreed, insisting that he himself would take charge of Appleton in their absence; so Louise and Gerard 'were enabled to go away for the last few weeks... we should have preferred to remain in our own home [but] it was

now an intense comfort to be relieved from all the cares of life and in rest and peace together to the last'.

Louise firmly believed that her formerly fit and healthy young husband had been worn down by worrying about the farm: 'I had many and bitter experiences in after years, but I minded this more than all... he might have recovered if this had not been laid upon him, adding to the natural depression of the illness, which at last drifted into hopelessness.'

Family rumour maintains that he had for a long time been suffering from clinical depression, perhaps even before his marriage, while his death certificate states the cause as bronchitis 'suffered over eight or nine days', following a much longer period of exhaustion. Whatever the full truth, Louise's husband, Gerard Oswin Cresswell, died on 27 October 1865. He was twenty-eight years old.

THE PRINCE AND PRINCESS OF WALES ON THEIR
WEDDING DAY, 10 MARCH 1863
(The Royal Collection © 2007,
Her Majesty Queen Elizabeth II)

NAMES

OF

THE INHABITANTS

OF THE

COUNTY OF NORFOLK

WHO PRESENTED

The Norwich Gates

TO

HIS ROYAL HIGHNESS

THE PRINCE OF WALES,

APRIL 7TH, 1863.

NORWICH:
PRINTED AT THE MERCURY OFFICE.

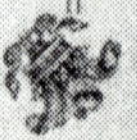

TITLE PAGE FROM 'RED BOOK' (p95)
(Chris Mackie, 2007. Book in author's collection)

LOUISE'S NEW HOUSE, BUILT 1864 (p100)
(illustration from first edition of 'Eighteen Years on Sandringham Estate', 1887)

MAIN ENTRANCE OF SANDRINGHAM HOUSE
AS IT LOOKS TODAY
(Chris Mackie, 2007)

GRAVE OF THE INFANT PRINCE ALEXANDER
SANDRINGHAM CHURCH (Chapter Six)
(Chris Mackie, 2007)

CHAPTER FIVE

Alone

Looking back at that time, Louise writes: 'It was long before we could realise, when the future seemed so bright and all our wishes fulfilled, that we were not to share it together. My husband bore it bravely as became one of Kingsley's "Englishmen", glad and willing to live, but not afraid to die. Our little daughter had gone before, now I and the boy were left alone.' [This is her only reference to Frances Dorothea and her first mention of her son.]

Gerard Cresswell died at the Bank House, as had his infant daughter before him, and he was buried near little Frances Dorothea in North Runcton churchyard. The *Lynn Advertiser,* for 4 Nov 1865, says that this 'untimely death is a source of sincere and general sympathy with his widow and relatives'.

As was customary, only men attended the actual funeral. Accompanying the hearse from the Bank House, riding in Mrs (Rachel) Cresswell's carriage, were Gerard's brothers, Frank and Addison, with the Reverend E. H. E. Hankinson (a great family friend, vicar of St Margaret's, who read the service); in Frank Cresswell's carriage came Louisa's brothers, Frederick Hogge and Captain Charles Hogge; Daniel Gurney's carriage held some Fry relatives, Somerville Gurney's carriage yet others, with four hired carriages bringing more. Many other friends and acquaintances, including Gerard's kinsman, Somerville Gurney, Esq., and Mr John Groom, his farming mentor, awaited the cortège at North Runcton, along with the Mayor of Lynn.

Two of Gerard's brothers were unable to attend the funeral: Gurney by this time was too ill, and youngest brother Lieutenant Ossie Cresswell had sailed, with the four HQ companies of the Cameronians, for India, aboard the ship *Dilawur,* the previous July. They had arrived in Bombay on 26 October, the day before Gerard died. It would be months before the tragic news of his brother's premature death reached Ossie.

For Louise, Gerard's death came as a devastating blow. Her lively young husband was gone, and all their dreams with him. Looking back in later years, she was able to view it philosophically: 'I suppose we all have as much happiness as we deserve... And as years pass by and the first sharp grief is over [we sometimes wonder] whether we would have willed it otherwise...' She muses whether the hoped-for prosperity would have brought the peculiar blessings which come with pain, and whether we should wish those who have gone before to remain and suffer other trials and infirmities, 'and the possibility that they might change towards us, or we towards them'.

But those thoughts came later. At the time, with her grief still raw, she was distraught. And bitterly angry.

After a bereavement, when the first shock and grief have begun to ease, human beings often find release in anger; they rail against fate and look around for something to blame for their loss and pain. Louise needed something to fixate upon, to help discharge her fury and frustration at the blow that fate had dealt her – this was not the way she had planned for her life to be, decked in widow's weeds with a baby son to bring up all alone. Whose fault was it? If one could not blame God, then what scapegoat could one find?

The nearest and most obvious cause of her pain was – yes, of course! – the hares. The Prince's hares! It was all their fault. Those detested hordes of furry 'kangaroos' had hounded and worried her beloved Gerard to his death, leaving her bereft, facing a lifetime of toil and penury. How she hated them. She never forgave them, or the men who reared them, or the master for whom those men worked.

Such reasoning soured the rest of her life.

Gerard's will

Did Gerard Cresswell have a presentiment of his own mortality? He made his will on 5 September 1865, only seven weeks before he died. At probate, the following January, his estate was calculated 'Under £8,000'. The will leaves to Louise all of her husband's movable goods and belongings, including her own wearing apparel and ornaments (which demonstrates how few rights women had in those days), but no monetary legacy, other than what she is entitled to under their marriage settlement. Other personal effects are to be turned into cash and invested, by selected trustees, for his son, young Gerard, in whose name the lease on Appleton is to be held, too. Trustees and executors are to be his 'dear wife' Louisa Mary Cresswell, his brother Oswald Cresswell (the army officer), and his second cousin, Somerville Arthur Gurney.

This is a fairly standard will from a man of no great fortune, but it left Louise with no additional capital or income. She had annuities, in the form of interest from her marriage settlements and legacies, but those hardly amounted to a fortune. Her main asset was the farm, for which she stood as trustee in her son's name. But Appleton, of course, was not her property: it was held on lease from the Prince of Wales, with rent due half-yearly.

A gift for a Princess
While Louise endured the first weeks of her deep mourning, at Sandringham Hall the royal pair held a house party to celebrate the Princess's twenty-first birthday. The ugly, draughty old house was full to bursting with relatives and friends, and everyone joined in a day of fun and feasting; schoolchildren sang, and estate workers devoured a lavish dinner treat.

Before setting out to bag a few pheasants, as a way of passing a merry morning, the Prince led his wife and all their guests out to the lawn, to show off the special gift he had ordered – a novel type of dog-cart, with a double seat in front and a single seat behind, where a groom could perch. The carriage was painted a rich chocolate brown, the harness dyed to match, with a high-stepping pair of matching bay ponies. The Prince himself climbed up and 'handled the dashing equipage in such a manner as to shew [sic] to advantage all its fine points', as the *Lynn Advertiser* noted.

The Princess was enchanted by the gift and, in after years, enjoyed driving herself about the estate, with silver bells merrily jingling to tell all and sundry that their much-loved lady was near.

Louise's choice

Louise, meanwhile, maintained a widow's expected seclusion. She needed to grieve, and she needed time to consider her future. What are you going to do, Louise? they asked her. You can't possibly stay at Appleton; you couldn't hope to run that place by yourself. It wouldn't be sensible. It wouldn't be… well, quite the thing. Not for a lady. Not a rational choice. My dear, you're in mourning, not thinking straight. Consider your boy…

But Louise Cresswell was not the type to fade into widow-weeded seclusion, nor did she relish the thought of throwing herself on the mercy of relatives; after all, she and Gerard had taken up farming partly to avoid becoming the perennial 'poor relations', openly pitied and secretly despised. She writes, 'now that the brightness of my life had passed away, the only future that seemed endurable was to remain in our house and carry out our plans. Unless it proved to be a positive necessity, I really could not go.' She had been warned that the house could not be let separate from the farm, but that suited her well enough: 'it was the occupation that I wanted, the sheer hard work as an opiate and distraction. If it had not been for the child, I think I should have gone into training in some London hospital, so great was the need of an all-absorbing employment… I resolved from the very first to give up all society, to lead as Robinson Crusoe an existence as if I had emigrated to the backwoods, to be wholly engrossed with my work, and do and think of little else from morning till night.'

Could she possibly manage a large farm? Appleton stretched across nearly 900 acres, with more than 1200 head of livestock (cattle, horses, sheep and pigs), and a large staff of labourers, both men and boys, to attend them. She says, 'It seemed a desperate attempt for a woman, and every possible argument was brought to bear against it, from the usual army of croakers to the opinion of disinterested friends…'

One of those 'disinterested friends' was the famous writer and churchman Charles Kingsley.

Charles Kingsley, 1819-1875

Born in Devon, Charles Kingsley studied at Cambridge and in 1842 became curate and later rector of Eversley, Hampshire, a post he retained until he died. He was a strong supporter of Chartism (an early labour movement) and a prolific writer. Probably his best known book is *The Water Babies,* which appeared in 1863 and, having as its hero a boy chimney-sweep, helped to outlaw the use of children for cleaning chimneys.

In 1860 he was appointed Regius Professor of History at Cambridge and soon found himself tutor to the Queen's oldest son. Though the professor declared himself nervous of the responsibility of educating the heir to the throne, nevertheless he found Bertie attentive and intelligent, 'a jolly boy', and grew very fond of him. After Kingsley died, his eldest daughter wrote to the Prince: 'Next to his own children I can truly say there was no human being my father loved as he did you.'

The affection was evidently mutual: Kingsley was frequently to be seen among the favoured house guests at Sandringham and at such times he often 'sang for his supper' by acting as guest preacher for Sunday service in the little church. He enjoyed wandering round the estate and often called on Louise Cresswell at Appleton, who recalls that he was fascinated by the historical resonances of the area.

This charming, cultured and gentle man, hearing that Louise was thinking of trying to keep the farm and manage it by herself, 'came down with his usual impetuosity to beg me not to think of such a thing'. Some of his own relatives had exhausted all their fortune on farming and Kingsley was terrified the same might happen to Louise. 'I can see him now, dressed like a scarecrow, stammering more than ever from nervousness, using no hackneyed words of consolation, but so sorry for me, and hardly able to say anything but "my d-dear lady, p-pray don't, you'll r-ruin yourself," and rushing away, hardly waiting to say goodbye, as if he could not stand it longer.' Perhaps she should have heeded his concern.

Most of her relatives and society friends also expressed their dismay at her intentions, but the farming community, including Farmer Groom, encouraged her to carry on. She attributes this to Gerard's influence: 'My husband had been so popular throughout the countryside, that everyone seemed willing to help me for his sake...' A great deal of expense had gone into improving the farm in those first three years and, as Mr Groom remarked, if she, with a private income and only one child to support, could not manage, then who could? Earlier that year, when Gerard had realised how seriously ill he was, he had asked Groom to watch over his wife and boy. She muses that if, as some believe, 'the dying are gifted with a peculiar foresight as to who will befriend those who are their last thoughts on earth, I can answer for the fidelity with which this trust was fulfilled'.

John Groom's obituary states that he was 'appointed to manage' Appleton Farm after Gerard Cresswell's death and, though I have found no other evidence to confirm this, it seems highly probable that he did have some official overseeing status, whatever Louise might imply to the contrary. She preferred to believe that she herself was officially in charge. Either way, with the ever-loyal Mr Groom guaranteeing his personal supervision, the last objections were laid to rest and, by the end of the year, Louise was, as she says, 'experimentally installed in the new position of lady-farmer *[sic]*'.

'Lady Farmer'… it was a sobriquet she cherished and encouraged, though she was not the only woman tackling work which might have been considered more a man's prerogative. Gerard's own grandmother, Elizabeth Fry, had worked hard to improve prison conditions; and Elizabeth Garrett Anderson became Britain's first female physician. Beside these more famous upper-class examples, not far from Appleton a young 'butcheress' followed her father's trade in Hunstanton, while Shouldham widow Elizabeth Gately carried on a blacksmith's business. Many women kept shops. Less common were female tin platers, watchmakers, newsagents, licensees, a woman plumber and glazier in Terrington St Clements, and a woman carrier who conveyed goods to Lynn. In the parish of Flitcham-with-Appleton itself, two female farmers – Keziah Griggs and Mary Burrell – had both taken over their farms after being widowed. However, none of these other local examples could claim the rank of 'lady'. That was what made all the difference as far as Louise was concerned – the others were working *women,* while she was that much rarer breed, a working *lady*.

A new steward for Appleton

Immediately after Gerard died, farm bailiff Tom Rumble slipped with pride into his new role of steward for his 'Missus'. He took the job seriously, frequently coming to the house for orders, to see if there was any extra task he might do, or to invite Louise to come and make sure all was as she wished it to be. However, other interested parties did not consider Rumble up to the task; in their opinion Louise needed more professional help on the farm.

These shadowy 'others' who wielded authority over her affairs (but whom she never names) were, firstly, her co-trustees under Gerard's will, particularly Somerville Arthur Gurney, director of the bank in Lynn and second cousin to the Cresswell brothers. Since the other named trustee, Gerard's youngest brother, Lieutenant Ossie Cresswell, was in India with his regiment at this period, Somerville Gurney may have called on his close friend and banking colleague, Frank Cresswell, to assist in giving advice (though Frank is never named in any of the documents concerning Appleton). Whatever she may imply in her book, Louise certainly did not make her decisions alone. Day by day she was on the spot at Appleton, taking an active part in overseeing the work in close liaison with Mr Groom, but always in the background were her husband's relatives, inextricably entwined with the bank that held her money, not to mention the men who kept close watch on behalf of her royal landlord.

These other forces decreed that poor old Tom Rumble must be denied a promotion to steward. Louise hardly knew how to break the news, but Rumble took it well and said he'd go on just the same and do the best he could. When the new man was appointed, less than two months after Gerard's death, Rumble willingly showed him about the place and tried to ensure a smooth changeover.

The new steward's name was James Thomas Mingay. Born in Thornham, he was about forty when he came to Appleton. Before that he had farmed in Suffolk, with his wife, children and his mother-in-law, Sophie Dodman, also a native of Thornham and probably related to Martin Dodman, the farmer, who leased part of his land from Helen and Edith Hogge and another part from Hunstanton's squire, Hamon le Strange. Since 1855 the Mingay family had moved three times, from Shepreth in Cambridgeshire to Newmarket in Suffolk, on to Thorrington in Suffolk, and now, in December 1865, they moved for a fourth time in ten years, to Appleton in Norfolk.

Louise refers to the man as 'Dinger' (changing the name to protect the guilty, presumably). He came with impressive references that practically crowned him with a halo – such glowing reports, in fact, that she did wonder how so many employers in so few years could have borne to part with such a treasure. But the man had a silver tongue, swiftly answering all her queries. Perhaps he took the newly-widowed Mrs Cresswell for a vulnerable, naïve woman, alone and easily bamboozled. She ruefully confesses to 'being a little apt to be taken in by plausible roguery well done', but she also desperately needed someone to take on the everyday management of the men and the fieldwork.

With his wife and four small children, Jim Mingay moved into a house at Appleton that December. All went well, the winter sowing, the new year's ploughing, the lambing... Even eagle-eyed Mr Groom seemed satisfied, and so Louise relaxed, believing her farm to be in good hands.

A difficult year

Bleak as 1865 had turned out to be, the following year proved even more difficult for Louise. Gerard's will, brought to probate in January 1866, offered little financial help. A few weeks later came sad news from Dover, where brother Charles's second son, Frederick Henry, was born on 26 February only to die three days later. Family stories say he was dropped by his nurse but, whatever the truth, it was a sorrow with which Louise could empathize.

As the hunting season ended and the spring began, the Prince's men concentrated on preserving a new crop of eggs, nestlings and leverets. The newly-appointed head gamekeeper, one Goss Overton, was a particularly officious, prickly brute of a man: at a sports day held between Sandringham estate workers and employees of Messrs Goggs & Co., the building firm working on the big house, the head gamekeeper beat all comers at putting a 24lb cannon ball.[25] This tough character, says Louise, 'took possession of the place in military style, and parcelled out my farm like policemen's beats. It was game, game, nothing but game…'.

Encouraged by Overton's bullying style, his under-keepers vied with one another as to who could raise the most game; the lazy ones would cover themselves by laying the blame for their own neglect on something the farmers had done. They could send in the most lying and libellous reports and have them believed. Being frequently a victim of these calumnies, Louise found one of the Prince's faults to be 'the fatal habit of listening to tales from any quarter, without taking the trouble to inquire into the truth of them, which I attribute to his not having passed through the wholesome discipline of a public school, where boys contract a horror of sneaks and sneaking…'

One of Louise's first letters to the newly-appointed royal land agent, Edmund Beck, is dated 19 March 1866.[26] Driven to distraction by worries and the shock of sudden widowhood, she told the agent that she was very sorry to be compelled to write, she had delayed doing so as long as possible, but 'the very large amount of hares upon the farm will cause such serious injury before harvest I am anxious to know if you will do anything to prevent it. With the understanding that only winged game was to be preserved at Appleton, we have, as you know, spent some thousands in bringing the land into order and had hoped this year (for the first time) to receive some return for the outlay, which cannot be the case if the hares remain any longer…'

A change of name – Hogge to Archdale
While Louise agonized over the damage caused by royal hares, her three surviving brothers changed their surname from Hogge to Archdale. George (now 48), Frederick (38), and Charles (33) each took out a separate deed poll to establish his legal right to make the change.

---

[25] *Lynn Advertiser*, 28 September 1867
[26] Royal Archive LAW/SHM/12/10/72A

Frederick's document, dated 5 March 1866, certifies that he claims the right to use the name Archdale by virtue of being descended, through the female line, from John Archdale Esq., of High Wycombe, a former owner of the Thornham Estate *(see Appendix C)*. The deed names Frederick as a banker (partner in Hogge & Lindsell) in Biggleswade, Bedfordshire; in Baldock and Hitchin, Hertfordshire; and in St Neots, Cambridgeshire; also as a merchant in Shefford. Under his guidance these family businesses were flourishing, which was just as well since his siblings and their Lindsell cousins derived at least part of their income from legacies invested in the family concerns.

The year moved on. Lambs fattened, cattle were herded down to graze on the marshes, the haysel was brought in, the corn ripened and the mangold wurzels grew fat under their green tops. Thousands of hares grew fat, too, eating the young corn and nibbling the fresh sprouting tops. The previous year, Gerard had worried himself to death over it; now Louise herself endured sleepless nights and restless days, joining her fellow tenants in complaints about prowling gamekeepers and marauding 'kangaroos'. How she hated them! She writes:

[The] "kangaroos" might have hopped and jumped to all eternity if they had not jammed down the crops in the process, and feasted themselves on the way, breakfasting upon the choicest swedes, cutting off the mangolds at a certain stage when the saccharine matter begins to form in the joints (for they are the daintiest brutes alive), devouring any delicacy that had been reserved for the lambs, gnawing the sainfoin, a very expensive plant, down to the ground... and biting off the ears of wheat... They were not quite so partial to barley and oats, making a raid on them now and then for a change, and on this principle would bark the young fruit and rose trees, decimate the vegetables, and leave not a crocus or any of the carnation tribe alone. Rabbits are not so bad in one way, for they eat straight on, clearing everything off as they go, and more easy to fence against, whilst the "kangaroos" frolic all over the place, turning up in every direction. When I rode or drove across the fields, they would start up at my pony's feet, gathering like a snowball, and run along before me like a little pack of hounds, while some of the most "owdacious" ones would stand upright on their hind legs with an air of irritating self-possession as if they knew they were Royal property and dared me to touch them... Sometimes from curiosity to see the number there, I would give a "view haloo!" at the corner of a wheat field, when up would jump a swarm of little brown ears in the corn, like a regiment of soldiers in ambush... I did not think I could have lived to hate any species of the animal creation so much...

I would have put down the hares quickly enough if any one in this Prince-ridden county could have been found to help me...[27] [I tried] every invention that could be thought of – tarring the runs, stuffing up the gaps with bundles of gorse, and one year I saved the mangold crop by cutting old canvas bags in strips, sewing them together and staking them round the field, which looked as if I had been taking in a gigantic wash for the county of Norfolk, and gave great offence at Sandringham, any attempt at self-protection being always resented.[28]

Though tenant farmers muttered together about the damage to their crops, what could they do about it, especially when their landlord happened to be the heir to the throne? Only a fool would argue out loud a fool such as Louise. She continued to complain about the massive numbers of hares; she complained about the extra costs accrued in digging out the foundations of the old house, about clearing away broken walls, and carting away builders' rubble; she had to make new pathways and bring in gravel for them, lay out gardens, plant new shrubs and fruit trees... She could not afford to do this additional work all at once; she and her late husband had already sunk too much of their precious capital into making immediate improvements to the sadly-neglected farm they had taken over. In his turn the Prince complained about the untidy state of Appleton, which created a bad impression when he brought his friends round to view his splendid new estate. As a consequence, says Louise, 'I lived in a sort of chronic disgrace...'

It all came down to 'vulgar money', in the end: 'had I had enough and to spare, how different my lot would have been; I could have afforded the game and not offended the Prince, and tackled the land agent, and remained in my house, and so on like the "House that Jack built".' This is the first time she alludes to

---

[27] Cresswell, *Eighteen Years...* p65-6
[28] Cresswell, *Eighteen Years...* p95-6

land agent Edmund Beck in her narrative. If she hated the Prince's hares above all, Beck was soon to become second on her list of *bêtes noirs*.

'Dinger' shows his true colours

For a few months, Appleton's new farm steward, Jim Mingay, lived up to his references, giving every impression of being the ideal man for the job. However, once Louise and Farmer Groom relaxed their close vigil, Mingay began to take advantage. Before long he was turning up late for work, or staying too long at market, or taking time off for yet another funeral – Louise began to wonder how many grandmothers one man could have. She made enquiries, discovering her steward to be frequenting 'an attractive "skittles and beer" establishment in the market town'. (The Wheatsheaf Inn, or 'Fiddaman's Hotel', on Norfolk Street in Lynn, was a popular ale-house and eatery near the cattle market, offering attractions such as gaming and pigeon-shooting.)

Louise tells us that she didn't act at once because she was confined indoors, 'recovering from a short illness'. Rising at last from her sick bed, she discovered the farm in such a state that she immediately sent for Mr Groom, who took a tour of the farm with both the steward and the lady farmer in train. What he found made him furious with both of them – Mingay for dereliction of duty and Louise for allowing it to get so bad without alerting him. She pleaded ignorance; it had all happened while she was 'sick and sorry' (like a scolded child, she often resorted to claims of ill-health whenever things went wrong). Groom's annoyance reached a climax when they came to a field of badly neglected turnips, thick with weeds. He ordered Mingay to leave the farm – at once, this very hour! – but, with his usual skill, Mingay turned on the tears, reminded them he had a wife and children to support, begged for proper notice… Groom relented, saying the man could stay until the end of the quarter, on condition that he behaved himself properly.

The delay (mid-July to October) gave the recalcitrant 'Dinger' ample time to build up a fine head of resentment. Just before harvest (the most crucial time of the farming year), he demanded better terms, threatening to quit at once unless allowed his own way. But he underestimated his lady employer: 'To his astonishment, I took him at his word, telling him that he not only might, but should go, and it was truly a relief to see him and his tiresome wife and children off the premises.'

However, Mingay paid her out for this summary dismissal by organizing a rebellion among a group of temporary harvest workers, who confronted their lady employer and refused to lift a scythe without the promise of a massive rise in pay. She told the rebels they could leave and she saw them off despite their sudden second thoughts, which occurred when they realized she meant what she said, for 'farm hands are as easily led away as a pack of children, only to repent of their folly afterwards...' When they had departed, she drove into Lynn to hire whomever she could find at that late stage to fill their places. A few men still hung about the market square and, having 'given them the shilling' (as a pledge of good faith) she hurriedly returned to the farm to organize bed and board for them in a barn. Inevitably, they were the dregs of the workforce – one villainous-looking man was wanted by the police, who arrested him and marched him off a day or two afterwards. Louise locked the rest up at night and let them out early, acting as her own steward, with her ploughman in the role of foreman – he was a Methodist preacher, his sober influence proving highly effective.

Louise hardly stopped during those weeks, beginning at dawn and often working until starlight. When the men had their 'levenses and fourses (meal breaks), she had other jobs to be seeing to – checking the livestock, overseeing the marsh farm, keeping an eye on the lambs... On Sundays, in church for morning service, she could hardly keep her eyes open. Her only recreation was an occasional nursery tea with her infant son in the nut walk. 'Yet when the last stack was topped up and it was time for the party to disperse, I was both sorry and relieved; we parted the best of friends in a chorus of harvest cheers, with a few extra ones for me and the child, and we hoped we should all meet again one day, which we never did.'

Only later did she reflect on what a risk she had been running, alone in lonely places with a gang of rough men, of whom she knew nothing, and 'enough valuables in the house to make it worth while to rob or murder me. On pay nights I used to drive home with a large sum of money from the Bank, past the woods and heaths; but no one meddled with me, I was neither robbed nor murdered.' This was, however, not the last time she faced physical danger. A few years later she had cause to sleep with a revolver under her pillow.

The miscreant Mingay had not yet finished with Louise. Having taken legal advice, he sued her for the balance of wages which he alleged to be due to him from 6 August, the day she dismissed him, to the end of the quarter at Michaelmas. First came a letter demanding payment of the wages; then a threat to take her to court. Louise refused to be bullied – she had in the meantime uncovered 'some still greater delinquencies... which would have fully entitled me to prosecute *him*'.

When the actual summons arrived, she called in her solicitor, Mr T. G. Archer, of Archer and Archer, King's Lynn, who worriedly informed her that Mingay had already hired the services of the best local lawyer. Mr Archer expressed dismay at her intention of appearing in person – it would be an unpleasant experience for a lady such as herself, and suppose she lost? But she didn't believe she would lose; she had no intention of paying money she didn't owe, and as for being a lady... 'I had carved out my own queer line of life and must take things as they came.' She instructed her solicitor to brief a barrister on her behalf and she left the office 'quite prepared to appear as defendant in the great case of Dinger versus the Lady Farmer'.

Mingay v Cresswell

The case was to be heard at the Norfolk County Court, a session held at King's Lynn on Friday, 23 November 1866, but there being too much other business, proceedings in Louise's case opened so late in the day that the judge ordered a postponement until the next sitting. Two weeks later, on Friday, 7 December, the protagonists gathered once again.

Louise says: 'The eventful day arrived and we were ushered into Court, my co-executor and brother-in-law as escort and body-guard, the lawyer, counsel and witnesses in professional attendance, and a tolerable array of spectators, it being rather a *cause célèbre* in a small way.'

The Lady Farmer of Sandringham (related by either blood or marriage to local notables the Hogges, the Cresswells, the Gurneys, the Frys, the Bagges, and the le Stranges) was already a well-known figure in her own small corner of the world. Her escorting 'co-executor and brother-in-law' were presumably that inseparable pair, Somerville Gurney and Frank Cresswell. (Heaven only knows what her relatives made of this all-too-public stand she was taking: 'There goes Louise, making a spectacle of herself again…')

The case of J. T. Mingay, farming steward, against Mrs L. M. Cresswell, of 'Appleton Hall', was an action brought to recover £14/4s/2d [about £14.21p], the balance of wages alleged to be due, heard before Judge Thomas Jacob Birch, with Mr Wilkin appearing for the plaintiff and Mr J. S. Ford (instructed by Mr T. G. Archer) for the defence. Among the witnesses for the defence, as named in the newspaper account of the trial, were Miss Fanny Hogge and Mr John Groom. In her own account, Louise mentions only the presence of 'Farmer Broome'; her supportive sister Fanny, as usual, she omits from her record.

The facts as stated in court, concerning the original altercation over the turnip field, agree in principle if not in detail with Louise's account. Mr Groom did not mention Louise's illness but said that she had called him in when he returned home after three weeks' holiday. Mingay, being confronted with his neglect, had consented to leave at once, leaving it up to Louise to decide about the wages due to him. But later the steward had begged Mr Groom for leniency, so that the farmer had persuaded Mrs Cresswell to allow the man to stay until Michaelmas and hopefully 'to redeem his character'.

Recounting Groom's evidence, Louise recalls how 'little Mr Broome stepped into the box, small in stature, but game to the core… Perhaps he treated the opposing counsel a little too much as a personal enemy…' The worthy yeoman destroyed the gravity of one important question by asking the lawyer 'to be so good as not to use them fine words' which he could not understand, but to use plain English. All in all, good old Farmer Groom proved an excellent witness for the defence.

Louise herself then entered the witness box, to be examined about the events and then closely questioned about statistics and duties on the farm. 'Fortunately my lonely evenings had been spent in studying the intricacies of my profession and keeping accounts...'

The main differences, between the incident as told in her book and the case as reported in the *Lynn Advertiser,* concern the arguments on 6 August, just before harvest, when Louise dismissed Mingay and had him, and his family, thrown off the farm. In her account, she says that he tried to blackmail her and sabotage the harvest; however, in court Mingay claimed that all he had done was grumble that Mrs Cresswell often consulted the labourers instead of himself; while she, in her evidence, said he had complained of her driving about the farm and keeping a close eye on him. She added, says the paper, that '[Mingay] said he would throw up his place at once, which, after consulting with her sister, she accepted, and refused to pay him any further wages.' Later, Miss Fanny Hogge deposed as to the truth of this account, she having witnessed the altercation between Louise and Mingay that day.

Louise recounts the hilarious witness given by her 28-year-old shepherd, Zachariah Mitchell, who, responding to demands that he should reveal his knowledge of the steward's where-abouts on a particular occasion, kept saying, quite truthfully, that he didn't know. Prosecuting counsel Mr Wilkin badgered him until the shepherd began to stammer, 'Well, sir...' At which the lawyer pounced: Aha! Thought so! You do know! 'Well, sir...' obliged Mitchell, 'he were *somewhere.*' Which caused laughter in court and the eventual breakdown of the plaintiff's case.

Mingay's neglect was proven, his absences from duty all retold and confirmed, together with other malfeasance, such as pilfering produce and selling meat to local butcher John Howard without accounting for it (the butcher gave evidence for Louise). Mingay had never had much hope of winning his case. No witnesses stood up to support his version of the facts, or to vouch for his character. The news report concludes: 'His Honor was about to give judgement for the defendant when Mr Wilkin said he would elect to be non-suited, which was done with costs.'

Louise had won the day. She comments, 'This really was the last of Dinger, so far as I was concerned, and I believe he afterwards emigrated to some more distant settlement, where he perhaps turned over a new leaf, and for ought I know may be a shining light in some new state of society unto this day.'

James T. Mingay emigrated to Ontario, Canada, and by the turn of the century his two sons were living in Michigan, USA.

The new rector

Early that year, residents of Sandringham estate had been saddened by the death of Reverend George Browne Moxon, rector of the parish for thirty-eight years and ten months (as someone with a gift for exactness recorded in the register of burials). He was buried on 3 February 1866. During the interregnum, other priests stood in at the pretty little church, the duty often falling to Revd Schofield, vicar of West Newton.

West Newton church, on the south side of Sandringham Park, was in a poor state: the north aisle had been demolished in 1805, the remaining archways walled over, and some of the windows were missing. However, thanks to the Prince of Wales, new buildings were rising to accommodate estate workers in West Newton and by 1881 major restoration work on the church would be completed.

Although West Newton is the nearest church to Appleton, Louise did not attend service there. Instead she regularly drove the pleasant couple of miles down the hill, through West Newton hamlet and across the royal park to the small church of St Mary Magdalene, standing on its little knoll some third of a mile from the big house. The church had been restored, in 1855, by Lady Harriett Spencer Cowper, in memory of her infant daughter.

To the white-gabled rectory just beyond Sandringham church, that summer, came the new rector, a gentle, caring man who was to become a great source of strength and support to the widowed Louise.

Revd William Lake Onslow (1820-1877)

Born on 10 May 1820, at Bishop Wearmouth (Sunderland, County Durham), William Lake Onslow came from a long line of Royal Naval officers. His grandfather was Vice-Admiral Sir Richard Onslow, his father Captain John James Onslow. His three younger brothers also joined the service but, tragically, all died at sea in early manhood.

Lake Onslow attended Yarmouth grammar school before going up to Emmanuel College, Cambridge, earning his BA in 1842 and his MA in 1845. He twice rowed at bow oar when Cambridge beat Oxford in the early years of the famous University Boat Race. Ordained at Norwich in 1843, he became curate of Witton and Brundall parish, a few miles east of Norwich. He and his mother Lavinia, with sisters Anne (b1822) and Agnes (b1840), resided in the village of Blofield (Anne married Revd J. W. Clapcott in 1847; Agnes remained single).

In January 1846 he became a Royal Naval Chaplain and served on various ships from the Americas to China, from the Baltic to the Cape. In April 1848 he was appointed to the flagship *Hastings*, and was a member of *Racoon*'s company in 1863 when he subscribed to the Norwich Gates wedding present fund. His association with the royal family began when in 1858, aboard HMS *Euryalus*, he acted as Special Naval Instructor to 14-year-old Prince Alfred (Queen Victoria's second son, later Duke of Edinburgh).

In June 1851, Revd Onslow was elected a Fellow of the Royal Astronomical Society (FRAS), a role he enjoyed for eighteen years. He was also, like the Prince of Wales, a keen Freemason and in the course of his life he acted as Chaplain of the Lynn Lodge, and Grand Chaplain of both Norfolk and all England.

The living at Sandringham-cum-Babingley, awarded to Onslow in July 1866, brought with it the honour of becoming 'private chaplain in ordinary' to the Prince and Princess of Wales. He was with them aboard *Ariadne* during their trip to Egypt and Greece in 1868.

He remained an officer of the Royal Navy until 1869, when he was placed on the retired list.

A lifelong bachelor, Onslow was forty-six, a decade older than Louise Cresswell, when, with his much-younger sister Agnes, then twenty-six, and their mother Lavinia, a lady in her mid-sixties, he moved into the Sandringham rectory, only two minutes' walk from the church. Louise remembers him as being a perfect gentleman of the old school, unselfish, kind-hearted and unaffected, with an endearing Pickwick-like knack of tumbling into trouble. But she felt he was always more sailor than parson, finding it hard to swap a life of cheerful naval society and world cruising for a quiet country parish and the courtly duties expected of him there.

All three of the Onslows would become great friends and allies for Louise through the trials which lay ahead.

Taking a stand

Louise's actions during the year following her husband's death demonstrate the depth of her grief and despair. A turmoil of emotions drove her to make ever more headstrong decisions, brushing aside the reasoned advice offered by her own and her husband's families. She had no time for the cautious, measured approach; her relatives' well-meant murmurings served only to infuriate her further. Her preferred adviser was good old Farmer Groom, whom, with a touch of condescension, she often dubs 'little Mr Broome'. He was, of course, only a yeoman. Still, low-born as he might be, she considered him her best, if not her only, true friend. That is, he was the only one who, more often than not, told her exactly what she wished to hear.

Kind-hearted, chivalrous Mr Groom hardly dared do otherwise; he had promised her husband that he would take care of her and that he did, as best he could. But all the evidence suggests that he was in thrall to her, in fear of her temper and in awe of her strong personality. Throughout their association, she manipulated him mercilessly.

As we have seen, her main grievance, woven throughout her story, stemmed from her firm conviction that, when Gerard took on the tenancy of Appleton Farm, definite promises had been made that no damages should be done by ground game. But customarily, all over England, landowners and tenants would agree some mutually satisfactory compromise regarding fair compensation for damages. Landlords, inevitably, protested at the sums involved and, with equal predictability, tenants complained of landlords' meanness; but as a rule no special written agreement was required. All the farmer had to do was submit a claim and it would be considered on its merits.

Louise herself implies as much when she says that she ventured 'in the most delicate terms' to request that her position could be established on 'a businesslike footing' rather than on the current tenuous 'gentlemen's agreement'. This request was denied with righteous indignation – was she doubting the Prince's integrity?! 'They' warned her darkly that she would be sorry if she attempted to 'go upon the commercial system'.

Who exactly was it who gave her such a dusty answer?

National newspapers of the time loyally proclaimed that the Prince of Wales himself managed his Sandringham estate, hearing and dealing with all complaints personally. His tenants could have argued: the Prince was charming enough on social occasions, having the felicitous knack of remembering one's name and small details of one's life (or a courtier at his elbow to murmur reminders), which in itself was enough to make one feel good; but Louise, in all her eighteen years at Appleton, never once heard of HRH actually *listening* to any of his tenants, not on serious business matters. True, he heard every last bit of tittle-tattle, and usually got it twisted, believing the first version he heard, but 'he was quite unapproachable on estate matters; and as "manners are manners", I could not when invited to his house, or when the Royalties came to Appleton, intrude subjects upon him that he did not choose to hear'.

Next in line of command came the elderly General Knollys, Comptroller of the Prince of Wales' Household, who lived at the magnificent newly-built Park House at Sandringham. Though nominally in charge of estate business, Knollys was burdened with many other duties, which frequently called him away from Sandringham. In practice, therefore, everyday management devolved on the Prince's more local subordinates, chief amongst whom came the land agent.

In her pamphlet *Norfolk and the Squires, Clergy, Farmers and Labourers, etc,* published in 1875 (while she was still ensconced at Appleton and obliged to be diplomatic), Louise declares that a landlord's agent is 'often another source of discomfort', though she adds, 'I am peculiarly fortunate in that respect'. However, five years later, in an article written as she was leaving the farm, she dipped her pen in acid to describe the type of agent who demanded more deference than the landlord himself *(see Chapter Eight)*. Truth was, she thoroughly despised and detested Edmund Beck. She would never have dreamed of turning to him for help.

She felt embattled. Gerard's death had left her responsible for the farm, as trustee in her son's name, and she had to make a success of it. But the healthy bank balance with which they had started out – and which had so impressed the Prince's lawyer – was beginning to follow her husband into a rapid decline. Her expenses continued to mount; her income proved ever more inadequate. That summer of 1866, as her problems escalated even further because of Mingay's poor management, with the harvest in danger, her feelings in a turmoil of grief and worry, and with her energy depleted by long hours of work, she must have been at her wits' end. And still the Prince's hares continued to breed by the hundred and run about trampling everything down and feasting with their voracious families on her most valuable crops. Those 'blasted kangaroos' were ruining her livelihood.

She had had enough! His Royal Highness must be made to pay for the decimation! But to whom could she turn for help? How could she make them understand the gravity of the matter?

The answer occurred to her when, in the midst of her tussles with her wayward steward, she received notification of the date of the August rent audit. Of course! What could be better? The rent audit would provide the ideal opportunity to confront both the land agent and the Prince's lawyer. She would use that day to make a firm stand for justice.[29]

Rent Audits
Sandringham rents fell due half-yearly, on 11 April and 11 October. Although the annual amount was fixed by the terms of the lease, the precise total due each six months depended on factors such as taxes, rates, and claims for damages. The 'audit' was a meeting when parties

---

[29] In her book Louise gives the impression that the court case and her stand at the rent audit took place in separate years, but historical records prove that it all took place in the same few months of 1866

involved might argue the case and agree a figure, such meetings taking place in February or March (for the period ending the previous Michaelmas, which payment came due on 11 April) and in August or September (for the period ended around Lady Day, 25 March, due on 11 October).

For Sandringham tenants, the formal audit meeting was preceded by a 'rent dinner' at which the Prince's London lawyer, Mr White, and the local land agent, Mr Beck, played host at the Prince's expense. Next day, suitably wined and dined, each tenant, or his proxy, was granted a private interview with the lawyer and agent, at which the due rent for the six months last ended would be agreed. These meetings took place at the Duke's Head Hotel, on the Tuesday Market Place in Lynn.

As a convention of the times, only men attended business meetings. After Gerard Cresswell died, Farmer Groom usually represented Louise, both at the Tenants' Dinner and at the audit – all that tedious business of haggling over 'vulgar money'. But in that bleak summer of 1866, driven by grief and desperation, she decided to attend the audit meeting in person to state her case. If she had consulted her friend the reverend professor Charles Kingsley, he might have advised her in the words of his poem: *'Be good, sweet maid, and let who will be clever...'* But Louise was far from being a passive 'sweet maid'.

Early on the August day appointed for the meeting, she went into her fields and armed herself with what she felt to be a rather telling stage-prop, 'a specimen bouquet of mangold tops that the hares had bitten off'. Thus equipped, she drove her trap into Lynn to meet with the three men who had agreed to act as escort and moral support. Mr Groom was one of them, the others she refers to as 'a brother-in-law and co-executor' and she later mentions 'dear old F –' [Frank Cresswell]; so we infer that the third gentleman involved was, yet again, Somerville Arthur Gurney.

When she appeared wielding her bouquet of ruined mangold tops, her husband's kinsmen, as she says, 'looked quite alarmed and wanted me to leave it behind; and it was "Come, Louise, you *can't* go with that thing; it looks exactly like a bludgeon. I declare if you do I won't go; you'd much better not, it will only make a row!" and other masculine arguments, for the men always think the women are going to make a disturbance and never give them credit for conducting things in a sensible fashion.'

She, however, had no intention of parting with her prize exhibit, or of letting the two gentlemen bankers escape when they had promised to accompany her to the meeting. And dear old Farmer Groom, regarding the mangold tops wryly, declared them, 'Not a bad idea.' So eventually Louise prevailed over the two more cautious men and 'succeeded in marching them off, a couple of victims, down the streets...' Out from the bank they went, Louise striding out with her crinoline swinging, bunch of wilting turnip tops clutched in one gloved hand, with Mr Groom trotting to keep up, while behind them trudged her extremely uncomfortable relatives-by-marriage, heads hanging, hoping no one would see them being obliged to follow, across King's Staithe beneath the squawk of seagulls, and over the bridge that spanned the smelly Purfleet (which had recently been partially filled in because of its unhealthy, noisome character, but riverward still gave harbour to several tall-masted ships), past the old Custom House and all the way down the broad cobbled King Street, with its fine houses and carriage yards (the street where Frank Cresswell had his home, opposite the house where Louise's older sister Fanny lived), on past the old medieval theatre of St George's Gildhall (doomed for the time to be a warehouse), past the popular Globe Hotel on the corner of Ferry Street, emerging on to the Tuesday Market Place in sight of Aunt Margaret Hogge's fine mansion, and thence across to the tall and imposing Duke's Head Hotel, where the headstrong and irrepressible Lady Farmer barged in yet again where angels might have hovered having second thoughts.

All four of them were ushered into the presence of the Prince's London lawyer (Arnold W. White, who had taken over after the death of his father Edward in 1865). This younger, sharper man bowed low, all politeness and 'compliments to the lady-farmer', though Louise suspected claws might be hidden not far beneath his smooth exterior. As for the land agent, Edmund Beck, he 'looked frightened and confused and fussed about getting us chairs; he always was fussing about and offering to do something for you, which took me in for years…'

She adds: 'Dear old F— planted himself well behind me and looked prepared for the worst.' Presumably the genial and mild-mannered Frank Cresswell expected his wilful sister-in-law to do something outrageous, but, in the event, as she recalls it, she merely laid her 'bludgeon' on the table and said she didn't know where the rent was to come from, 'for my wheat is cut to pieces and here is a specimen of my mangold crop'.

After what she terms 'a long parleying and pros and cons', the lawyer agreed that damages – for that one half-year, Michaelmas 1865 to Lady Day 1866 – should be assessed and paid. Louise felt this to be a great step forward and she allowed herself to be persuaded to hand over a cheque for the rent. Frank Cresswell was so relieved that he started 'provokingly prompting' from behind that, 'It will be all right, Louise,' which the lawyer took as a signal to terminate the interview. He bowed his visitors out, with the 'obsequious land-agent opening the door for us and looking as if the door handle was his very best friend'.

We have only Louise's version of this meeting: it seems unlikely that she remained as calm and reasonable as she claims. It's clear that she held Frank Cresswell and Somerville Gurney to blame for persuading her to pay the rent at that meeting (in fact the cheque she handed over was for only part of the sum, not all), and for edging her out before things were properly agreed. She leaves the impression that the pair of them, cringing with embarrassment, couldn't wait to get out; but, considering her nature and the stress she was under, perhaps they had good cause to feel uncomfortable.

The incident was far from ended, however. More angry letters were soon in the post, some of them winging their way to the Houses of Parliament.

First Sandringham Flower Show

Even then, only three years after Bertie and Alix were married, their country estate had become a huge draw for tourists and celebrity-watchers. The first 'Horticultural Fete' at Sandringham, held on Thursday, 20 September 1866, drew two thousand people to pay the one shilling [5p] entrance fee. (Today the annual Flower Show, held in July, draws many more thousands to admire not only floral displays but crafts, fruit and vegetables, and to rub shoulders – almost! – with members of the royal family.)

The lonely Princess

In late autumn, while Louise was embroiled in the court case brought by her steward, the Princess of Wales and her two small sons, Eddy and Georgie, came to Sandringham alone. Bertie had gone, at his own insistence, to Russia – the first time he had visited that country – and, though Alix would have loved to be with him, being pregnant again she was not considered well enough to make the long trip. Her first two children had been born prematurely and were not robust, much to the Queen's disgust (she blamed Alix's Danish heritage for it); so this time the mother-to-be had orders to take good care of herself.

The gentle Princess had grown to love Sandringham. Its wide skies and wind-swept landscape reminded her of her Danish home, where she had been raised in unpretentious style. She was never entirely happy at the Queen's court, especially knowing how her mother-in-law despaired of her. And being slightly deaf (Alix suffered from osteosclerosis, a degenerative disease of the middle ear), too much company was increasingly a trial. At Sandringham she could relax and be herself, setting aside the pomp and ceremony. She and Bertie often broke all the rules of protocol, going out and about their country home like ordinary people, preferring *not* to be 'Your Royal Highness'd' at every turn – 'sir' and 'ma'am' were quite sufficient. As a result, the people of Sandringham loved their 'little missus' and would hear no wrong of her.

To celebrate her absent husband's twenty-fifth birthday, on 9 November 1866, the Princess made sure that the usual dinner was held for the labourers on the estate. One hundred and thirty of them sat down in the coach house to a meal of beef, mutton and plum pudding, supplied by the Globe Hotel in Lynn. That evening a celebratory bonfire blazed from Balaclava Heights to proclaim the birthday of Sandringham's royal master. It being a clear evening, the flames could be seen for miles around, certainly from the windows of the big house as the Princess and her invited house guests dressed for dinner. It was to be a small party; additional guests Revd William Lake Onslow and his sister Agnes drove over from the rectory.

That evening was a poignant occasion for Princess Alix. Not only were she and Bertie far apart on his birthday, but, a mere two days before, he had attended the wedding of her younger sister Dagmar and the Tsarevitch Alexander (later Tsar Alexander III) in the Winter Palace at St Petersburg. Alix herself, because of the child stirring in her womb, had been denied the pleasure of seeing her sister wed. As she played the gracious, smiling hostess at draughty Sandringham Hall, her mind roamed to the glittering palaces of far-away Russia. How was Dagmar enjoying her marriage? More importantly, what was Bertie doing? With whom was he spending his days? In whose arms was he dancing the evenings away?

The Princess knew all about the rumours; every time her husband went off without her – for an evening, a weekend, or a longer trip such as this one to Russia – gossip had him meeting and dallying with other women. Outwardly, the Princess simply refused to listen to such ugly talk. Inwardly, she felt as badly as any young woman would after only three years of marriage, the birth of two sons, and with another child on the way. But, for the lonely Princess Alexandra, the bad times had only just begun.

The Prince of Wales returned from his enjoyable visit to Russia in early December, after which, as had become their habit, he and Alix came back to Norfolk. They spent a few days at Oakley Park, near Diss, returned to London for Christmas with the Queen, and travelled again to Norfolk to celebrate New Year with the Earl of Leicester at Holkham, where they remained for the first ten days of 1867.

But the Princess was not well, complaining of pains in her hips and legs, which grew worse after the family returned to London. Immured at Marlborough House, she endured one of the worst health crises of her life.

Winter work

At Appleton, still trying to assuage her grief and loneliness, Louise applied herself to learning by experience. Following the fiasco with Jim Mingay, she hired a new steward, Robert Faircloth, to supervise the farm. Faircloth, in his mid-thirties and with a French wife of similar age, proved a much more trustworthy and efficient lieutenant than had his predecessor. Louise says he would even help in the crew-yards if she needed him, 'but [he] had quite enough to do on the land, whilst I preferred keeping the management of the stock entirely in my own hands'. She enjoyed working with the animals, though her insistence on personally overseeing every aspect of the work was not always appreciated by her labourers.

That winter in Norfolk was bitterly cold; heavy falls of snow blocked the roads and made travel over any distance near impossible. Work in Appleton's fields stopped for a while, but on a farm there is always something to be done – threshing in the barn; carting mangolds from their clamps to the feed store, and manure from crew-yards to dung heaps; cutting up turnips and chaff to feed the stock; and caring for the animals' health and welfare.

Louise writes knowledgably and entertainingly about the work. Young horses and bullocks, brought back from the marsh in October, were settled in warmer winter quarters. Sheep were kept folded, some destined for the butcher while others awaited their lambs. Much work went into doling out the correct feed, to fatten up the bullocks and sheep for market while making sure the gravid ewes ate a diet designed to bring their lambs on in good health. The first lambs might appear in January and from then on more and more arrived; caring for them all proved problematical. The shepherd usually lived in a hut on wheels close to the lambing pens, so that he was available day or night, and often he followed the old tradition (or superstition), going unwashed and unshaven until the last ewe and lamb were released from the pen as the spring came.

In Norfolk, the even older tradition of horse-mastery made the head teamsman a force on many farms; he knew ways of handling horses that seemed magical to the uninitiated.[30] At Appleton, the head horseman did not believe in keeping working horses in stables, even in winter: they were taken inside only for grooming and feeding, and through the winter they slept in a well-littered yard, 'which makes them less liable to chills than if brought straight out of a steaming stable', or so the Lady Farmer informs her readers. In summertime, the team horses enjoyed the freedom of a grassy field once work was done.

As for the beef cattle, the best bullocks would be selected early in the winter and kept in loose boxes with separate compartments, 'where they can't prod one another or fight over the food... There was a pathway between the boxes with bullocks on each side, and roofed overhead, a sort of Burlington Arcade, only much more interesting...' Here Louise and any company who had made it through the snow-drifts might stroll on a Sunday afternoon, to sit on the straw bales, kept warm by the presence of the bullocks.

Accessible from this covered avenue were outhouses, for storing turnip and chaff, meal and cattle cake, and the farm engines – small, steam-driven affairs, which throughout the winter added their chuntering and chugging to the farmyard melodies. 'We had fixed up some very useful machinery which turned two small mills for cake and meal on one side, and cut the straw and hay into chaff on the other, which fell through troughs into their respective compartments below...' She tried to keep up with advances in technology, though the machines often proved expensive and took a long time to earn their outlay.

Louise herself oversaw the distribution of feed and the care of the animals, but she believed she had the best yardman in the country. 'Trusty' Trundle, as she calls him, was able neither to read nor write, but 'he stayed with me till the last... feeding the home stock, milking, bringing up the calves, poultry, pigs and sundry other work, with the necessary assistance... he was so

---

[30] For much more on the fascinating subject of horse-mastery, which in Norfolk goes back at least to the Iron Age, see the 'oral history' books by George Ewart Evans (pub Faber and Faber)

kind and clever with the animals, did not mind what trouble he took, or how often he sat up at night...' (George Trundle lived in a cottage on Church Hill, West Newton, with his wife, one daughter, and seven sons.)

...and still more hares...

Inevitably, the hares remained a sore trial, ever increasing in number. And further trouble stemmed from those winter days when shooting took over, when all work on the farm had to stop and everything must accommodate the sporting enjoyment of the Prince and his guests. Louise's description of a shooting day at Sandringham has been used many times by other historians, but I make no apology for repeating it here as it gives a most vivid picture of what the shoots were like and how she felt about them:

A shooting day at Sandringham

For the benefit of the uninitiated, I will describe a Royal battue in the open. The fields were cleared for action early in the morning, and I had to stop the work and keep the men at home, field machinery, &c., at a standstill...

A complete silence having been secured for miles round, the day was ushered in by a procession of boys with blue and pink flags, like a Sunday School treat, a band of gamekeepers in green and gold, with the head man on horseback, an army of beaters in smocks and hats bound with royal red, a caravan for the reception of the game, and a tailing off of loafers to see the fun, for H.R.H. is very good-natured in allowing people to look on at his amusements, provided they do not interfere with them, and, if it could be conveniently managed, would perhaps have no objection to everybody's life being "skittles and beer" like his own.

At about 11 o'clock, the Royal party arrive in a string of waggonettes, and range themselves in a long line under fences or behind shelters put up for that purpose, each sportsman having loaders in attendance with an extra gun or guns... The boys and beaters are stationed in a semi-circle some distance off, and it is their place to beat up the birds and drive them to the fences, the waving flags frightening them from flying back. On they come in ever increasing numbers, until they burst in a cloud over the fence where the guns are concealed. This is the exciting moment, a terrific fusillade ensues, birds dropping down in all directions, wheeling about in confusion between the flags and the guns, the survivors gathering themselves together and escaping into the

145

fields beyond. The shooters then retire to another line of fencing, making themselves comfortable with campstools and cigars until the birds are driven up as before, and so on through the day, only leaving off for luncheon in a tent brought down from Sandringham, or on very cold days it is carried into the nearest house…

The hares are dispatched upon a still lower scale of slaughter, and they might as well have fired into a flock of sheep in a fold…

A wild open country was the proper place for these military manoeuvres instead of highly cultivated farms; for on the partridge-driving days, if the Royal party did not do any individual harm, the village boys made it a Carnival, enjoyed trampling down all before them, breaking fences and gates, and doing as much mischief as they could…

When riding round after the invaders had retired, seeing the general air of devastation left in their wake, the empty cartridges strewed about, and listening to the mournful chirruping of the poor little birds for their lost relatives, I felt it to be a "dree" [sad and sorry] accompaniment to my solitude.[31]

Louise was not alone in hating those days when practically every living thing that hopped, darted or flew became a target for well-bred and well-fed gentlemen exercising their marksmanship. Even Charles Kingsley, himself a keen huntsman who enjoyed a day's outing in pursuit of a fox, was shocked by the extent of the slaughter during one particular shoot through Wolferton woods. Revolted by the sight of a bloody carpet of dead and wounded hares, some of them still screaming in terror and pain, he rounded on the gathered band of 'sportsmen' (including the Prince of Wales) and castigated them for their profligacy and cruelty.[32] Chastened, they must have wished the ground would open and allow them a hole in which to hide the smoking guns they were still holding.

But nothing stopped the slaughter. The Prince loved shooting above all sports and on his country estate he indulged his passion to the full. Which meant that his gamekeepers raised more and still more hares…

---

[31] Cresswell, *Eighteen Years…* p68-72
[32] St Aubyn, Giles: *Edward VII: Prince and King* (Collins, 1979) p137

HOUSE IN RUTLAND GATE, KNIGHTSBRIDGE, LONDON
Rutland Gate was once home to Louise's father
(Chris Mackie, 2005)

BANK HOUSE, KING'S LYNN
Home of Francis and Rachel Cresswell
(Courtesy of Norfolk Library and Information Service)

THE NORWICH GATES, SANDRINGHAM
(Chris Mackie, 2007)

APPLETON HOUSE (date unknown)
(Author's collection)

SANDRINGHAM HOUSE AND LAKE
(Chris Mackie, 2007)

SANDRINGHAM CHURCH AND RECTORY
(Chris Mackie, 2007)

THE 'LOW ROAD' AS SEEN FROM APPLETON FARM
(Chris Mackie, 2007)

'A BIG SHOOT AT SANDRINGHAM HOUSE, 1871'
by Thomas Jones Barker
*(The Royal Collection © 2007,
Her Majesty Queen Elizabeth II)*

LOUISA MARY CRESSWELL (date unknown)
(Courtesy of Jan Lavelle)

CRESSWELL GRAVES, NORTH RUNCTON

Upright cross, centre, is monument of Louisa Mary Cresswell.
Front left is her infant daughter; front right her husband Gerard
Oswin Cresswell; similar grave behind, Frank J. Cresswell and
his wife; third low grave, Addison Cresswell
(Chris Mackie, 2004)

THE AUTHOR AT LOUISA CRESSWELL'S GRAVE,
NORTH RUNCTON
(Chris Mackie, 2007)

HOUSE IN ABILENE, TEXAS
Home of Gerard F.O. Cresswell from 1926
(Prof Fred Bailey, 2005; courtesy of Geri and Mack Jones)

CHAPTER SIX

Lady of letters

Correspondence from the first few months of 1867[33] gives a clear insight into Louise's volatile nature and illustrates the increasing animosity between her and the Prince's land agent, Edmund Beck. The letters mainly concern her continuing efforts to obtain proper redress for depredations caused by the detested hares, but, while Louise veers between threats and pitiful pleading, often laced with sarcasm, Beck tries to maintain a dignified distant politeness. It is hardly surprising that eventually he, and others, grew weary of trying to mollify the woman they began to refer to simply as 'the widow'.

After her dramatic appearance at the rent audit, assessment of the actual amount of damage done by game at Appleton was carried out by John Groom, aided by another of Louise's friends, her close neighbour John Hebgin. Mr Hebgin, who sounds a delightfully Pickwickian character, was an eccentric whom Louise calls the 'last of the Norfolk Farmers'. He drove around in a 'high vehicle of ancient build [wearing a] beaver hat with broad buckle and band, wide expanse of shirt front and frills, ponderous chain and seal and spotless top boots'. Having given up his own farm to his son he had moved onto a property adjoining Appleton and 'good-naturedly came across to help in all emergencies'. He and the loyal Farmer Groom estimated the damage done to crops, under-woods and so forth as amounting to a massive £575/16s/- (more than half the annual rent of £1,029). Louise forwarded this assessment to the agent on 22 January, reminding Mr Beck yet again of the agreement over game, made (she insists) when the farm was taken on, with the 'rent fixed accordingly'.

Receiving no immediate reply, she wrote again four days later: 'I cannot help writing to entreat you to do all you can with

---

[33] Letters in this section are from Royal Archive LAW/SHM/12/10/72/A-P

the Prince about those wretched hares, for although in your official capacity you are obliged to oppose me, I know you do not really approve of it. It is an <u>incessant</u> anxiety to me, not for the sake of the money, but I have had so much sorrow and to bring up the child in the home his father had planned is the only earthly pleasure left to me, but of course if his property is destroyed year after year I must be ruined and sold up, which (though people think I have courage for anything) would be more than I could live to bear. Pray explain the business part of the case fully to the Prince, and how we were induced to take the farm trusting to his good faith…'

Mr Beck was taking care to refer everything concerning Appleton to the farm's co-trustee, Somerville Gurney; perhaps the agent preferred doing business with a rational male banker rather than the emotional and unpredictable Lady Farmer. On 5 February, Louise wrote to inform him: 'Mr Gurney has given me your corrected papers of the rates and taxes that were forgotten at the audit and as you wish the rent to be paid before the compensation I beg to forward you a cheque for the same and shall be obliged by your sending me the amount of damage, estimated at £575/16s/- as soon as you possibly can.'

In the same post as this formal missive, another letter, strongly marked **Private,** says, '…Mr Gurney tells me you will see me if I like before you leave for London and I am sincerely obliged to you for the offer but as <u>fire</u> and <u>gunpowder</u> do not meet on easy terms, and the subject is such a peculiarly irritating one, I think we had better leave it alone. Please do not go on persuading the Prince not to send me the money, you know I have been a good tenant and even if I were not it is hard to have one's property destroyed and then be grudged the damages besides… is it likely myself and Mr Groom and Mr Hebgin would combine to extort money from HRH? However, I won't begin to quarrel again, so will end this. Yrs…'

In a PS she refers to someone who recently came to check on her story but found very few hares at Appleton. In mitigation, she adds, 'I too had remarked the mysterious disappearance of all the hares on Saturday… It is an old gamekeeper's trick and I quite expected it,' and she repeats her request for privacy: 'This letter <u>really is</u> private, please…' She was anxious not to have these petty, nit-picking matters brought to HRH's notice.

Beck replies the following day: 'I have received your official packet containing the cheque, and your second letter. I enclose a stamped receipt for the rent and beg to thank you. With regard to the claim, I shall see the General [Knollys] on Saturday and will write to Mr Gurney and yourself as early as I can. You may rely upon it that I will do all that I can for you as far as I consistently am able. But I must respectfully and firmly say that I cannot recommend the payment of £575/16s/-.'

In view of Louise's constant griping about hares, it is interesting to note from archive sources that, even before these letters were exchanged, the Prince of Wales had granted permission for all his tenants to engage in hare coursing, from 1 February to 5 March that year. Beck wrote to inform everyone of this concession, which meant they were free to engage in some sport themselves and kill down some of the dreaded hares. Louise, however, rather petulantly refused this privilege, whereupon Beck commented that her late husband had 'always looked upon the liberty of coursing as one of the greatest boons that could be granted to the tenantry and urged me to obtain it'. As always, seeing herself losing an argument, she backed down: there had been a misunderstanding, could she see him…

In her book, Louise frequently bemoans the Prince's lack of understanding, his obsession with shooting and his refusal to allow anything to interfere with his sport. Nowhere does she mention being granted permission to course after hares, or feeling free to ask outright for certain numbers to be killed off by the gamekeepers: 'will you order 2 or 300 hares to be killed directly on Appleton Farm,' she wrote on 11 March.

Meanwhile, the dispute over the promised compensation continued. Edmund Beck turned once again to Somerville Gurney, appealing with him to reason with his co-trustee over the huge amount she had claimed. Eventually, on 5 March, Gurney conceded: 'On second thoughts it might be *better if you forwarded that money to me* [emphasis added] and I will place it to Mrs Cresswell's account.' By return, the grateful Beck sent a cheque for £250, adding, 'I sincerely hope we shall hear no more of it... I cannot close this without thanking you for the patience and trouble you have had in assisting me to bring about the settlement of this unpleasant matter, in which I am sure both the Prince of Wales and General Knollys most heartily join.'

Gurney agreed: 'much obliged and hope this is the last we hear on this subject.'

They underestimated Louise's tenacity.

Furious with Somerville Gurney for going behind her back, she wrote to inform Beck that she was away from Appleton, detained, 'on account of the child's illness. I enclose receipt for the £250... and hope you will send as soon as possible a cheque for the balance of three or four hundred pounds, if not I shall expect interest upon it...'

She sent again to Beck, on 8 April, pointing out that her receipt, and Mr Gurney's, were on account of the £250, which was only part of the agreed sum and therefore she expected payment of the balance. Since the matter had been agreed by mutual consent 'we are both bound by law and honour to abide by it'. However, amid all this contention something must have made her wonder whether her belief in that 'special agreement' was based on fact; in the same letter she asks, somewhat belatedly, for a copy of the Appleton lease, which she admits she has not yet seen.

In fact, on the subject of game, the original lease says only that all rights are reserved to the landlord; perhaps seeing this for herself gave Louise pause. But she remained incensed over what she considered the Prince's reneging on her claim for damages. As she comments in her book, 'their bogus, the "British Public" stood between me and my due; the payment for damages was proof of damages, and they did not want those figures to go before the country; a quite unnecessary terror; I can hold my tongue where interest demands it...'

Whether she held her tongue or not is debatable, but she certainly took up her pen. A paragraph or two later, she says, 'I had named my difficulties to a Member of Parliament [and] through some misunderstanding he considered himself at liberty to bring the case before the notice of government... I was rather startled one morning to find that my letter giving all

particulars… had been read out in the House of Commons…'
Was she really so naïve as to believe that she could write to an
MP detailing her grievances and not anticipate his taking action?
Yet again she is obfuscating.

The man to whom she wrote was Clare Sewell Read, the
farmers' champion, and he did indeed read out two extracts from
her letter to underline his argument during a Commons debate on
the game laws on 21 May 1867. He did not name Louise, the
Prince, or Sandringham, referring only to 'a widowed lady' who
was tenant on 'an estate in Norfolk in which the public took great
interest', but that would be enough for the scandalmongers who
dogged the Prince's footsteps. In her letter, Louise had told the
outline of her story, how eager the agent had been at the outset to
secure 'a man of character, education, and capital' for the farm;
how 'the rent was fixed at a high rate, and there was hardly a
hare to be seen'; and how her husband 'was assured he would
never be injured by game'. She recounted how, after she and her
husband moved to Appleton, the hares multiplied until they were
destroying everything, but when she put in a claim for damages
only half the total was paid. Mr Read commented that 'if this was
the way enterprising farmers were treated on the estate of such a
landlord, what could they expect from small and needy
landowners?'[34]

The daily newspapers failed to report on these proceedings,
but an agricultural weekly picked up the story and, according to
Louise, someone rushed to inform the Prince. The Lady Farmer
was both thrilled and horrified: 'after all their precautions the
murder was out, and through me!' She tries to have it all ways –
she might have exonerated herself by laying the blame wholly on
Mr Read, oh, but she couldn't do that, after all, it was all true, oh,
but if she had known he would bring it up in public she would
never have… She adds, 'The very worst must have been made of
it to His Royal Highness, who scowled at me in true Henry the
Eighth style whenever he chanced to meet me; and if Kings had
power of life and death in these days… I know where my head
would be.'

---

[34] Hansard, Vol. 187; columns 908-10. Debate on the Game Preservation
(Scotland) Bill

Alexandra's illness

While Louise exchanged heated letters with Mr Beck, the Princess of Wales suffered a serious bout of rheumatic fever, during which she went into a prolonged and painful labour, giving birth on 20 February 1867 to her first daughter, named Louise Victoria Alexandra Dagmar. The child was premature, as had been her two brothers, but this time it was the mother's health that concerned the doctors. Alix was fevered and in immense pain, her mouth so swollen she could hardly bear to eat, and she developed 'white leg', a painful form of thrombosis. In mid-March, when the King and Queen of Denmark hurried to their daughter's bedside, the people of Britain feared the worst. Even her disapproving mother-in-law was moved to observe that the Princess's condition was 'heart-rending'. Only Bertie refused to believe that his wife was critically ill. While appearing suitably concerned in her presence, the moment he left her he was off, continuing his dalliances and usual rounds of pleasure. The royal honeymoon was decidedly over. Even Alix knew it.

She was ill for so long that the new baby's christening had to be delayed for three months, until May. On the evening of the baptismal day, the Prince departed for Paris, one of his favourite haunts. He was to represent the Queen at the opening of the Great International Exhibition, but this royal duty provided a good excuse for him to return to the company of various mistresses and some of his more dissolute friends. Not that he needed any excuse; he no longer tried to conceal his excesses and as a result the British people were beginning to mutter against him.

During her slow recovery, the Princess was obliged to use a wheelchair for some months, but by the end of the summer she was well enough to undertake a journey, with her husband and children and the usual entourage, to Wiesbaden in Germany, where the baths were supposed to be efficacious against rheumatism. But the spa waters didn't help, and Bertie's frequent absences – off to the races or for a day's shooting – only added further stress. Alix's health never properly recovered. Nor did her marriage.

The illness left her lame. Even after she was able to leave her wheelchair, and set aside the two walking sticks that followed it, she always walked with a slight limp (some idiot ladies in society adopted the same halting gait, thinking to flatter her, but they had underestimated their Princess, who found their sycophancy irritating). She taught herself to dance again, eventually, and she rode to hounds despite her mother-in-law's disapproval: she even gave Bertie three more children. But she was never again the same healthy young woman, nor quite the same adoring, unquestioning wife. Her deafness increased, too, leaving her ever more isolated. She retreated into herself, into the simple pleasures of her home, her children, her animals, and to caring for others in distress. And, as always, she found deep consolation at her beloved Sandringham.

Sorrow untold

Also in May, that year of 1867, as Mr Read, MP, drew national attention to Appleton farm and its widowed tenant, Louise's mother-in-law Rachel Cresswell (now aged sixty-four) quietly travelled to Norwich to sit beside the sick bed of her second son, Addison. He, who had been such a splendid young blade in big buttons and a tandem gig, had been suffering from disease of the heart and kidney for some two years. He died of congestive heart failure on 1 June, aged forty-three, and was brought to rest in North Runcton churchyard.

Rachel hurried straight back to the bedside of another ailing son, naval hero Gurney. For almost four years he had been languishing at home, growing slowly weaker; now his long struggle was ending. His mother recorded how she and Gurney 'spent six quiet loving days together, he quite himself, though unable to speak, his face full of response and expression. Then came a few hours of strife and trial, and he was gone – August 14th, 1867.'[35] Captain Samuel Gurney Cresswell, RN, died a few weeks before his fortieth birthday. (His death certificate gives the cause as 'cerebral softening ending in serious effusion' and confirms that he had been suffering from this illness for five or

---

[35] Harrod, D (Ed): *War, Ice, and Piracy* (Chatham, 2000)

six years. This form of words was a euphemism for syphilis, a horrible disease whose name no respectable family would dare breathe aloud.[36])

Unlike the more public grieving for his father, and for his brother Gerard, Gurney's funeral was a quiet, private affair, attended only by his nearest relatives, including (unusually) the ladies of the family. He was laid to rest with other deceased members of his family, in the Cresswell vault at North Runcton. (Today, this local hero is commemorated by a blue plaque on the Bank House, his parents' home, where he was born and where he died.)

Louise says nothing of these tragic events, but she cannot have remained aloof. Surely she at least visited the Bank House, to comfort the invalid and provide moral support for her mother-in-law. And surely she was among the 'ladies of the family', who gathered to say farewell to the sailor hero. Perhaps, when she came to write her book, she decided it was not appropriate, or relevant, to mention these deeply personal sadnesses. But she must have been affected by the untimely loss of two more of Gerard's brothers, and by the distress visited yet again on her mother-in-law.

However devout a Christian Rachel Cresswell may have been, to lose her children in this way, mown down one by one, must have been a severe test of her faith.

Rachel Cresswell, widow
Though she had broken away from the Quaker way of belief, Rachel Cresswell remained a practising Christian; throughout her adult life she made a habit of actively working for, and contributing financially to, many local good causes. She was, for a time, secretary of the Lynn and West Norfolk Hospital, and of the new women's refuge which she had helped to set up for 'fallen and repentant women'; she was a cornerstone of the Lynn District Visiting Society, encouraged clothing and thrift clubs, championed the welfare of the fisher-folk of the North End, and established a girls' school in Broad St, in memory of her

---

[36] By the late nineteenth century one Briton in ten was infected with syphilis. Prostitutes were blamed and the Contagious Diseases Act of 1864 sentenced them to prison if found to have the taint

young daughter Harriet (the school remained active for thirty-two years, until elementary education became a privilege extended to all children). She loved flowers; she liked to draw and make water-colour sketches (a talent Gurney inherited and used to advantage on his foreign voyages); she taught illiterate fishermen how to read and write; she gave Bible study lessons; she brought unwashed urchins off the street into her garden, had her servants make them clean and tidy, fed them and read to them. The grateful poor of Lynn's North End referred to her as 'Lady Cresswell'.

She was not alone in performing charitable works; many a wealthy matron gave her time and money to help less privileged people, but Rachel's list is exceptionally long and varied. It seems that, despite their disagreements in earlier years, she turned out to be a true child of her mother, Elizabeth Fry.

Beneath the mourning clothes which fate decreed she should wear almost constantly, Rachel the woman was increasingly lonely and saddened. Only two sons remained to her — her oldest, Frank, and her youngest, Oswald. Soldier Ossie, now twenty-seven and still a bachelor, was far away, stationed in India with the 26th Cameronians, but Frank and his family lived close by at 3 King Street, just a few minutes' walk from the Bank House.

Frank was now in his forty-seventh year. He had given up the Rifle Corps that January, but he still enjoyed boating: he designed and raced a succession of four yachts, all called the *Wild Duck,* and all built in Lynn. In off-duty time from the bank, he was often to be found on and near water, in the marshes when duck-hunting season came around, or racing his yacht in one of the local regattas. With this affable sportsman lived his wife, the Hon. Charlotte, and their four children – Charlotte Rachel Frederica (15), George Frederick Addison (14), Edith Frances Louisa (13), and Cresswell Augustus (10). They must have been a comfort to their ageing grandmother.

And out at Appleton lived the other Cresswells – Rachel's youngest grandson, Gerard (almost 3), and *his* mother, Louise. How did Rachel feel about this other, somewhat problematic daughter-in-law of hers? Ambivalent, one suspects.

And what of Louise's feelings for her mother-in-law? Was Rachel a shining example much admired, or far too saintly a being for any normal, fallible woman ever to hope to emulate? Louise herself is silent on the subject. In later years she did make some efforts at helping the poorer children in her own neighbourhood, but she was mostly occupied about the farm, trying to make ends meet. Not for her the luxury of lifelong service to others, even had she been so inclined.

Little by little, a rift was opening between Louise and the other Cresswells. The gap would only widen with the years.

Louise and her son both benefited from legacies left by Addison and Gurney – Addison left £1,000 for Louise, with a further £1,000 for young Gerard when he attained his majority. Gurney left Louise only £10, but his inheritance from his father's estate, which would come due when his mother Rachel died, was assigned to his infant nephew, Gerard Francis Oswald Cresswell.

Fire!

Under steward Robert Faircloth's guidance, the Appleton harvest came safely home and, once again, golden mounds in the stack-yard promised equally-golden profits for Louise's bank account. But fate had not done with her yet. On the afternoon of 8 September 1867, a Sunday afternoon, around tea-time, 'a stack of meadow hay on the farm of Mrs G. O. Cresswell was found to be on fire and the flames communicated to an adjoining stack of sainfoin. The alarm being given, the Prince of Wales's small but powerful fire engine was quickly brought from Sandringham, with a good supply of hose, and accompanied by an efficient staff from the stables, etc, and a large body of water was poured upon the burning mass' – so said the *Lynn Advertiser.*

Some of Sandringham's early fire engines are still on display in the stables' museum. The device used at Appleton would be horse-drawn, with a long hose that could be unrolled and the end fed into the duck-pond, from where water would be siphoned by a team of men on each side of the engine pumping the two handles. The report doesn't say how the fire might have started but haystacks did occasionally combust spontaneously from the heat that built up inside them. Thankfully, because of the prompt response by the Prince's staff – stable-hands, gamekeepers, whoever was available – three other stacks close by were saved. If the whole yard had gone up in smoke, it would have meant a further loss for Louise of some £500, and if the fire had spread… It didn't bear thinking about.

As she watched her men clear up the wet, blackened, stinking mess, what must Louise have been thinking? Did she doubt her ability to cope with the farm after all? Nothing went right for her. Her husband taken, and recently two more of his brothers, her crops destroyed, her profits decimated, her hay and expensive sainfoin gone to ashes… It was yet another black day. And not the last for Louise.

Stormy winter

For four months, from November 1867 to February 1868, Norfolk was battered by fierce winds and thunder-storms. On Princess Alix's birthday, 1 December, gales uprooted several large trees along the Dersingham avenue at Sandringham, and in March a great part of the Hunstanton cliffs, weakened by hurricanes and deluging rain, fell onto the beach.

When the royal pair and their entourage arrived at Sandringham on 17 November, the Prince promptly set about his usual round of shooting and fox-hunting. His wife, still not fully recovered in health, did not attend church until Christmas Day: she said the church was too cold. But she did drive out most days, well wrapped up, slowly resuming her normal routine, much to the relief of everyone. As had become their wont, the Prince and Princess spent New Year week at Holkham with the Earl of Leicester, before returning to Sandringham, where they remained that year until 15 February – a long period, giving the Princess time to recoup her strength. It was to be their last winter in the old house.

If his wife's illness failed to sway the Prince to mend his hedonistic ways, it did at least motivate him to admit, at last, that the damp and terminally draughty Sandringham Hall needed major renovation. It might have been wiser to pull the place down and build anew, but Bertie was reluctant to alter too much – for one thing he wanted to keep the chimneys (the architect Humbert persuaded him to settle for replicas), while the Princess wished to keep her small sitting room, which she adored (she had her wish). Compromises were argued over for months before the builders, Goggs of Swaffham, began on the demolition and rebuilding.

It would be three years before Their Royal Highnesses returned to the remodelled house. When in Norfolk during that interim period, they stayed with aristocratic neighbours, or for brief periods with General Knollys at his splendid new residence, Park House, not far from the church at Sandringham.

Brother Charles moves to Norfolk

After sixteen years in the army, Louise's youngest brother, Captain Charles Wells Archdale, aged thirty-five, retired to civilian life and brought his family to Norfolk, late in 1867. They stayed temporarily in the new town of Hunstanton St Edmund, taking over brother Frederick's fine holiday home, Cliff End House[37], with its unimpeded views across the Green to the beach promenade and the sea (the pier was not added until 1869). Charles Archdale's third child, Mary Caroline, was born there on 13 January 1868; the new church in Hunstanton St Edmund having been badly damaged by the fury of November gales, her baptism took place in the more ancient church at 'Old' Hunstanton village.

Later that year, Charles Archdale removed to Grove House, in Coltishall, a picturesque village on the River Bure, on the edge of the beautiful Norfolk Broads, some fifty miles away from Appleton. The family remained there, producing four more daughters and, finally, another son. The income from various inheritances allowed Charles to live the life of a Gentleman, and in his spare time he made use of his military expertise by captaining the 6th Corps of Volunteers in nearby Aylsham.

---

[37] Cliff End House (now Pierpoint House) stands on the corner of the Green below the Princess Theatre, behind the more modern shops and ice cream parlours..

Death of Aunt Margaret Hogge

At the annual general meeting of the Lynn and District Visiting Society, in mid-February 1868, members – including Somerville Gurney and society secretary Frank J. Cresswell – formally recorded their sorrow on hearing of the failing health of the widow Mrs George Hogge. In their minutes, they recalled her unbounded generosity, her ceaseless care of the poor, and her tender sympathy with the sick and suffering.

Margaret Hogge died the following Tuesday, 18 February, aged seventy-eight, having been a widow for twenty-one years. She was a wealthy woman in her own right, a daughter of the Ainslies of Staffordshire and Cumbria; her will was valued at near £50,000, most of it coming from shares in the Harrison Ainslie company, who manufactured iron and gunpowder. She left the bulk of this personal fortune to her own brothers. Two Hogge godsons each received £50 – one of these was Louise's brother George, now Archdale – and a few pounds each went to three of her husband's nieces, including Louise's sister Eliza who had £10. Louise herself is not mentioned.

However, the properties left by Uncle George Hogge to his widow had been hers for life only. Her death released the Lynn properties to the ownership of Louise's oldest surviving brother, George Archdale, while Thornham, finally, came entirely into the hands of Louise's sister-in-law, the widowed Helen (Mrs William Samuel) Hogge and her daughter Edith. Edith, now seventeen, would inherit the manor of Thornham when she came of age in September 1871; however, since Aunt Margaret had owned all the furniture and contents of Thornham Hall, and bequeathed those to her own family, the empty house was let to the farmer who held lease on most of the land. Mrs Helen Hogge and her heiress daughter resided mainly in London at this time.

Quieter times

Following the altercations of 1866/7 – Louise's stand at the rent audit, her letter to MP Mr Read, and the Prince's resulting fury – for three long years she lived in what she calls 'an atmosphere of misrepresentation, black-lettered, labelled dangerous, looked upon suspiciously by courtiers from within and without'. This ignominy occurred 'to the great concern of my good friend Mr Onslow, Rector of Sandringham and Domestic Chaplain to their Royal Highnesses, who was distressed to see me in such a position'.

Reverend William Lake Onslow was the kindest of men, open-hearted and anxious to fulfil his calling, helping all who came to him with troubles. He could not fail to respond to the appeal of a thirty-seven-year-old widow with a small child, alone, embattled, and rapidly losing friends, both because she had dared to upset the Prince of Wales and because of her own spiky nature – sadly for her, Louise had a talent for alienating people. The three Onslows, the rector and his mother and sister, frequently invited poor Mrs Cresswell over for afternoon tea, or for dinner; the rectory became her second home, where she could pour out her heart and be sure of a sympathetic hearing.

Being a genuinely caring soul, Revd Onslow also grew increasingly concerned about the welfare of Princess Alexandra; he knew the secret sadness she endured, and he worried about her depleted health.

Prince Albert Edward, too, sought to remedy his wife's lingering debility. Having ordered the rebuilding of Sandringham Hall, in an attempt to cure its dampness and cold draughts, he decided that he and his wife should undertake a long trip through Europe, which might help to restore some colour to Alix's pale cheeks. Of course, he himself loved to travel, and when abroad he could escape the insidious whispers of scandal that were beginning to attach to his name like sticky cobwebs; so the trip would suit his purposes very well, too. It would be one long round of pleasure.

They left London on 17 November 1868, the eve of the election which brought Gladstone to power for the first time as Prime Minister. Since Princess Alix wished to spend Christmas with her own parents in Denmark, she and Bertie took their three children (Eddy, George and Louise) with them, despite Queen Victoria's disapproval. But first they must visit Paris, Bertie's favourite city, where the velocipede bicycle was much in vogue, a craze soon spreading in Britain too. They stayed for eight days before beginning a slow progress across Germany to

Copenhagen. After six festive weeks with the Danish royal family, on 16 January 1869 the three children were sent back to England, while their parents went on through Berlin, Austria and Prussia, to Trieste, where HMS *Ariadne* was waiting, fitted up as a yacht (with Revd W. Lake Onslow aboard her as chaplain).

They sailed for Egypt on 27 January, took a six-week trip up the Nile, came back to Cairo and went on to witness the Suez Canal under construction (it was to open eight months later, November 1869). At the end of March, *Ariadne* set off again, via the Dardanelles to Constantinople, where the royal company visited the Crimea. They re-embarked on 15 April, for eleven days in Greece, returned by train to Paris and came home to London on 12 May 1869. They had been away for seven months.

New premises for Gurneys' Bank

For most of that time, Louise's oldest surviving brother, George Archdale, had been busy disposing of most of the family properties and businesses, which had devolved to him when Aunt Margaret Hogge died. Among them, the mansion on the corner of the Tuesday Market Place in Lynn had become the new location of Gurneys' Bank.

On 7 June 1869, the bank's co-directors, Frank Cresswell and Somerville Gurney, with their clerks, moved from the old counting house premises on King's Staithe, adjacent to the Bank House where Rachel Cresswell dwelt, and opened offices in the much grander and more central building which had belonged to four generations of Georges Hogg(e). The last of that line, now turned Archdale, was ending the long association of his family with the town.

The one business in which George Archdale retained his interest was the brewery at Setch, with its spread of pubs and hotels in the area. In time, being childless, he passed this on to another George – his nephew, George Fitzroy Archdale, Frederick's second son.

Summer of 1869

The summer of 1869 was a great time for social gatherings. Many companies of Norfolk Volunteers attended a camp in the grounds of Hunstanton Hall, with parades and sports and evening entertainment in a marquee. Somerville Gurney led the 5th Corps, from Lynn, while Charles Archdale headed the 6th Corps of Aylsham. Frank Cresswell and his elder daughter Charlotte (aged seventeen) were among the audience for the evening's fun.

A rather more gala occasion saw the opening of Lynn's new Alexandra Dock, by Their Royal Highnesses the Prince and Princess of Wales, on 7 July 1869. At the sumptuous dinner held afterwards, Revd Onslow and his mother were among the chief guests. Frank Cresswell and his wife had declined the invitation, she being unwell. With Sandringham Hall still under renovation, the royal pair stayed overnight with General Knollys at Park House.

In August, Hunstanton held its annual regatta, though, as the *Lynn Advertiser*, always ready with dry wit, reported, 'enjoyment of the occasion was considerably marred by the execrable band that annoyed the visitors in the enclosure'. During the yacht races, Frank Cresswell won the St Edmund cup in his yacht *Wild Duck*. He and his family were spending two weeks at Brenda Lodge, another holiday home with wonderful views, just a few strides higher up the hill than the Railway Hotel. Happily, since the newspaper recorded all weekly visitors, we also know that, over the ensuing five weeks, this same Brenda Lodge was rented by 'Mr C. Magniac and family, from Coleworth House (Beds)' – Charles Magniac had come to Norfolk to stay within easy reach of his widowed sister Helen Hogge, who was spending the summer at the Cottage, Thornham, with daughter Edith. Happy holidays!

Unfortunately for Louise, while her friends and family enjoyed themselves, in her own life yet another brouhaha was brewing.

Fox cubs and pheasants
The new headaches arose through a misunderstanding with the overbearing and, as Louise observed, 'formidable-looking' Goss Overton, the burly head gamekeeper at Sandringham. Once again, letters of the time tell a story slightly different from the one she gave in her book, though all agree on the main facts.

The fracas began and ended with the Prince of Wales.

Out riding with the West Norfolk Fox Hounds on a day when foxes proved elusive, HRH, with his usual bonhomie, invited the Master to try his luck over Sandringham estate, where foxes were sure to be found. They rode for hours, but the hounds raised not a single fox – hardly surprising on an estate dedicated to the production of game birds, rabbits and hares, where keepers did their utmost to eliminate everything that might want to eat eggs, birds and coneys. But the Prince, furious at being made to look foolish, ordered that, next time he offered a day's sport to his neighbours, there had better be some sport to be had! Trying to obey such contradictory orders must have been stressful.

Since Overton fiercely objected to having foxes anywhere near his precious pheasant coverts, the Prince had instructed his land agent, Edmund Beck, to supervise the building of an artificial earth, and in spring 1869 the local hunt gave Beck four orphaned fox cubs, to be raised by hand for the first few months of their lives, until mid-September, by which time they would be old enough to fend for themselves and could be turned out to live in the purpose-built brick earth. Meanwhile, as they grew, they had to be kept confined and tended. Mr Beck asked Overton to supply some rabbits to feed the cubs, but the head gamekeeper refused, on the excuse that he needed all his available rabbits for his pheasants,[38] so instead (as the agent informed the royal solicitor that November), 'Mrs Cresswell volunteered, and fed them at her own expense, kept closely confined...'[39] Beck himself kept a watchful eye on the young cubs' progress.

Louise maintains that Beck came and *asked* her to raise the cubs, because she 'understood all about them. It seemed rather strange to be asked a favour when in disgrace [but] I had no objection to take charge of the little "beasties," and said I would not let them out until I had an order from head quarters. They

---

[38] Keepers fed the young 'poults' four times a day with a mixture of cooked rabbit meat and hard boiled eggs, finely chopped and mixed with biscuit meal
[39] Royal Archive LAW/SHM/12/10/16

were a great deal of trouble to keep in, and began to burrow under the walls of the place where they were kept...'[40]

Goss Overton remained unhappy over the presence of the adolescent carnivors. While they were still under Louise's care, in July, he wrote to General Knollys complaining that Mrs Cresswell had let out some foxes that could threaten the welfare of the Prince's hares. When Knollys enquired, agent Beck assured him this was not so – the cubs were still confined in their nursery. Alas, Beck gossiped about the gamekeeper's fears to his friend Somerville Gurney, who in turn took the story to Louise, and she, as agent Beck later reported to the royal solicitor, 'went and gave Overton her mind and threatened to imprison him if he ever circulated another libel about her. I believe Overton was entirely cowed as he scarcely answered a word.'[41]

Louise wrote to Mr White in her own defence: 'I felt so hurt and indignant that a gamekeeper should be allowed to write untruths of me...',[42] but, she adds, she took no notice except to tell Overton that if he did it again she would sue for libel.

The incident passed. But as the summer of 1869 drew on and the foxes grew ever closer to maturity, Overton's paranoia escalated.

To Louise's relief, in the third week of September Mr Beck instructed her to turn out the troublesome 'beasties' into their earth, which had been built in a leafy copse on the edge of her farm. She received 'profuse thanks for the trouble I had taken...' and she naturally believed the incident was ended.

A month later, horror struck in Sandringham woods when the keepers found seventy-one pheasants torn to bloody pieces.

When his under-keepers brought news of the massacre, an apoplectic Goss Overton hastened over to Gunton Hall, where the Prince happened to be staying with Lord Suffield. HRH was relaxing with friends when the bullish Overton burst in and declared for all to hear that Mrs Cresswell's foxes had killed seventy-one of the royal pheasants.

---

[40] Cresswell: *Eighteen Years...* p 87-93
[41] Royal Archive LAW/SHM/12/10/16
[42] Royal Archive LAW/SHM/12/10/14

Louise says, 'The explosion that followed must have been terrific. H.R.H., having been so industriously prejudiced against me for years, was ready to believe anything; and though I did not hear particulars of the epithets invoked upon my head, a little leaked out through one or two of the county people there, who said they had never heard such a row in their lives.' She adds that among the group gathered around the Prince at Gunton that day were the Duke of Cambridge (the Queen's cousin, Commander in Chief of the army), her good friend Revd W. L. Onslow, and that venerable sportsman 'General Hall of Six Mile Bottom, with whom I had some acquaintance'. After some gentle persuasion from the more rational men in the party, the furious Prince ordered a full enquiry, and Lake Onslow obligingly agreed to act as a kind of investigative officer and 'write down all particulars' in order to present them for the Prince's consideration.

It was Reverend Onslow who brought the news to Louise. She was taking tea with the rector's mother, Lavinia, when the rector himself came in 'looking nervous and uncomfortable'. When he told the shocked Louise that she had been accused of this heinous crime – the slaughter of seventy-one of the Prince's pheasants – her first reaction was, she says, to 'cut up rusty' and allow HRH to believe what he liked. But, out of consideration for her friends, she eventually condescended to justify herself.

Arnold White, the Prince's solicitor, became involved. Letters of explanation flew between him, Edmund Beck, Louise, and General Knollys at Sandringham.

On 6 November Louise put her side of the case to Mr White, ending, 'If you and Mr Beck were not so just and kind to me, and that I believe it would almost break my heart to leave my home, I <u>could not</u> remain upon the Prince's property another day. Perhaps after all if I am to be exposed to this incessant persecution it may be better for me to go, but can decide nothing at present and of course must consult my friends. Yrs faithfully... PS I hope you will excuse my troubling you with this, I have been ill lately and am so wearied with never being allowed to live in peace that I cannot help telling you of it.'[43]

---

[43] Royal Archive LAW/SHM/12/10/14

The lawyer communicated this to Edmund Beck, who, on 12 November, replied, 'You are quite right in conjecturing Tis the Old Tale, but as you intend speaking to the Prince...' He goes on to explain events and says that the Prince was angry not only with Mrs Cresswell but with him [Beck] too, 'as he imagines I have shown some encouragement to the widow'. He adds that when Mrs Cresswell heard that Overton had accused her, she came frantic to see Beck and then wrote to comptroller General Knollys, who called Beck in and obliged him to explain yet again. Then Beck went to see Overton, who now opined that the pheasant fatalities had not, after all, been caused by Mrs Cresswell's cubs but, as Beck writes with understandable scepticism, 'by some Tame Fox. Query what truth and proof! He has however made mischief enough and I am very sorry the thing is now in the mouth of everyone [and is] damaging to the name of the Prince. He [Overton] is a good keeper but becoming a nuisance. None of [the tenants] respect or like the man, simply owing to his manner... I assure you I do not take the Lady's part, as you know by previous transactions, but I can assure you Mrs Cresswell is the Best Tenant upon the estate...'[44]

Louise would, no doubt, have been gratified by this final comment.

She tells how Revd Onslow bravely undertook to approach the Prince with the results of the enquiry, which had concluded that her cubs had certainly not been responsible for the dead pheasants – they were too young, too far removed from the scene of crime, and anyway, with their earth situated in a leafy copse aswarm with young rabbits, the little foxes had no need to go foraging after pheasants. The real culprit was obviously the wily old dog fox that had been eluding the hunt for years. Or so someone had decided.

However, Louise knew that, for dear Mr Onslow, taking this news to HRH would be 'no pleasant task, as the Royal anger had not yet subsided, for I heard of my misdeeds in all directions, even in London via Marlborough House and elsewhere...'

---

[44] Royal Archive LAW/SHM/12/10/16

She describes the final act in this drama, 'a grand Court-martial being held in the Prince's presence, with the Lord Lieutenant of the County [the Earl of Leicester] as cross-examiner and umpire, Mr Onslow to represent me and my interests, and the keeper, agent, and some non-official spectators.' She herself was not present at this meeting, but 'the evidence in my favour was so overwhelming that a verdict of "Not Guilty" was speedily arrived at…'

The Prince, she adds, eventually conceded that the whole thing had been 'a misconception of truth' – more like 'a misconception of lies', says a bitter Louise.

In a letter written to Louise four years later, 18 Oct 1873, Lake Onslow recalls a confrontation with the Prince of Wales: 'that day when she [the Princess], yourself & Mrs William Grey [the Princess's favourite lady-in-waiting] stood together on an occasion which cannot be blotted out of the book of memory…'[45] Is he referring to one final private scene in this drama, when, perhaps, the Princess and the rector, together, took up cudgels on Louise's behalf?

Royal scandals

Another new princess, named Maud, joined the Wales household on 26 November that year of 1869. However, for her parents those times were fraught with anxiety, mostly because of the gathering scandal of the Mordaunt divorce case. Admitting to adultery, the sad and possibly mad Lady Mordaunt had reeled off a list of suitors, including the Prince of Wales. HRH, subpoenaed to appear in court, was officially cleared of culpability, but the scandal, like splattered mud, cast another stain upon his reputation and caused yet more grief for his family. When Princess Alix went out alone in public, she was cheered and applauded – the crowds loved her and held her faultless; but if her husband appeared at her side, boos and catcalls followed the pair of them.

The scandal gave a boost to the faction who despised the Queen and her 'brood of Germans': republican clubs sprang up

---

[45] Letters in private hands, copies in author's possession

and anti-monarchist pamphlets littered the streets. One of the leaders of the movement, Charles Dilke, at his most vitriolic, cried 'Let the Republic Come!' and even Prime Minister Gladstone commented in private that this ill-feeling was not to be wondered at, for it seemed to him that the Queen was invisible and the Prince of Wales not respected. Fearing anarchist attacks at Sandringham, the police offered official protection to all the main tenants, though the farmers deemed this excessive. It was during this time that Louise slept with a pistol under her pillow for fear of anti-monarchist hooligans.

Many people blamed the Queen for the rise of ill-feeling – she kept herself aloof and apart, still wallowing in self-imposed, self-indulgent mourning for her beloved Albert, though, as everyone knew, she frequently enjoyed the intimate company of her favourite ghillie, John Brown. As for the Prince of Wales, he spent far too much time chasing earthly pleasures, having too little real work to do, besides being indiscreet. Even his mother didn't trust him to handle affairs of state.

With all of this gossip to contend with, little wonder that the Prince and those close to him found Louise Cresswell's constant nagging and nit-picking a tad annoying at times.

Departure of Overton

Louise was still not happy, still agitating and arguing. Having belatedly perused her lease, she instructed her local solicitor, T. G. Archer of Lynn, to ask for a proviso about the increase of hares. This was not approved, but the Prince's camp did concede on the question of rabbits, which might be kept down by means of ferrets and purse nets – but not traps, which could injure game birds.

Rabbits took over from hares as Louise's latest obsession.

Edmund Beck, writing to Mr White from his farm at Oxwick on 16 January 1870,[46] observes that Mrs Cresswell has made a grave mistake in allowing her bailiff to shoot rabbits in standing crops of corn. She has written to say that the number killed by that means was nearly 400, though Beck can hardly

---

[46] Royal Archive LAW/SHM/12/10/19

credit this. None of the other tenants have complained and 'you know the kind of Lady Mrs Cresswell is'. He agrees she was badly treated by Overton's slandering her to HRH, but 'as Lord Leicester remarked, *if she had not been injudicious also* [emphasis added], more good could have been done on her behalf'. He adds, 'There is now very bad feeling between the tenants and the head gamekeeper...'

The unpopular head keeper was replaced the following year by a much more amenable man named Charles Henry Jackson. And Goss Overton, as Louise says, 'was promoted to the charge of the Queen's preserves in Windsor Park, and the friendship of Mr John Brown...'

These upsets had a salutary effect on everyone involved. With Overton gone, Louise and the other Sandringham farmers had fewer reasons for grievance; the new man, Jackson, a far more reasonable chap, did try to keep the hares under control, one way or another. The flow of letters, claims and accusations dwindled and Louise settled down to become a proper farmer. At last it seemed that she was to be allowed some peace.

Frank Cresswell widowed

Louise refers in her usual oblique way to 'a gentleman whose yacht was often moored for months together in the creek [at Wolferton] for the wild winter shooting...' This description fits her oldest brother-in-law, banker Frank J. Cresswell, who in his spare time loved nothing better than being out on the marshes or in the Wash with his boat *Wild Duck*. Now he was embarking on a new business venture.

The opening of Lynn's capacious Alexandra Dock, in 1869, had brought larger vessels, bearing heavier cargoes, into the port; consequently stronger tug boats were needed, to guide them through the notoriously tricky channels in the Wash. The newly-formed Lynn Steam Tug Co., of which Frank Cresswell became a shareholder, began business with a tug named *Spindrift*.

Trips aboard the *Spindrift*

Off-duty, the tug acted as a pleasure cruiser, taking crowds of trippers out to the cockle sands, or from Lynn to Hunstanton, or across the Wash to Skegness. By the early 1880s the boat was a popular attraction. Day trippers left Skegness pier at 8.30 a.m., to steam for a pleasant two and a half hours over to Hunstanton pier, from where they could take a charabanc ride to gawp at royal Sandringham, and sail home to Lincolnshire by 8 p.m., perhaps pausing at the Lynn Well lightship to collect mail and deliver fresh fruit and veg., and newspapers.

Hunstanton St Edmund had become a popular destination for local trippers, by rail or by sea, while longer-staying holidaymakers filled the boarding houses. Invalids also came to the resort, hoping to benefit from the curative properties of sea bathing and ozone-rich air, highly recommended by doctors.

That summer, Frank Cresswell's wife, who had been unwell for some time, stayed in the new town for several weeks, hoping to recover her health. Unfortunately the sea air didn't help her; only a few days after returning home to Lynn, on 18 August 1870, the Hon. Charlotte, Mrs F. J. Cresswell, died. She was forty-six. She left behind her husband (48) and four teenage children, first cousins to six-year-old Gerard at Appleton.

Refurbishments at Sandringham

The Prince's remodelled Hall, rechristened Sandringham House, was declared habitable just before his twenty-ninth birthday, 9 November 1870. The house had been enlarged and much improved, with the latest materials and all modern conveniences, including fireproofing and up-to-the-minute sanitary facilities – these last installed under the supervision of the famous Thomas Crapper. The 'his and hers' bathrooms, lit by gas, had identical fittings except that his bath was made of black marble while hers was of white.

The Waleses arrived, with a train of guests, on Saturday, 26 November. For the County Ball the following Friday the guest list included: four local MPs, among them Clare Sewell Read and his wife; Mr and Mrs Somerville Gurney; Revd W. Lake Onslow; Mr Frank and Miss Cresswell; Mrs [Rachel] Cresswell; and, named beside them, Mrs Gerard Cresswell.

Louise had felt disinclined to go: 'when you get into the habit of living in a serge gown and thick boots you feel comfortable in nothing else, and get out of the way of dressing yourself, particularly for a Court Ball.' But the Onslows prevailed on her to accept the invitation, to make it clear she did not harbour ill feelings, and she found herself 'routing out a trousseau gown that had hardly been worn, and some old lace, and sending them to London to be done up' (shades of Scarlett O'Hara!). She had not seen HRH since the 'court-martial' over the dead pheasants, but now he came up to her and actually condescended to shake hands with her. 'I always felt that were it not for the game and the mischief-making I should have got on very well with the Prince... [It] was very hard to be so persistently misrepresented.' How easily she could be swayed!

She was especially relieved because this invitation signalled her return to royal favour, and thus her reimmersion in the social swim of the county. She attributes this largely to the help of Mr Onslow, who was dubbed her 'Knight and Champion' by some facetious court wag. Other invitations followed and, though she couldn't afford to keep buying new dresses, and hadn't the time to socialize too often, when she did appear at the big house she was graciously received. She recalls, 'The next few years after "me and Wales" had made it up... were the happiest and most prosperous of my Sandringham life.' With HRH all smiles again, so the courtiers began to veer round too, as did the royal lawyer, and 'as for the little agent, you would think he had been created for the express purpose of studying my interests and making magnificent promises that were never fulfilled...' She still heartily despised Edmund Beck.

At home at Appleton, though, she was entirely contented, for young Gerard's former nurse, Lucy Sparrow, had taken over the housekeeping, while the boy's governess acted as social secretary, writing letters, doing the flowers and other such refinements. Other household servants performed more menial chores, 'and lastly the child completed the party. I indeed grudged the days as they passed... I never wanted to go away...'

More sadness

Early in 1871, Frederick Archdale lost his second wife Emily; she was only thirty-four. She died at their home in Christchurch, Bournemouth, leaving Frederick with seven children to bring up, one son having died as an infant. Emily had borne these eight children during twelve years of marriage.

After the funeral, Frederick and his brother-in-law, Henry Fitzroy, travelled up to Norfolk to stay with Louise for a while, leaving six of the children at home with Grandmama Fitzroy and her younger daughter, Emily's sister, Adela (19). Frederick's oldest son, William Frederick (10), was at boarding school in Brighton. Childless George Archdale and wife Mary, domiciled in Kensington, were also in Bournemouth at the time, lending support to the bereaved family.

That year, the Prince and Princess of Wales came home to Sandringham on 4 April, intending to spend Easter there. Alix was again heavily pregnant, nearing her sixth confinement, but – unbelievably, in view of all her earlier problems with premature births – nothing was ready when, on 6 April, she abruptly went into labour and produced another son. It soon became clear that he would not survive and so, late that night, they sent for Revd Onslow to come and perform a baptism. When morning came, the baby prince was dead.

Sandringham parish records tell the story with graphic simplicity: 'Wales, Alexander John Charles Albert, son of HRH the Prince and Princess of Wales, of Sandringham Park *[sic]* born and baptised on 6 April 1871, died on 7 April.' A note at the bottom of the page, says 'baptised privately being in danger of death' and is signed with initials: 'WLO'.

Louise would have preferred to stay away from the funeral, but, she tells us, she and the rector's sister, Agnes Onslow, were commanded to attend. The service was conducted, without any regal pomp or ceremony, by the Dean of Windsor, resident chaplain to the Queen; Louise approved of the simplicity of the occasion, 'the tiny coffin covered with flowers and carried with reverence and care by an old family servant, the mother crying at home, and the father and children the only mourners'. They interred the tragically small casket close beside the church; much better, thought Louise, for the baby to be at rest in a country churchyard, near its home, rather than in any grand royal vault.[47]

This was to be the last child for Princess Alexandra. She had been married for eight years, during which time she had endured six difficult pregnancies; she had a husband who openly vaunted his relationships with other women; she was lame, deaf, prey to painful rheumatism… and she was still only twenty-six years old. Little sympathy came from Her Majestic mother-in-law, however; Queen Victoria considered that Alix acted like an irresponsible young girl instead of a mature married woman with five children. And she still blamed the Princess's Danish blood for the inherent weakness of the royal offspring.

Later that year, the rector lost his mother, Mrs Lavinia Onslow; she was buried in the churchyard at Sandringham, on 19 August 1871, not far from the gate that leads from the churchyard to the rectory which was her home for five years.

America, land of opportunity

As the years passed, Louise took an increasing interest in America and its affairs. One shocking story told of a massive fire that had left half of Chicago in ashes: 'the severest fire that has ever occurred in any city in the United States,' said the *Lynn Advertiser*. With the war between North and South now ended, and the indigenous peoples mostly 'pacified', the huge country was opening up. The two transcontinental railways had met, linking east coast to west, in 1869, and now homestead land was being given away. With virgin prairie for growing corn and vast ranches producing beef cattle, America was truly the land of opportunity. Europe's poorest saw the place as El Dorado, but wealthier people also seized the chance for adventure and profit: Louise's father had invested in lands in Ecuador and New

---

[47] The tiny grave still attracts the sympathetic interest of thousands of visitors who come to see the little church. Next to Alexander lies another lost prince, John, youngest son of George V, who suffered from epilepsy and who died, aged 14, at Wood Farm, Wolferton, in 1919

Granada [modern Colombia/Panama] a year or two before his death, and her illegitimate cousin, Fred Safford, owned orchards in Colorado and at least two properties in California.

In her book, Louise frequently mentions the New World, calling the United States 'the most businesslike nation in the world'. She considered 'the Yankees' to be the people to emulate and compete with: 'I have a great regard for our American cousins and an especial admiration for their fair countrywomen, who are becoming so ornamental and attractive an addition to English society [but] I do not like to see my farmer friends so completely outwitted by them, and wish with all my heart they would rouse up and beat them in return...'

The Prince falls dangerously ill

Another grand, glittering 'County Ball' celebrated the thirtieth birthday of the Prince of Wales that November. As usual he was entertaining a houseful of elevated personages, including several Royal Highnesses, a couple of Earls, a Marquis... the list of guests ranged through all ranks of aristocracy and gentry, plus a score and more of reverend gentlemen. Many familiar names appear – Gurneys, le Stranges, ffolkes, Bagges... Edmund Beck was present, as was a certain Miss Keppel; there were Fountaines from Narford (relatives of Louise via her great-aunt Mary Fountaine, née Hogg), and, naturally, several Cresswells – Frank with both of his teenage daughters and his mother Rachel, and also Louise, accompanied this time by her sister Fanny, Miss Hogge. 'The company began to arrive at about ten o'clock,' said the *Lynn Advertiser*, 'and by the time the ball commenced there could not have been less than 300 present.' Dancing began soon after the royal host and hostess appeared with their house guests, around half past ten, and to the music of quadrilles, lancers, gallops and valses, played by Messrs Coote and Tinney's band, the dancing was 'kept up with great spirit till three o'clock'.

Celebrations continued, with fox-hunting at Congham on Saturday, Divine Service conducted by Revd W. L. Onslow on Sunday, and on Monday many of the house guests repaired to Narford to enjoy a day's shooting on the famous preserves kept by Andrew Fountaine, Esq. After that, the royal pair left for a visit to Woburn, planning to spend a further few days with the colourful Sikh Prince, the Maharajah Duleep Singh, who had acquired a country home near Thetford. But this last excursion was cancelled when Bertie felt unwell. Doctors believed at first that he had nothing more than a cold.

However, on Thursday, 23 November, an official bulletin announced the terrible truth: 'His Royal Highness the Prince of Wales is suffering from an attack of typhoid fever.' He appeared to have caught the disease during a visit to Lord Londesborough, who felt this a calumny on his name and strongly denied any uncleanness in his home or his water supply. But Bertie was not the only one of the party to be stricken – the Earl of Chesterfield went down with fever a few days later, as did one of the Sandringham grooms, Charles Blegg.

As the days passed, the news grew ever more grave. The Wales children were sent away to Windsor and the extended royal family, from across Europe, began to gather at Sandringham, filling both the big house and the outlying mansions of the estate. Even the Queen was moved to stir from her solitude; she came to Sandringham, visiting her son's country home for the first time, on 29 November. However, the Prince's symptoms appeared to be abating and, after two days, his mother departed back to her own home and her royal duties.

Louise sent someone over now and then to see what was happening, her thoughts with the Princess and the children; she herself had been through a time of grief and loss, so she could empathize with the agonies Alix was suffering. She recalls how the 'tumult of anxiety that it aroused throughout the British Empire was in remarkable contrast to the silence and stillness that prevailed [here at Sandringham]. We heard of the excitement from without like the surging of the sea in the distance, for those who lived near or came from afar to hear the latest news were awed and hushed with the solemnity of all around, and walked or drove with measured steps. Even the very wheels seemed to have a muffled sound as if they feared to disturb him… And the weeks went by until the time came when we hardly dare ask for news, or look to see if the flag was still flying from the tower of Sandringham church.' In that church, on Sundays, the congregation hardly dared to look at the Princess, 'but could hear her sobbing as if her heart would break'.

Anxiety grew deeper after the Earl of Chesterfield died and, when a few days later the Sandringham groom followed him, the prospect of a sensation brought the gentlemen of the press crowding to the Norwich Gates like carrion crows. The newsmen kept their pens poised, anticipating each new bulletin; at this stage, the latest news was posted at the gate twice daily, at 9 a.m. and 5 p.m. Ordinary people gathered, too, and across half the world people awaited the latest news. The name of Sandringham became a household word during those dark days.

For the first week of December, Bertie's condition remained serious but stable; then on 8 December came renewed anxiety when doctors noted 'considerable increase in febrile symptoms'. The Queen and other close members of the royal family took to the trains again, Her Majesty with a morbid certainty that her oldest son was doomed to die exactly ten years after his father. As the dreaded date, 14 December, approached, everyone prepared for the end.

But the day passed. The symptoms began to ease. Bertie would be weeks convalescing, but by Christmas his eventual recovery seemed certain. Everyone rejoiced.

Few of the Sandringham people could attend the great Service of National Thanksgiving, held in St Paul's Cathedral, but they did organize a small ceremony of their own, presenting, 'an address and memorial to the Princess, who had not quite got over the long strain and anxiety. She broke down in the speech she made in return, and Mr Onslow nearly did the same, and I think we all felt – I do not know exactly how.' Even the usually articulate Louise found the right words elusive.

To aid his convalescence, the Prince and his wife went on a tour of France and Italy, travelling incognito (if such a thing were possible) under one of their lesser titles, Earl and Countess of Chester. They were away from 9 March to 1 June 1872.

During that period, on 27 April, the kindly rector Lake Onslow wrote to Louise, who was staying in Lynn with her sister Fanny, 'I have had a letter this morning from the fascinating Francis Knollys [the Prince's private secretary, son of General

William Knollys] dated the 23 of April from Venice: all was well, the Prince of Wales quite himself again. The Princess sent me a very sweet message, as I sent her some flowers from her little son's grave; a thought struck me, she would like such a memo of the past and away from home here...'[48]

One thing was sure – the tide of rejoicing that followed the Prince's recovery completely swamped the threatening swell of Republicanism.

Death of Ossie Cresswell

While the country celebrated the renewed health of the heir to the throne, at the Bank House in Lynn Rachel Cresswell was nursing yet another of her sons through the last difficult months of a long and terminal illness.

In 1868 Lieutenant Oswald Cresswell had been obliged to leave the army because of failing health: like his naval officer brother Gurney before him, Ossie had contracted syphilis and was doomed to suffer a gradual and inevitable decline into fever, paralysis and dementia. After five years of this slow torture, thirty-two-year-old Ossie died, on 20 May 1872. He joined his father, sister and four brothers in the churchyard at North Runcton.

This latest tragedy left Rachel Cresswell, who was now sixty-nine, with only one son remaining – her first-born, Frank.

Ossie's named trustees were his brother, Frank, and his second cousin and friend, the ubiquitous Somerville Gurney. He left small bequests to the closest members of his family, including £100 for Louise, but the bulk of his estate was to be shared among his nieces and nephews in two portions – one half divided among Frank's four children, the other half to young Gerard of Appleton.

---

[48] Letters in private hands, copies in author's possession

CHAPTER SEVEN

Happier years for Louise

Apart from the brief years of her marriage, the early 1870s were the happiest of the eighteen Louise spent at Sandringham. Hares continued to breed far too prolifically for her peace of mind, but their numbers were not quite so overwhelming as before and new head keeper Jackson turned out to be far more congenial than the bully Overton. It was a time of contentment, of cream teas in the best parlour, a curtain of vines over the windows and the munching of cows and sheep outside. Friends and family, seeing Appleton in the idyll of a warm summer day, envied Louise her life, forgetting the hard work, the long hours, the freezing winters and, not least, the constant poking and prying of tourists who came 'gawking after anyone connected with Royalty… poor Mr Onslow bears the brunt…' (Even then, royalty provided a spurious thrill for sensation-seekers.) The rector was too kind and well-mannered to turn people away, but Louise had less patience with the intruders: 'I believe I often gave offence when their raids upon my valuable time were but coldly received…'

Invitations to dinner at the big house came occasionally, but she felt unsure of herself in such intimate parties, which meant making small talk, over food, with Dukes or foreign royalty, politicians, Lords Bishop or intellectual giants: 'I never had that honour without remembering afterwards that I had done or said the wrong thing.' She felt more at ease receiving such exalted personages in the familiarity of her own house, 'particularly when the Princess and her children walked down to call'.

Less demanding opportunities to dress in one's best evening frock and mingle with the cream of county society were more welcome, if rare. They included the County Ball which was held at Sandringham in February 1873, the first since the Prince's illness. But one of the most spectacular balls took place over at

Hillington Hall on Thursday, 21 November 1872, when Sir William ffolkes *[sic]* attained his twenty-fifth birthday.

Grand Fancy Dress Ball at Hillington Hall

Nothing quite like this party had been seen for thirty-five years; it brought local residents crowding eagerly onto the galleries above the grand hall to witness the gaiety. Happily for us, the *Lynn Advertiser* for 23 November 1872 noted both guests and costumes: Sir William ffolkes appeared as Sir Walter Raleigh; his two brothers came dressed as a Danish pirate and the Duke de Rohan; Hamon le Strange, squire of Hunstanton, was a Mexican Ranchero, while his wife Emmie personified 'America'; Somerville Gurney was Lord Darnley; Frank Cresswell went as 'Major Bridgnorth, 1661', his two daughters portrayed Puritan Ladies while his older son, George, assumed Turkish dress (younger son Cressie, aged fifteen, was away at school). Revd W. Lake Onslow wore court dress with medals and orders; his sister and her friend were Spanish ladies; there was a fairy; a personification of 'Twilight', and 'Little Bo-Peep, without her sheep', and down the list came Mrs Gerard Cresswell and her sister Miss Hogge – Fanny dressed as a 'Marquise, Louis XIV', and Louise togged out as a Spanish Duenna.

What fun! No wonder the locals came crowding to see.

While such occasions provided light relief now and then, the farm occupied the bulk of Louise's time. She writes lyrically and knowledgeably about the turning seasons, the year's work of seed-time and harvest, of birthing and marketing for her animals, and the daily routine – being about the yards, or poring in the evenings over account books in her office. 'The autumn skies and sunsets are magnificent... if you want scenery in the Eastern Counties, you must look up instead of down, where with a little imagination you will discover Alpine peaks and mountains and Turneresque colouring to your heart's content. Creeks ending in miniature harbours wind in and out of the marshes... The villages are noted smuggling resorts, and you may still see lonesome public houses and outlying farm premises suspiciously near the harbours, where the horses would be found in the early morning reeking from some midnight expedition…'

She entered her livestock in agricultural shows, locally and sometimes at national level. She also began to experiment, very successfully, with breeding pigs – her improved Norfolks were little beauties, 'round balls with no noses to speak of, "fit for a parlour" as the dealers said… they sold to the Royal Farms of England, Denmark and Greece…' Indeed, the Prince of Wales took a consignment of Appleton pigs out to Athens aboard HMS *Serapis* on his way out to India in 1875.

Although Louise was not making much profit, at least the farm was paying its way, and when obliged to economise she made light of it. She comments ruefully that the trap in which she drove about the farm, or to market and Tuesday lunch at the bank, had no equal in the county, having been 'patched and mended by local talent until there was hardly any of the original structure left… once it collapsed through the bottom coming out, and when too rotten to hold a nail was tied up with string.' She named the ramshackle vehicle 'Agricultural Distress'.

Reverend Onslow and his sister Agnes continued to provide companionship and support. After Louise had spent an evening at the rectory in April 1872, Onslow wrote concerned that she had elected to walk all the way home: 'I much fear you were quite done [in] yesterday… you have ever a brave spirit but you cannot do too much: so please remember there is always anchorage here.' He adds, 'Gerard is a mathematician and his conversation delighted me not a little yesterday.'[49]

The boy Gerard, now six and a half, had been riding since he was quite small and, set free by his governess and mounted on his pony, would accompany his mama about the farm, or 'career in the hunting field', as she puts it. His life was a paradise of ponies, dogs, birds, kittens, and birthday trees and treats. 'He was a great favourite with the village people and everyone around; and the only shadow in the distance, for me at least, was the dreadful separation for school which must come in time…' When young Gerard went to boarding school, she felt, she would

---

[49] Letters in private hands, copies in author's possession

be 'truly alone' for much of the year – a sentiment with which every mother may sympathize. However, Louise's adult friends and relations were never far away, chief among them her sister Fanny, Mr Onslow and his sister Agnes at the rectory, and the invaluable Farmer Groom.

Mr Groom had by this time moved some nine or ten miles away, to Ashwicken Hall, taking on an extra 500 acres, though he also retained his much larger farm at Congham. His elderly parents still lived there and his oldest son, John Edmund, now in his early twenties, managed the place, with Farmer Groom keeping an overseeing eye on both properties. However, despite this added work, and even though Ashwicken was twice as far from Appleton as was Congham, he continued to provide advice and encouragement for Louise, and when she needed a man to represent her interests – at rent audits, or business dinners – it was Groom who assumed the mantle.

Before long, however, even good old Farmer Groom's inherent patience would be sorely tried.

Although a few years remained before the final storms broke over Appleton, across rural England an ominous shadow haunted the horizon; in the last three decades of the nineteenth century, the Agricultural Depression began to bite everywhere, affecting towns as well as countryside. The causes were manifold, but all stemmed from the Industrial Revolution.

The Agricultural Depression of the 1870s

The growth of the 'dark satanic' mill towns in the north of England had increased the demand for food while depleting the labour force in the countryside. Mechanization on farms helped to narrow the gap, and improved methods of transport brought more markets within the farmers' reach, but competition from abroad grew ever more intense, and emigration drew more of the labour force away, to seek a better life in the New World.

Steam-ships and steam-trains rushed produce from all corners of the world to feed the growing markets in Europe. Cheap wheat came from vast corn-fields opening up on the prairies of America, while new methods of refrigeration brought in beef from the Argentine and mutton and dairy products from the Antipodes, while armed conflicts and financial depression affected the whole world and sent prices tumbling.

At home, the demands of the embryo farm labourers' union, agitating for higher wages and fairer conditions, put a further strain on farmers' bank balances, along with new chemical fertilizers and the need to buy and maintain expensive threshers, reapers and steam ploughs, machinery which could be dangerous if handled carelessly by men more used to hoes and horses.

Nature herself seemed to turn on the British farmer. From 1875 a series of cold, wet summers ruined five harvests in succession. In 1877 the cattle plague rinderpest returned, and in 1879 liver-rot destroyed millions of sheep.

All these forces conspiring against them drove many farmers to bankruptcy. The rest struggled on, desperately scrimping to keep up payments on their rents, mortgages and overdrafts. The banks themselves had to balance their books with care; they began to refuse credit, or foreclose on property used as security for loans.

It was a terrible time to be a farmer.

Writing in 1875,[50] Louise Cresswell predicted the eventual extinction of small farms and their replacement by huge, food-producing manufactories owned by public companies. She knew her world was changing, but she failed to foresee how soon she herself might be caught in the whirlpool and dragged down.

She was not alone in her hopeless fight to stay solvent; many other farmers were struggling just as she was, and many of them also complained bitterly of the depredations caused by hares; the difference was that Louise, rather than admit that the general depression might be her main foe, clung stubbornly to the notion that her problems lay mostly at the door of the land agent, the Prince, and the game question. The moment things went wrong for her, she sharpened her pen and went on the attack again.

Family affairs
In summer 1873, Louise took a short holiday in the Isle of Wight. Her good friend Revd Onslow also happened to be on the

---

[50] Cresswell: *Norfolk and the Squires, Clergy, Farmers and Labourers, etc'*, pamphlet, p12

island, a guest at Osborne Cottage, one of the smaller dwellings in the grounds of the Queen's residence, Osborne House. Onslow had accompanied the Prince and Princess of Wales on a visit to the west country, which included a trip on the Royal Yacht, much to his delight. He wrote a long letter to Louise: 'Dear Cousin, I was indeed glad to see your handwriting and to find that you are also in this pleasant island and not bothered with cough or anything save the coming parting with your boy. I think you are quite right not to take him to school yourself... to see him after a time would be far better.' After indulging in some harmless gossip, he sends 'love to Gerard' and signs off, adding a PS: 'I am so glad to hear the wedding is coming off on Wednesday.'[51]

The wedding was that of Louise's niece, Edith Eliza Hogge, lady of Thornham, and Captain Lionel Neville Frederick Ames of the Grenadier Guards (soon to be Ames-Lyde when he inherited Lyde family property in Ayot St Lawrence, Herts.). Edith was twenty-two, her husband just seven months older, when they married, on Wednesday, 27 August 1873, at St Peter's church on Eaton Square, London, and in far away Norfolk the good folk of Thornham celebrated with decorations of banners, flags and mottoes, and a roast beef and plum pudding dinner for all 160 children of the local school. The event, paid for by the young lady of the manor, was hosted in her absence by her land agent, Edmund Beck.

Less than a month later, on 24 September, the Hogge family welcomed another new member when Louise's brother, the wealthy banker, brewer and merchant Frederick Archdale (46), married his third wife, Fanny St Quintin (35), in her home village of Harrold, Bedfordshire. They set up home in Baldock, Hertfordshire, where in 1875 Frederick acquired an imposing town house named 'The Wilderness'. (The property consisted of not only the house but also two large plots of land, one opposite the house and one to the rear, encompassing the area now occupied by the Knights Templar School. The house is long gone – a large road junction occupies the place – but the gardens

---

⁵¹ Letters in private hands, copies in author's possession

provide a green recreation park for the people of Baldock.) Fanny Archdale presented her husband with at least three more children, the final one in 1882, when she was forty-four.

While Frederick continued to prosper, a long-standing dispute over their grandfather Wells's legacy had soured his relationship with Louise. She believed that he and the other trustees of Samuel Wells's estate were not handling the money as astutely as they should, which meant that she and the other legatees, her siblings and Lindsell cousins, were not receiving sufficient interest on their investment. The matter having been in lawyers' hands since 1872, Louise fully intended to take it as far as the Court in Chancery if she was forced to it.

This disagreement clouded the background of her life. As always, it came down to that 'vulgar money': she simply did not have enough of it.

The adorable Alix

Though everyone at Sandringham adored their 'little Missus', the Princess Alexandra of Wales remained a mass of contradictions, childlike in many ways, and empathetically tender toward children, animals, and anyone in trouble. Some courtiers thought she lacked intelligence, but Alix's charm soon made most people forgive her, especially for her knack of appearing sublimely unaware of any problem she might have caused by her habitual lateness, or her increasing deafness. Even her formidable mother-in-law, stern and critical of the younger royals' hectic social life, lack of discipline and light-mindedness, relented whenever she found herself in Alix's merry company. Alix enjoyed practical jokes, as did her husband, but where his humour had a hard, bullying edge which made others the butt of his jokes and never himself, she enjoyed more child-like games such as using tin trays as sledges to whiz down the staircase, making apple pie beds, and playing hide and seek.

Her deafness may have been the reason some people considered her unintelligent, though she had learned to hide her infirmity, often holding conversations with a whole group at a time, though not really hearing anything anyone said. She preferred a one-to-one situation, when she could properly give attention and hear almost every word – that was why she enjoyed visiting Louise at Appleton; and for the same reason she loved being with horses and dogs, often going out to the stables or kennels to take titbits to her favourites.

'Our dear Princess will be here on the 3rd Nov – bright, rejoicing and good creature!!!' wrote Lake Onslow to Louise on 18 October 1873. He had been at Balmoral with the royal pair and on returning home to his 'den' he penned a letter full of gossip about various romances and upsets among the courtiers, concluding with a paean of praise for his royal lady: 'How much I have seen of her this time, twice a day in the school room with me… Peerless woman, what a jewel for his coronet!!'[52]

Louise, too, writes with fulsome admiration of the Princess: 'the embodiment of all that poets have ever dreamed in their dreams of fair women… she looks well in everything… in full dress with rows of priceless pearls… in a quiet serge dress with her favourite Danish cross… in a bonnet… in her sailor's hat or riding habit or rough Ulster and cap, driving the miniature four-in-hand of ponies that might have been Cinderella's… You finally give up all comparisons and discover what England found out long ago, that the fairest of daughters is Alexandra of Denmark, Princess of Wales… I do not think I am quite sane upon the subject… It never occurs to me that she is a woman at all, but some exquisite little being wafted straight from fairyland, to say and to do the kindest and prettiest things all the days of her life…'

However, being Louise, she tempers this saccharine praise with a touch of tartness when discussing the decline in morals: 'Without wishing the Princess of Wales to become strong-minded or lose her unique identity, an occasional stand against some of the more notorious characters, instead of ignoring, condoning, and receiving all alike, might be desirable in the interests of morality; and though the Princess suits the nation so well the Duchess of Edinburgh [Russian wife of Prince Alfred] would perhaps make a better leader of society… her Romanoff

---

[52] Letters in private hands, copies in author's possession

temper and determination would soon make a clean sweep within the precincts of the Court, which, as the Court reigns supreme in all social matters, might lead to better things.'

Among the delights of the Sandringham winters, which included the various balls, the hunting and shooting, and visits from VIPs who liked to wander round the estate and chat with the tenants, Louise remembers the evening skating parties with especial fondness: 'the lake and island illuminated with coloured lamps and torches, the skating chairs with glow-worm lights, and the skaters flitting past and disappearing into the darkness... The Princess usually wore a grey Siberian style of costume and cap, and looked – but I must not go into raptures every time I name her!' The Prince allowed the villagers to gather on the banks at the far end of the lake and look on at the gaiety, but Louise herself stood nearer to the house and on one occasion HRH himself brought her a tumbler of 'negus', a hot drink of spiced port with sugar and lemon. 'Those sort of things make it impossible not to like the Prince in a way,' Louise concedes, 'though I cannot say I quite approve of him altogether.'

She obviously relished these personal encounters, though she is scathing about acquaintances who were jealous of her closeness to royalty: 'women who are friendly and pleasant in a general way will look black and queer, and make a tart remark or preserve an ominous silence, if you are incautious enough to name having been to a party to which they were not asked...' She claims total disinterest in such petty one-upmanship, saying that it might have mattered to her if she had 'gone in for' society, but as it was 'it made no difference to me whether I was first or last, looked up to or down upon, liked or disliked.' So she says.

At this period, Louise led a fairly quiet and solitary life. She had reached her forties, but still gave most of her time to the practical work of farming. From dawn to sunset she tended the stock or drove round the fields, overseeing her labourers and frequently irritating her steward by interfering in his area of expertise; she met and haggled with salesmen, went to market with her pigs and cattle, and after dark, when the housemaid lit the lamps, she passed the lonely hours by working in the farm office. She tried music, but the sound of her piano echoing round the empty rooms only succeeded in making the house feel emptier than ever. When the affable Duke of Cambridge visited Appleton one time, he asked Louise what she did with her evenings and she replied, 'I have the accounts, Sir, and the work to think about.'

She was still struggling to make ends meet and, for much of the time, she was alone with a few house servants and the nurse-turned-housekeeper, her old ally, Lucy Sparrow. Young Gerard had been sent off to his first boarding school in autumn 1873, a few weeks prior to his ninth birthday. But he came home for Christmas and summer holidays, going fishing and ratting with his friends, and helping his mama teach the village boys rudimentary lessons – until state schooling for all became the law. Not that Louise approved of that innovation: too much education gave country boys notions above their station, teaching them things they did not need to know. In her opinion village lads should start full-time work at age nine or ten: 'they can pick up quite enough book learning by that time and keep it up at the evening school, and religion on Sundays.'

Her own son's education was another matter; he was due to go up to the famous public school of Harrow when he was fourteen.

Frank Cresswell and his family

Louise's son was still too young to join in his Lynn cousins' social activities. By now Frank Cresswell's oldest three were beginning to enjoy more adult social outings, being noted at various balls in the area, usually accompanied by their father. In January 1874 they threw a party of their own, a 'Blue and White Dance' for forty-six guests, when everyone dressed in the specified colours and many of the girls giggled over dousing their hair in old-style violet powder. The jolly Troubridge siblings, living with grandfather Daniel Gurney at Runcton, joined in the fun that evening. The youngsters were all close friends as well as being second cousins – sharing Christmas at Runcton Hall, they had enjoyed dressing up, with twenty-year-old George F.A. Cresswell costumed as an Algerian pirate, while his cousin Geoffrey 'Gee' Gurney wore 'a very jolly red and gold uniform of Ozzie *[sic]* Cresswell's'.[53]

Later that year, the King's Lynn town council elected Frank J. Cresswell to the Mayoralty. He himself did not attend that particular meeting but after taking time to consider he declined the office and also decided to resign from the town council. This formerly active, easy-going man had never properly recovered from a boating accident three years before, when he severely injured his right side. Now, reaching the age of fifty-two, he felt the time had come to curtail some of his official activities.

However, in 1875 he was fit enough to give away both of his daughters in marriage, settling £10,000 on each of them. Younger daughter Edith (21) wed Charles Edward Thorneycroft on 21 April in St Margaret's church, Lynn (where only a few days earlier the Prince and Princess of Wales had attended a service to mark restorations to the church paid for by money raised in thanksgiving for HRH's return to health). Then, in August, Charlotte (23) married Commander Gerard Henry Motred Noel, RN: this wedding was a quieter, private affair since the groom had recently lost his mother. His father was rector at Stanhoe, not far from Lynn.

In time, Frank's oldest son George F.A. Cresswell followed his father and grandfather into the offices of Gurney & Co. Bank, and, also like his father, he took command of the 5th Battalion of the Norfolk Volunteers. As an enthusiastic observer of wildlife, George Cresswell founded the Wolferton Wild Birds' Protection Society and was later awarded a CVO.[54] He married, in succession, two of the Gurney girls: Constance Gurney, of Keswick, became his wife in November 1878, but died only two months later; then in 1882 George took Eva Gurney, daughter of the North Runcton rector William Hay Gurney, as his second

[53] Hope-Nicholson, Jacqueline (ed): *Life Amongst the Troubridges: Journals of a Young Victorian 1873-1884,* by Laura Troubridge (Tite Street Press, London, 1999)

[54] Watson, Alfred T: *King Edward VII as a Sportsman* (Longmans, Green and Co, London, 1911)

wife. They had two sons, the older of whom was killed at the battle of Mons in 1914.

Frank's youngest child, Cresswell Augustus Cresswell, variously referred to as 'Cressie', 'Gussy' or 'Cripps', went up to Oxford in October 1875, aged eighteen. He studied at Magdalen College and was, for a while, part of Oscar Wilde's set. In 1877 Wilde wrote to his friend, William Ward, 'My greatest chum, except of course the Kitten [Reginald Harding], is Gussy, who is charming though not educated well: however he is psychological and we have long chats and walks.'[55] 'Psychological' was then a euphemism for 'homosexual'. C.A. Cresswell eventually (1893) married another Gurney girl from North Runcton rectory, his sister-in-law Eva's sister, Kathleen Laura Alicia Gurney. He became a stockbroker and made his home in London.

Louise in print

When the Earl of Leicester offered a prize for the best essay on recent improvements in agriculture in Eastern England, Louise sat down to write an entry. Realizing that her expertise did not extend beyond Norfolk, she 'gave up all hope of the Prize' but still went on to complete and publish her essay, full of expert comment on farm machinery, expenses and rearing of animals, and also rich with her own acerbic opinions on topics of the day. Under the title *Norfolk and the Squires, Clergy, Farmers and Labourers, etc,* it appeared in pamphlet form (40 pages, price one shilling) in 1875, while she was still ensconced at Appleton and having to be diplomatic.

Though being careful not to criticize the Prince of Wales openly, she drops acid hints, aimed at landlords in general but based on her own specific grievances. A friend had asked what guarantee she had for recompense, regarding improvements she had made at Appleton which had 'considerably raised the value of the property'. Her answer, 'My landlord is a gentleman,' seemed crazy to him, but in her opinion it worked where honour and tradition still applied. She cites 'the former owner of Sandringham [Charles Spencer Cowper], that perfect landlord,

---

[55] McKenna, Neil: *The Secret Life of Oscar Wilde* (Century, 2003, <u>et al</u>)

neighbour and friend to all who had the privilege of knowing him, [who] made it a <u>sine qua non</u> upon the sale of the estate that it should pass into good hands, and all England knows how he kept his word.' (Did she intend the ambiguity in this last phrase?)

In general, she believed the sport of shooting to be a right which the landed aristocracy should be allowed to enjoy, for everybody, rich and poor alike, enjoyed the excitement of a shoot: 'cold beef and beer, cracking jokes, and the love of sport born in every Norfolker, makes a red-letter day in the rural calendar' (which belies the scathing descriptions in her later book).

While not particularly religious, she held decided opinions about the way the church was going and the kind of clergyman it employed: the Church of England would be everyone's preference if it stopped being so hide-bound; Methodists love money and are not to be trusted (though their women are better housewives than most); and the histrionics of the Ranters provide 'quite a little opera' for working-class people who have been driven to worship at chapel by the dullness of the church.

As for assistant gamekeepers, the 'Velveteens' were a formidable vehicle for mischief when so disposed, making ill-will between landlords and tenants. However, there were exceptions, such as 'on the estate where I have the honour to reside, where the present head game-keeper affords splendid sport, and yet is courteous and considerate to all...'

She calls the recently formed Labourers' Union 'a violent, communistic attack upon property', and its leader Joseph Arch[56] 'a rabble-rouser, cunning and clever'. Her own men were at first 'desperately offended' by her opposition to their Union but now she and they agree to differ. She praises her farm workers, who stood by her when she needed them: 'I would rather have one on

---

[56] Joseph Arch (1826-1919), farm labourer, became a preacher in the Primitive Methodist 'fire and brimstone' tradition, often using his sermons to point out the injustice of the farmworkers' situation — very long hours and very poor pay. Gaining a reputation as a radical reformer, he founded the National Agricultural Labourers' Union in 1872 and went on to become Liberal MP for north-west Norfolk. A strike by Suffolk farmworkers in 1874 culminated in an eighteen-week lock-out of unionists in the eastern counties

my side in a witness box than anyone I know, and would answer for his baffling the best lawyer on the circuit.' However, her rant about the general improvidence of the labouring class could have been written by some of today's wiseacres – working people are feckless, they spend their wages on fast living, don't save, have too many children, and then rely on state charity, often telling lies to get the most money they can…

Louise had opinions on everything and few qualms about expressing them. She also provided answers to most of the country's problems – if only someone would take heed! All her writing is lively, informed, immensely readable, and often imbued with dry humour.

Her book, *Eighteen Years on Sandringham Estate,* has a chapter titled 'Social Convulsions' in which she writes much more about the troubles caused by Labourers' Union agitators: 'there were some queer characters about, and an unfortunate farmer's daughter was dragged, out of revenge to her father, into the woods one evening and terribly maltreated.' The culprit got a sentence of penal servitude and a flogging, thanks to 'a no-nonsense judge'. People who, like herself, openly opposed the Union, were in greater danger than they realized: 'In consequence of some friendly warnings that had been conveyed to me, I slept for some weeks with a revolver in my room, and took it with me sometimes when obliged to be late in the evening, and let everyone know I should use it pretty freely, if attacked; and a farmer near having two policemen on guard one night, it could not have been an unnecessary precaution. I preferred the revolver; it wanted neither beef nor beer, and couldn't make love to both maids at once.'

Harbingers of doom
In January 1875, Canon Charles Kingsley died. The news saddened Louise, who admired and liked him, but it was only the first in a succession of yet more bad omens.

That summer the weather turned foul; the harvest came in wet and difficult, with poor yields. Some of the wheat rotted in the stacks before it could be threshed. Winter followed with storms and gales; floods threatened the sluices along the Ouse, and more chunks of the soft, chalky, tri-coloured Hunstanton cliffs went crashing onto the rocks below. In January, eighteen degrees of frost held the land in thrall, and in March more storms prevented any work on the fields; spring sowing had to be put off until April, and many farmers abandoned hopes of growing any wheat at all that year, planting beans or barley instead.

The adventures of the Prince of Wales, off on an expensive seven-month junket to India, served only to increase general criticism of his spending habits, and when he came home, in May 1876, he faced ugly rumours about his relationship with the adulterous Lady Aylesford. Though he may have been innocent of any physical impropriety, he had certainly written some imprudent letters; but his wife and his mother stood by him, put on a united front, and once again the scandal passed into history.

The weather continued to harass the farming community. Spring storms and floods turned to June drought; young green shoots, already delayed, paused in their growing; even the trees looked half-bare, while the land lay parched, with deep cracks spreading. The wheat crop was meagre, harvested in weather almost too hot for working, and before all the corn could be garnered more violent storms left the land sodden, delaying the sowing of winter wheat and blighting potatoes in their clamps.

The dark, damp skies of October 1876 accompanied a time of deepening uncertainty for Louise. Her lease on Appleton expired that month and no one proposed that she might sign a new one; instead, she and Somerville Gurney, as co-executors and trustees, became 'tenant(s) on sufferance until payment of Rent at the previous rate, when a new Tenancy from year to year was thereby created, upon the terms and conditions as in the expired Lease...'[57] This meant, in plain language, that if she failed to pay the rent on time she could be summarily evicted.

Happily for Farmer Groom, his own financial affairs were on a sounder footing than some of his neighbours'. Now well established as squire at Ashwicken Hall, he played host to the West Norfolk Fox Hounds on 10 February 1877, affording them

---

[57] Royal Archive LAW/SHM/12/10/58

some excellent sport, as the *Lynn Advertiser* recorded: 'the constant supply of foxes here is remarkable and shows great care and forbearance on the part of the owner, in the interests of fox hunting, for Ashwicken is surrounded by game preserves and fox traps' (including those at Sandringham, of course).

But while Groom prospered, moving up a few rungs in county society, at Appleton Louise despaired. Born to comfort and wealth, she had firmly believed that her life would continue in that way, and though she had been prepared to work and do without – by her standards – she had always believed that such deprivation would prove temporary. The looming shadow of yet more debt dashed all her hopes and began to affect her reasoning. The small profit she had made over the few years of contentment dwindled again towards the red, and the bank in Lynn began to jib at handing out loans to tide her over. Growing anxious for her future, she knew she must find some other source of funds. If the farm could not support her, the returns from her investments must be increased.

For some time now, she had been convinced in her own mind that her capital – inherited mainly from her maternal grandfather, Samuel Wells, and from her father, William Hogge – ought to be providing a better income. In fact, she had formally accused the estate trustees of mismanagement and her legal representative, Mr Archer of Lynn, had been preparing a case against them for at least five years. This must have caused some awkward moments at family gatherings since the principal trustees were her two older brothers, George and Frederick Archdale. Actually, with George sequestered in London among his more bohemian friends, the onus fell largely on Frederick, who was still managing the Bedfordshire businesses.

In the spring of 1877, with her financial situation ever more bleak, Louise once more took up her pen to contact her family's solicitors, Messrs Hooper and Fletcher of Biggleswade:

Appleton, Sandringham
April 25th 1877

Sirs,

I trust you will excuse my writing to you personally instead of through a Solicitor and particularly as Mr Archer received no reply to his last communication to you.

Ever since I received a Deed of Release sent to me in the year 1872 for signature by the Trustees of the late Samuel Wells the case has been placed in the hands of legal advisers, but owing to the mass of evidence to be collected from various sources, and *my own ill-health*, the arrangements for *taking the case into the Court of Chancery* have not long been completed [emphasis added].

I need hardly say that I have had eminent and strictly disinterested legal advice – taking care on my part to bring forward every fact and circumstance that would probably be brought in evidence against me. The opinion of Counsel is that there is no doubt whatever of a breach of Trust having been committed, through which I have lost a considerable sum of money, and that I have as good a chance of receiving the same in the Courts of Chancery as anyone may have who decided to run the risk of the law.

Being anxious to prove in Court that I only resorted to the law as the last remedy, and also because a peaceable settlement of every dispute is desirable if possible, I write to propose submitting the case to arbitration...[58]

Interesting to see that she pleads ill health yet again.

Charles Dickens' satirical slant on the slow grindings of the Court of Chancery, in his novel *Bleak House* a few years before, had not deterred Louise. She had undertaken a crusade and was determined to see it through, however long it took.

The legalities ground on, and on, a wearying backdrop to her life.

For a third year in succession, capricious weather affected the crops, with gales and hail delaying everything before milder weather encouraged a spurt of growth, only for rain and sleet to turn the green shoots sickly yellow. April frosts heralded May hailstorms, and a deluge of rain on St Swithin's Day lent credence to the old superstition when a wet, cold season followed. The harvest began fitfully, interrupted by long spells of cold and damp. Before it ended, fate struck more cruel blows for Louise.

---

[58] Bedfordshire and Luton Record Office HF/45/14/5

'My doom was sealed...'

A chest infection, contracted early in 1875, had brought Lake Onslow so low that his sister Agnes and their friends, including Louise, feared for his life. The rector fought off the infection that time, but it left him weakened and, though he bore up with cheerful stoicism, two and a half years later, as a third dreary summer ended, his strength began to ebb for the last time. Louise's faithful 'Knight and Champion' died at his home, the Sandringham rectory, late in the evening of Thursday, 30 August 1877. He was fifty-seven.

'The loss to me was irreparable,' writes Louise. 'I felt my doom was sealed and that I should no longer be able to cope...' Lake Onslow had, she felt, been her mainstay against the adverse forces that surrounded her. Without him, her enemies would surely close in.

On 4 September, the tiny Sandringham church was filled to overflowing with men who had known Onslow in his various guises as churchman, naval officer, Freemason, and amateur astronomer. Sir Dighton Probyn, recently promoted Comptroller of the Prince's Household, represented his royal master and mistress, along with agent Edmund Beck. To signify both Onslow's long service as chaplain of one of HM ships of war and his years of distinguished work as a Freemason, they draped a Union flag across his coffin and laid on it his sword, hat, medals and epaulettes, along with his Masonic insignia.

Four chief mourners followed the coffin, led by Onslow's brother-in-law (his sister Anne's husband) Revd J. Clapcott, and Master Gerard Cresswell. Young Gerard, a month short of his thirteenth birthday, was performing one of his first solemn adult duties as he watched his old friend being laid to rest, only a few yards away from the gate to the rectory and the path along which he had so often walked.

Later, a plaque in memory of William Lake Onslow was placed prominently on the wall inside the church by 'his friends afloat and on shore to record their high esteem and affection for one who while faithfully discharging his various duties endeared himself to all by his kind and gentle disposition'. (This tribute was moved in 2005 to make room for a memorial to Queen Elizabeth the Queen Mother and her husband George VI; it can now be seen on the wall at the base of the bell tower.)

Young Gerard shot

The day of the funeral was a sad day for Onslow's unmarried sister Agnes, waiting behind shrouded windows inside the dark rectory, along with Louise and the other ladies. Agnes was by this time thirty-seven; she had shared the rectory house with her brother for eleven years and now she was thrown on the mercy of friends and distant relatives.

Louise grieved too, having lost the man she felt to be her only ally at Sandringham. But that mournful September day had another shock still in store.

Only a few hours after Onslow's funeral, young Gerard was handling a gun which went off and shot him in the hand. With the bloody wound swaddled in clean cloths and with his frantic mother beside him, he was bundled into a carriage and rushed to the hospital in Lynn. There, to his mother's great distress and horror, surgeons amputated the second finger of his injured left hand. Later, when he was up to the short journey, the boy was taken to his grandmother's home, the Bank House, to be nursed back to health.

This is one of the very few personal incidents that Louise mentions in her book, though she does so in passing, not linking it with Onslow's funeral but using it instead as an excuse for an oversight of hers. That autumn, she says, she was being blamed for every petty ill and irritation that affected the even tenor of life at Sandringham. During a shoot, one of her men had 'got in the way between the drives' and the Prince of Wales, observing him, saw fit to 'anathematise' Louise in front of everyone, as if she had done it on purpose. She excuses herself by revealing that G— (as she refers to her son) had received 'a severe gun-shot wound that endangered his life' and she, being called away from his Lynn bedside by news that the Prince wished to shoot over her land, may not have given clear orders to her men, owing to her 'severe shock, and being rather worn with the nursing'. She adds, 'as the Princess said afterwards, "What <u>did</u> you do? Only think, your precious boy to be shot..." '

Once again, her memory appears to have blurred the facts to serve her own purpose. It is certainly true that Gerard lost a finger – his grandchildren remember that about him. Also, the *Lynn Advertiser* carried the story, on 14 September 1877, under the heading 'Gun Accident': 'We are glad to learn that Master Gerard Cresswell, who on the 4th inst. accidentally shot his hand (necessitating amputation of the second finger) is progressing favourably.' The odd thing is that usually the paper took care to record every royal visit, but it says nothing of the Prince's being present at Sandringham in early September that year; besides which pheasant shooting, requiring the drives Louise mentions, does not start until 1 October.

She recounts another incident, when illness struck the Prince's oldest son and heir, the teenage Eddy (Prince Albert Victor Christian Edward[59]) and, fearing that he had contracted typhoid, everyone panicked. Since the royal children had lately been staying at Sandringham, where a water tower serving the big house had recently been erected on the hill behind Appleton, someone at court had accused Louise of allowing her farm drainage to poison the spring. When Edmund Beck called at Appleton with this news, Louise in typical fashion sat down at once to address an admonitory note to the courtier involved. He returned, as she says, a 'most emphatic denial', thereby creating 'another unsolved mystery'.

Suspecting forces at work against her, she concluded that all the unpleasantness must stem from a single source, some secret enemy who kept inventing 'petty trumperies... incidents so ludicrous and incredible that I long to relate them... Perhaps I may reproduce them in a little private and confidential edition, when I have scribbled this one off... I instinctively felt that it was the intention to make me appear an intolerable nuisance to His Royal Highness, who hates being bored, and forgets that it is often the talebearers who are at fault...'

---

[59] Prince Albert Victor, Duke of Clarence, died years later, of influenza, in January 1892, a few days after his twenty-eighth birthday

To add to her feelings of paranoia, the dreaded hares began to increase yet again, riddling her crops as in former years. She estimated the cost as running to several hundred pounds but in answer to her demands the agent paid a measly fifty pounds compensation. It was too much to bear!

Like a vixen driven into a corner, Louise leapt out with fangs bared. But this time the hounds were ready for her.

CHAPTER EIGHT

Endgame

As 1879 began, in the middle of one of the coldest and snowiest winters for years, fourteen-year-old Gerard Cresswell prepared for his first term at the exclusive, and expensive, Harrow School in Buckinghamshire. In common with other parents down the years, Louise put on an encouraging face, but inwardly she was terrified by the downward-spiralling trend of her overdraft; the £500 legacy she had received from her uncle, Fred Hogg, in 1878, had been a help, but not enough to save her. Knowing she would not be able to pay the next period's rent on time, she appealed to Edmund Beck for a reprieve. The agent immediately agreed to defer the coming rent audit.

In a letter dated 10 January, Louise writes to Beck saying she is very much obliged for the delay in the audit, being so burdened with rent, taxes, cost of labour and depredations of game that she hardly knows what to do… she's having to live entirely on her private income and is 'quite frightened' at her present losses. Regrettably, she doesn't leave it at that; instead she spurs up her latest hobby horse: 'You are… aware of the extravagant way in which the West Newton people dress and live, and expect to do less work for more pay than any other village, also that if dismissed or reproved, for theft or any other fault they have a good place given them on the [Royal] Estate at once… Ground game is still in excess… although I was very glad of the £58 you gave towards it last year it did not make up for the £360 of visible damage… I do not intend this letter as a complaint, I feel quite overpowered just now.'[60]

Four days later Mr Beck answers that the tone of her letter causes him much regret, 'because it conveys the impression you wish either to relinquish your farm or that you must ask HRH for a considerable reduction of your rent…' He notes that she claims

---

[60] Royal Archive LAW/SHM/12/10/34 A

not to be making a complaint, but he cannot reconcile that with the tenor of the letter: perhaps he might show it to Sir Dighton Probyn?[61]

Lieutenant-General Sir Dighton Probyn, VC, Comptroller and Treasurer of the Prince's Household, was a much-decorated cavalry officer of great heroic repute, a tougher opponent by far than his courtly predecessor, Sir William Knollys, who had retired in March 1877, aged eighty. The tall, full-bearded Probyn was now forty-six, three years younger than Louise.

Beck's invoking of Probyn's name evidently gave Louise pause; she replied in haste, to emphasize that her previous letter was not to be taken as an 'official' complaint, she ought to have made that clear; she would never take such a serious step without consulting her co-trustee [Somerville Gurney]. 'Consider my letter private for the present [ie don't show it to Probyn]'. But she cannot stop herself making yet more complaints about recent damage by frost, her expensive sainfoin ruined... 'I cannot but think [HRH] would wish us to have a fair chance of remaining... It is the game and the labour that is the difficulty.'[62]

Beck arranged to call and see her, but the encounter proved stormy. The tone of his ensuing letters grows sharper: if she is considering leaving Appleton, she should first seek advice from her co-trustee Mr Gurney, and will she please do so swiftly as Beck wants to put the matter to Sir Dighton Probyn before HRH leaves Sandringham.[63] At this, Louise protests again that her original letter was a private statement: 'I cannot but feel that your anxiety to represent it to Sir Dighton Probyn as a notice to quit is a proof that you are extremely anxious for me to leave...' She says she never troubles Mr Gurney if she can possibly avoid doing so; she also adds a PS, claiming that Beck has taken her original letter in a very different light from that intended and she requests him not to show it to anyone.[64]

---

[61] Royal Archive LAW/SHM/12/10/34 B
[62] Royal Archive LAW/SHM/12/10/34 C
[63] Royal Archive LAW/SHM/12/10/34 E
[64] Royal Archive LAW/SHM/12/10/34 F

On 1 February 1879, Beck replies: 'I… regret that you so unfairly misjudge me… I am glad [the problem] is not the rent and that you have all the labour you require… the whole complaint now rests on the excessive quantity of game.' However, her allegations are so grave that any impartial person would agree that it was an agent's duty to bring the matter to the notice of the proprietor. Or does she now wish to withdraw the criticism? He strongly advises her to consult Mr Gurney and he adds that Sir Dighton Probyn would wish to be involved too. 'I have from the first been most anxious about the success of your farming and am very sorry to know too well the losses – and trials which have during the past three seasons beset you… [but] I could not let it go forth uncontradicted that you were being ruined from excessive rent, cost of labour, and game damage, nor should I have acted honestly to HRH if I had done so. I can only add that I have never expressed a wish that you should leave.'[65]

Two days later, Louise writes: 'As I must entirely differ from your letter, I leave it unanswered for the present. Up to this time I have always consulted Mr Groom and then referred to you officially. In this case I thought it might be better to send you a <u>private</u> statement and have the opportunity of consulting with you without troubling anyone. In this I have been mistaken… I did not anticipate that you would act in so unfriendly a manner.'[66]

Beck answers: 'I beg to acknowledge your favour… I can only again repeat that I have not acted in an unfriendly spirit towards you and have not the least intention of so doing.'[67]

The frosty formality of this note persuaded the Lady Farmer to sheathe her claws for the time being. However, she continued to be exercised on the subject of marauding ground game and, on 31 May, she addressed a brief note to head gamekeeper Jackson, asking for more hares to be shot.[68]

---

[65] Royal Archive LAW/SHM/12/10/34 G
[66] Royal Archive LAW/SHM/12/10/34 H
[67] Royal Archive LAW/SHM/12/10/34 I
[68] Royal Archive LAW/SHM/12/10/72 R

By this time, all correspondence concerning Appleton was being kept, copied, and sent to royal solicitor Mr White; wary of the Lady Farmer's capricious temper, the Prince's advisers were gathering evidence to be used if needed. The Earl of Leicester's comment about her 'injudicious conduct' proved increasingly apt, but such was Louise's nature – when she had what she felt was a righteous cause she acted on impulse, with the instincts of a wildcat.

Sadly for her, she no longer had full control of her emotions, or her reason. She persisted in blaming the hares for her troubles: she loathed them with a passion and would have killed them with her own hands had that been possible.

At least the hares were tangible enemies; other adversaries, such as the effects of foreign competition and foreign wars, and above all the continuing foul weather, could not be controlled. Conditions had been bad enough in previous years, but 1879 broke all records for low temperatures and never-ending rain, the coldest year in four decades, the wettest summer, with twice the average rainfall. How could you plough oozing mud? How could crops grow when seed rotted in the ground before it germinated? British agriculture groaned under the burden. Undercut by American competition, many farmers gave up even trying to grow wheat and many more simply went to the wall. Louise was not alone in her bitter despair.

Another rent audit loomed, and she had not yet raised what was due for the previous period. She was already on dangerous ground, for under the terms of the new, yearly tenancy, in the event of non-payment of rent the landlord had the immediate right to claim the property and turn the tenant out. On 18 July 1879, Louise wrote asking Edmund Beck if he would agree to defer the payment until after harvest. Beck replied that he would consult Sir Dighton Probyn about postponement of the audit, and at this Louise panicked; terrified of Probyn, she protested that she was asking only for deferment of her own payment, not for the entire audit to be delayed.[69]

---

[69] Royal Archive LAW/SHM/12/10/30 (A-C)

But that year's harvest proved worse than ever, bringing little if any financial profit. Already owing six months' rent, and aware that pretty soon that figure would double, Louise was half mad with worry, her state of mind vividly illustrated by the brief, malicious letter she hurled in her brother Frederick's direction:

Appleton
Aug 28th

[No salutation]

Owing to ill-health I have been unable to proceed at present with the Chancery suit for the recovery of the sum of money that you have deprived me of.

I am afraid that nothing but compulsion will ever induce you to return it, although you are perfectly aware what a cruel, miserable business it is.

I can only say that if by your continuing to withhold it I am unable to continue in my home here, and my boy's prospects are injured for life, I am quite certain that some terrible judgement will fall upon your own children.

Louisa Mary Cresswell.[70]

This missive, virtually cursing her brother and his family, reached Frederick when he was staying in Lowestoft. On 6 September he sent it on to his solicitor, T. J. Hooper, in Biggleswade, with a letter of his own which says in part, 'Mrs Cresswell sent me the enclosed a few days ago – I suppose the best thing to do is to take no notice of it. Her plea of ill health cannot be true, as I hear she is well enough to be out farming all day, and blows up her men, etc, in fact she won't let her Foreman do much. My idea is she is losing money by farming, and hopes to get some out of me to help her to keep on…'[71]

A few days later, after hearing from Hooper, he writes: '…Mrs Cresswell cannot with truth plead either want of money or ill-health. Some of her brothers-in-law left money either to her or her boy… If you think I should tell my brother George I had better send him a letter. I have been uncertain as to where he is,

---

[70] Bedfordshire and Luton Record Office HF/45/14/5
[71] Ibid.

but I see by the Bournemouth paper he has taken a house there... It is rather hard lines having this threat of a Chancery suit hanging over one so long, it is I think ten or twelve years ago that Mrs Cresswell first talked of beginning it. We have not had much rain, but the weather is rough and squally...'[72]

Frederick's laid-back, disinterested attitude infuriated Louise even further. She went to see Somerville Gurney at the bank, trying to enlist his help, and he in turn met with Edmund Beck and informed him that, unless Mrs Cresswell's rent was considerably reduced, by around £400, she would not be able to stay at Appleton. In reply, Beck made it clear that this figure would not be entertained; however, needing time to consult the others, he promised to think the matter over. Writing to Arnold White to keep him informed, he added an interesting comment: 'Things get worse every day and next year will I fear finish many more tenants... Captain Lyde is finding the money but I am sorry to say he has notice of another falling in 1880.'[73] (He is referring to Captain Neville Ames-Lyde [husband to Edith, lady of Thornham, Louise's niece], another land-owner for whom Edmund Beck acted as agent.)

Despite her claim that she never bothered Somerville Gurney unless forced, Louise had evidently begun to use him as her intermediary. On 18 November, the banker wrote to ask Beck to make 'considerable concessions', without which Louise would not be able to stay at Appleton: 'HRH knows how sorry Mrs Cresswell would be to be obliged to leave Appleton both for her own sake and that of her son.'[74] Beck's reply, hurriedly scribbled on top of the letter, says he'll pass the message on.

Fact-finding in the USA
That champion of all agriculturalists, Clare Sewell Read, along with fellow MP Albert Pell, had departed the previous August to study methods in the United States and hopefully to find a way to combat the depression in British agriculture. In an exhausting

---

[72] Bedfordshire and Luton Record Office HF/45/14/5
[73] Royal Archive LAW/SHM/12/10/31
[74] Royal Archive LAW/SHM/12/10/32A

three-month tour, they travelled on average 120 miles per day, examining systems of cultivation, transportation across land, and ocean shipping of provisions, grain, live animals and dead meat. They arrived back in Norwich three days before Christmas.

Their findings, published on forty pages of close-printed, tightly-packed columns, held immense amounts of information but, boiled down to a nub, offered little cheer: American lands were so vast and their surpluses so enormous that the small islands of Britain could hardly hope to compete.

With their own livelihood failing and little prospect of better things to come if they remained in England, Louise and her teenage son had begun to wonder whether their own fortune might lie over the ocean. Young Gerard in particular was inspired by the promise that lay in the wide open spaces, the rich prairie lands of the American West.

Last Days, 1880

In the end, Louise believed, she was ruthlessly hunted down. She describes it in her book: 'I would have stayed and fought through everything if the money losses that were forced on me had not brought me to a standstill. The bank dare no longer continue the advances, and suddenly called in those already made... Not one single concession would they make... They saw their opportunity and were down upon me with, "go, go, go," in all directions... I was to send in my resignation, giving any but the real reason for leaving, saying that I placed my case entirely in the Prince's hands, from whom I might expect the most liberal treatment in return... I wanted no charity, only my lawful due... I would not play their game and whitewash matters over...' When friends asked why she was leaving, she stated it plainly: 'Because I could not remain unless I killed down the Prince's game from Monday morning to Saturday night, and reserved Sunday for lecturing the Agent.'[75]

Her sense of persecution grew deeper. Having been accused of speaking against the Prince openly – in a railway carriage! – she determined to get to the bottom of it all. She went to see

---

[75] Cresswell, *Eighteen years...* p232

Edmund Beck and he, 'in his terror, thinking I knew more than I did, let it all out… if ever a woman longed to be a man with a hunting whip, that woman was myself!' So, Edmund Beck was revealed as her 'secret enemy'. To her fury, she also learned that the agent had 'reported that I was letting down the land and neglecting the flock… Even my rooted prejudice against legal proceedings could not hinder me from threatening an action for libel…' (This is rich when, as we have seen, she threatened people, including her own brother, with law suits at the least provocation.)

Louise saw it all as clear-cut, black and white – she the innocent victim, unjustly persecuted; they the evil villains, out to destroy her. The actual correspondence sheds light of a more varicoloured hue.

Crown solicitor Arnold W. White, having been drawn deep into the fray, met with Somerville Gurney on 1 December 1879, to discuss Mrs Cresswell's demand for what amounted to a one third reduction in her annual rent. The participants spent another month debating the matter. In a letter written at New Year, 1880, Mr White apprises Somerville Gurney of the outcome: royal estate agent Beck has told HRH that the present rent is fair and reasonable; all other Sandringham tenants pay similar rents without protest; so HRH suggests that the other tenants might be asked to judge; he would regret it if Mrs Cresswell had to leave, but a £400 reduction cannot be entertained. Her request last audit for a delay was readily granted, though she has yet to pay that debt; however, a huge permanent reduction in rent is another matter entirely.[76]

Immediately after New Year, on Saturday, 3 January 1880, Mr White arrived at Sandringham and was accommodated in Bachelors' Cottage (later renamed York Cottage), from where he wrote to inform Louise that he would be pleased to call at Appleton the next Monday, to see her or Mr Groom, or both. Sending this note on to Mr Groom, Louise added in her ink-heavy, forward-slanting hand: 'This is very satisfactory. I think we shall get him to ourselves. I have said 12 o'clock. If there is

---

[76] Royal Archive LAW/SHM/12/10/36 B

an alteration will let you know. Pray be here a little before [as] Sandringham 12 o'clock is 11½ with us.'[77] (Sandringham clocks were always kept half an hour fast, perhaps to allow the Prince to take full advantage of daylight for shooting; or was it because Princess Alexandra was notoriously unpunctual? Whatever the truth, 'Sandringham time' was well known to be different from the rest of the country.)

The meeting at Appleton duly took place, though we have no record of what was said. Three days later, after Mr White returned to London, Louise wrote to him to claim that she had had no idea the bank would withhold the rent money; indeed, if she had known she would not have asked for any deferment. She hopes Mr White's personal regard for her will not be affected; she can hardly contemplate the pain it would cause if she had to leave Sandringham and she hopes something may yet be arranged, particularly as it appears that HRH 'has no personal wish for me to leave'. In an obsequious PS – 'I trust you will not think it prejudiced of me to ask' – she begs him *not* to tell Edmund Beck about this communication and she concludes with a caveat that this is the last *non-official* letter she will write.[78]

Mr White must have baulked at this veiled threat. He replied saying that he would have to show her letter to the Prince, which gave her pause: 'Would you prefer me to see you in London after my boy's holidays are over?' she writes on 14 January. 'I may not have expressed myself clearly as to the 'non-official' nature of my last, but I do not in the least mind the Prince seeing it if you think it proper, but would prefer it not to go further…'[79] And two days later: 'Gerard goes back to school on Wednesday. I had intended to go into Town with him but the following week would be much better. I trust you will not send me notice to quit or wish me to do so before Lady Day, March 25th, which is I believe the usual time. Time is of great import to me for reasons I'll name if

---

[77] Groom family records
[78] Royal Archive LAW/SHM/12/10/38
[79] Royal Archive LAW/SHM/12/10/39

you think proper.'[80] (The records don't tell what these reasons might have been.)

In the event, Arnold White was already planning another visit to the Prince at Sandringham, so he arranged to meet Louise towards the end of the month.

These contacts with the royal solicitor ran concurrent with a flurry of correspondence between Louise and the Prince's head of household, that straight-talking soldier Sir Dighton Probyn. Letters exchanged from 15 to 18 January 1880[81] mainly concern Louise's threat to bring a libel action against Edmund Beck.

She writes to the Sandringham comptroller: 'I have been obliged to give Mr Beck notice of an action for libel for I can really endure his mischief making no longer. I should be sorry if HRH and yourself were displeased with me for doing so, but now that Mr Onslow is dead I am quite friendless and alone on the place and how can I have redress? I ought to be allowed to confront Mr Beck face to face and have it fairly out. As an officer and a gentleman I think you will admit I have a right to be heard in my own defence? Yrs truly…'

Probyn replies that he has already seen her letter to Beck and is exceedingly sorry for it: 'I could only view such a step with sorrow as I saw that it was bound to bring harm either on Beck or yourself. The Prince, I felt sure… would never allow such a threat to be held over his agent by one of his Principal Tenants, without having the accusation enquired into, the result being grief either on the agent or the tenant.'

He adds, 'For the life of me I cannot think on what grounds you bring an action for libel against Mr Beck – I can honestly declare that to the best of my recollection I have never heard him say an unkind word against you. He has expressed his regret to me at your losses, regret in which I have sincerely joined, but nothing libellous or derogatory to your character as a Lady… I know what a kind friend Mr Onslow was to everybody who applied to him, and how willingly he gave his advice, but I

---

[80] Royal Archive LAW/SHM/12/10/40
[81] Letters on this page: Royal Archive LAW/SHM/12/10/43 (A-B)

cannot help thinking that were the poor dear old gentleman now alive he would strongly deprecate the rash step you are now taking. It is not my business to interfere but having, like my royal master, the interest of his tenants at heart, I regret you did not consult Mr Gurney before threatening Mr Beck with an action for libel…'

Louise avows that she doesn't want to bring the action, indeed she had planned to see her adviser in London next week, but will defer in hope of some more peaceable arrangement. However, 'I do not consult Mr Gurney upon anything. We are old friends but there are others in whose judgement and opinion I have more confidence. I am very much obliged by your letter…'[82]

On 'Friday night, 16 January', Sir Dighton Probyn replies in surprise: from previous letters he had assumed she had already taken out an action. He feared for *her* sake only and is glad she has not yet taken this rash step. 'But do not let me deter you from consulting with your legal adviser… I only ventured to mention Mr Somerville Gurney because knowing him to be a gentleman of honour and believing him to be a friend of yours… In the reply you authorise Mr Somerville Gurney to make… (which you must pardon me for saying I think had better be soon) you will of course be at liberty to urge any grievances, real or imaginary… but be careful and not bring any accusations… which you are not quite certain of being able to prove. It appears to me very doubtful if he [Beck] can afford, considering the position he holds, to allow to pass unnoticed even the threat you have already held over him'

Beginning to feel out of her depth, Louise asks Probyn to see Mr Groom, who can explain so much better than she could. 'I trust Mr Beck will not suppose that I retract anything, only if I can counteract the injury I consider he has inflicted on me by any other means than a prosecution for libel, I should prefer it, although I do not know that I should not bring an action against him under <u>all</u> circumstances… As to his anxiety for an enquiry, I

---

[82] Royal Archive LAW/SHM/12/10/43 (C-E)

do not think he would find it so satisfactory as he imagines. I trust you are better this morning, although the weather is so severe.'

Sunday, January 18, Probyn to Louise: 'as you are aware, Mr White is, by the Prince's orders, endeavouring to come to some understanding with you through Mr Somerville Gurney...' He adds that he would be going far out of his province if he were to discuss her business with Mr Groom or anyone and he asks her in future to address all correspondence to do with her tenancy through Mr White. Groom can contact the solicitor too if he wants to. Probyn is sorry to note her continued bitter tone towards Mr Beck, though of course she is at liberty to take whatever steps she pleases. 'But again I warn you... [you] are treading on very dangerous ground in making these charges... I believe Mr Beck to be a thoroughly honest good servant of the Prince's and His Royal Highness is... well satisfied with him'. He ends by saying that since he doesn't feel justified in 'carrying on a private correspondence, with you or anybody else, on the Prince's business without HRH's knowledge, I [should] mention that I have felt it my duty to acquaint His Royal Highness of this correspondence. Thanks for your kind enquiries about my health, I am quite well today...'[83]

Making a bundle of these letters, he sends them to Mr White with a note saying that these are what 'the Lady Tenant' has forced upon him. 'I was obliged to be civil to her but I thought it *time to stop her at last* [emphasis added]. Yesterday she paid me a visit – nothing worth recording... *She cried, of course* [emphasis added], and said that her great grievance against Beck was that he had damaged her reputation as a Farmer! – that was precious to her! I told her I would not let her abuse him before me – I warned her too that she had better be careful as Beck would never submit to her slandering him and telling all the people in the County she had prosecuted him for libel. I told her she talked nonsense when she asked to be let off 4 or 500 a year

---

[83] Royal Archive LAW/SHM/12/10/43 (F)

rent, that we felt sure we should have no difficulty in finding another tenant if she gave up Appleton.'[84]

The bundle went via the Prince's private secretary, Francis Knollys, who added a note reminding Mr White that it would not do to allow Mrs Cresswell to claim that she had withdrawn her libel charge against Beck at the request of either the Prince or Dighton Probyn.[85]

The row had not quite ended. Even as Knollys scribbled his note that Monday, Louise was writing again to Probyn, frantically back-pedalling, thanking him for granting her an interview, and for his advice: 'I do not expect or wish that anything I send to you should be kept from the knowledge of His Royal Highness and feel that it will pass through safe hands. I am very glad indeed to hear that you are well again and with kind regards to Lady Probyn... [PS] I did not intend to write bitterly of Mr Beck although he has done me a grievous injury. My character as a Lady can take care of itself, but anything that affects my agricultural reputation or the care taken of my animals touches a very tender point. This may seem very absurd but would an Officer like to be reported for neglect of his duty to the Commander-in-Chief? The farm is <u>my</u> "Regiment".'[86]

Probyn did not reply to this piece of impudence, he only forwarded the letter to Mr White with a brief note: 'I think this is the last of it – just received – to it I send no answer, of course...'[87]

At this point, having inflamed the opposition's ire, Louise retreated, leaving her mess of hot potage in the hands of loyal Mr Groom – though obliging him to stir it with a spoon which she provided. Groom had an appointment to meet Mr White when the latter came again to Norfolk, but the royal solicitor's visit was delayed by a bout of illness. Dighton Probyn wrote from Marlborough House on 21 January to express his concern: 'Sorry

---

[84] Royal Archive LAW/SHM/12/10/42
[85] Royal Archive LAW/SHM/12/10/44
[86] Royal Archive LAW/SHM/12/10/46
[87] Royal Archive LAW/SHM/12/10/45

to hear you are unwell... The Prince [wanted to see you at Sandringham] from Saturday next till Monday... HRH wants you to have a talk with old (Dr?) Robertson who will be there, and also **to settle Mrs Cresswell**!' [This last is writ large in thick black ink and heavily underlined].

'I have just mentioned to the Prince that you were unwell and not able to come here today – he said he thought perhaps that change of air to Sandringham would do you good... If not this Saturday then next week.' He adds that the Prince would like to see copies of all correspondence concerning Mrs Cresswell.

On a miserable Monday, 26 January 1880, Louise Cresswell and her old friend John Groom met with her banker and co-trustee, Somerville Gurney, to discuss the gravity of her situation. Later that day, Gurney wrote to inform the royal camp that 'Mrs Cresswell is quite unable to pay her rent and she now wishes to leave it entirely in the hands of His Royal Highness the Prince of Wales.'[88] This is the formula Louise claims was forced upon her, but she left it to her financial adviser and co-trustee to pen the weasel words. She herself, meanwhile, was still picking away, enquiring of Dighton Probyn whether she should apply to him or to Mr White 'to know whether I am to be allowed or am to be refused the opportunity of clearing myself from the charges brought against me by Mr Beck...'[89]

This was too much for Probyn, who replied curtly that Mr White was expected the following day and she must address all business communications through him.[90] Then he sent copies of both letters on to White with a note: 'The enclosed you may digest at leisure in the train tomorrow. It is an impertinent production. I hope you will certainly see her before you leave.'[91]

Mr White finally made it to Sandringham at the end of that week. His meeting with John Groom, fixed for high noon on Monday, 2 February, turned into a 'long interview' involving

[88] Royal Archive LAW/SHM/12/10/49
[89] Royal Archive LAW/SHM/12/10/51 A
[90] Royal Archive LAW/SHM/12/10/51 B
[91] Royal Archive LAW/SHM/12/10/50

both the farmer and Louise. After it, he consulted with HRH and on Thursday informed Groom, 'I am now instructed to inform you that as Mrs Cresswell avows her inability to pay her rent, of which two half-years payments are now due, and makes no proposal for an extension of her tenancy on the terms indicated in my letters to Mr S Gurney, it necessarily results that she must leave the Farm.

'*The alternative which Mrs Cresswell suggested, that she should be allowed to continue on the Farm without paying Rent* [emphasis added], could scarcely have been seriously made, and, as you can easily understand, could not possibly be entertained.

'It is impossible not to sympathise with Mrs Cresswell's attachment to a place where she has lived so long, and with her reluctance to give a notice to quit, which I confess I thought would, from her point of view, have been the wisest course for her to have adopted. Any proposal proceeding from her for an extension of time for payment of the Rent, or for an allowance in respect of bad seasons, would have met with the most favourable reception; and, as I said before, His Royal Highness would have been quite ready to consider an extension of the tenancy on the conditions named in my letters to Mr S Gurney. But, a simple announcement that a tenant cannot pay her Rent, unaccompanied by any such proposal, can only be considered as equivalent to a notice to quit though it may involve the necessity of the Landlord giving the formal notice instead of the tenant.

'Such being the light in which it seems to me Mr S Gurney's communication <u>must</u> be regarded, I am commanded to say that His Royal Highness is most anxious to consult Mrs Cresswell's convenience and interests as to the time and terms of her leaving Appleton.

'Mr Beck will be instructed to meet you to consider these points, and Mrs Cresswell may rest assured that there is every desire to meet her wishes in all reasonable respects.

'For convenience I have used the name of Mrs Cresswell alone but, as you are aware, the Executors of Mr Cresswell are legally the tenants.'[92]

---

[92] Royal Archive LAW/SHM/12/10/54

Louise elected to send John Groom to meet with Edmund Beck and discuss the situation. This he did, on 12 February, though since he had the Lady Farmer peering, metaphorically, over his shoulder and whispering stubborn advice in his ear, the encounter settled nothing.

As Beck informed Mr White later that day, Groom's main aim had been 'to try and find out what sum the Prince would give Mrs Cresswell. I told him that your letter alone was the only basis upon which I could act and that my duty was simply to ascertain if the rent would, all or in part, be paid, and if not to ascertain through Mr Groom what steps under the circumstances would tend most to the comfort and advantage of Mrs Cresswell?' This brought the reply that Mrs Cresswell could not pay but that there were *friends who would come forward and help* [emphasis added], also that Mrs Cresswell would not give any notice of her quitting but that 'she would put the onus of so doing upon the Prince, and that she would go upon the day she was desired. Mr Groom then went on to speak of the widow having lost her all which was due to game damage and excessive rent. He speaks of public sympathy and all that kind of feeling, and finishes by telling me tis *[sic]* my duty to modify and smooth matters down. From his admission I fear the poor woman is not solvent and I therefore pointed out the madness of her attempting to remain… I do not anticipate that we shall get much help from Mr Groom as I find he is not endeavouring to make her have any more friendly feeling towards the Gurneys than she has for myself.'[93]

Louise describes how an 'old friend' offered her sufficient capital to pay off the bank and start again, on the condition that 'arrangements would be made at Sandringham which would give me a fair chance…'[94] She says Sandringham refused to comply, but she gives no clue to the identity of this 'old friend', or the timing involved. The vague remark by Mr Groom, noted above, is the only other reference to this generous offer of aid.

---

[93] Royal Archive LAW/SHM/12/10/55
[94] Cresswell: *Eighteen years…* p231

To add to the growing file of evidence concerning the Lady Farmer, Edmund Beck contributed a bundle of correspondence from his own files (which we have seen in context earlier). In his accompanying letter he mentioned two occasions when Louise had declined the offer to do some coursing and instead had asked the head gamekeeper to shoot some hares. He had shot forty, all of which she took as gifts for friends. 'If Mrs Cresswell is so much injured,' Edmund Beck observes, 'I cannot imagine how it is that the two Flitcham tenants do not suffer equally. Stanton tells me that the number of hares now on the farm is most scanty.'[95] (Mr Stanton's farm adjoined Appleton and, when spring coursing after hares was allowed, by kind permission of HRH, Louise generally invited him to avail himself of the sport on her land.)

The Prince's camp put the facts to Charles Hall, a lawyer engaged to act as arbitrator in the case, in a document which explains that, under the proviso contained in the Lease, in the event of non-payment of rent, HRH the Prince of Wales is entitled at once to re-enter and take possession of the farm. In fact, HRH *does not desire to avail himself of this power* [emphasis added], but is anxious that notice should be given to Mrs Cresswell, or whoever may now be considered the tenants of the farm, to quit at the earliest period that she or they can legally be required to do so.

Counsel Mr Hall appends his judgement: 'I am [of the] opinion that the Agricultural Holdings Act 1875 applies to the tenancy and that the tenants are entitled to one year's notice expiring in Oct 1881... The notice should be given to both the Executor and the Executrix...'[96]

A formal Notice to Quit was duly drawn up.

Mr Groom's last stand

Louise's contention that she received no help from anyone, 'not one single concession', is demonstrably untrue: the Prince and his advisers gave her every opportunity to ease her own path; she

---

[95] Royal Archive LAW/SHM/12/10/71
[96] Royal Archive LAW/SHM/12/10/56

simply refused to help herself, would not 'back down', as she saw it, nor allow 'them' any way out except, in the end, officially to force her out of Appleton. When she saw how badly things were going for her, she employed her usual defensive tactic, withdrawing to the sidelines and nominating someone else – usually good old 'Farmer Broome' – as her front man. Groom found himself in an unenviable position, caught between the irresistible force comprising the Prince of Wales and his advisers, and the immovable object known as the Lady Farmer.

Aware that a crisis loomed, Edmund Beck invited John Groom to 'come and talk matters over'[97] with himself and Mr White at the Globe Hotel, on 5 March 1880, the occasion of the Tenants' Dinner and the spring rent audit. This might have provided a chance to meet on sociable terms and perhaps come to some amicable arrangement, but Groom chose to refuse the offer and, instead of attending the dinner, sat down in his study at Ashwicken Hall and wrote to Mr White in his own blunt manner:

> Many thanks for your kindness and also Mr Beck for the invitation to dine with the Sandringham tenantry. As Mrs Cresswell is not in a position to pay her rent, I could not with any comfort accept.
> Mrs Cresswell has lost all the large sums invested in Appleton farm from the following causes:
>   1st   from the large quantity of ground game
>   2nd   from very bad times during the last 4 or 5 years
>   3rd   from the large increase of labour
> I enclose Mr Faircloth's estimated account of damage done by Game during his stewardship[,] also one since. The enclosed statements I have shown to Mr Beck who said Mr Faircloth he always considered an honest and straightforward man.
> I also enclose a statement of Mrs Cresswell's expenses.[98]

He enclosed three documents,[99] two of them drawn up by Louise's farm steward Robert Faircloth and addressed to Mrs Cresswell. In the first, dated 24 January 1879, Faircloth certifies

[97] Royal Archive LAW/SHM/12/10/62
[98] Royal Archive LAW/SHM/12/10/63
[99] Royal Archive LAW/SHM/12/10/64 and 65

damage done by game during the time he was employed at the farm, November 1866 to October 1874. He calculates these at £1600. The second document, dated 30 April, details crop damage observed by him, at Mrs Cresswell's request, from 23 January to 31 March 1879: 'Turnip crop – sufficient injury done which otherwise would have fed 465 sheep for 14 days. Wheat crop – damaged considerably, in places by the plants closely eaten off to the surface of the ground. Rape crop – 17 acres entirely destroyed...' And so forth. The steward doesn't attempt to quantify the sums of money involved.

Groom's final enclosure for Mr White is written in Louise's own characteristically assertive, oblique hand, comprising three pages headed 'List of expenditure which has been directly or indirectly of benefit to my Landlord's property from 1862 to 1868-9.' [This last date is a slip of the pen: she obviously meant to include her whole time at Appleton to the end of 1879.] Judging by the untidy handwriting, the list was dashed off in haste, and probably in tears of despair and fury. It includes such items as 'cake corn and manure consumed by stock and sown on the land'. Total spent on such items over fifteen years is £20,703/4s/1d; 'besides a large quantity of hay'. Carting for new buildings, £225; for fittings, £57/9s/11d; bricklayers, carpenters and glaziers bills, £137/18s/4½d (this calculating down to pennies and halfpennies is pure bathos). For some items she doesn't attempt to estimate a cost: 'making rough field barn, there being none on the farm; laying out flower, shrubbery and kitchen garden, gravel walks and planting with shrubs and fruit trees... making new roads... clay, mould and marl carting... cleaning land which had been "run out" and was a wilderness of rubbish and weeds... removing old stumps and trees...'[100]

This renewed defiance served only to harden attitudes in the Sandringham ranks and, back in his London office the following Monday, Mr White replied to Mr Groom:

---

[100] Royal Archive LAW/SHM/12/10/66

> 12 Gt Marlborough St. W
March 8th 1880
>
> Dear Mr Groom,
>
> I was very much disappointed at not seeing you on Friday – I could understand your disinclination to dine at the audit dinner, but considering the position of affairs and the kind way in which H.R.H. the Prince of Wales has behaved to Mrs Cresswell, I think it would have been in better taste had you come frankly forward to meet Mr Beck and me, to state what Mrs Cresswell's position was, and what proposition she had to make as to liquidating her debt, and to ascertain what were His Royal Highness's views and wishes.
>
> You have thought fit, instead, to write me a letter which it will be my duty to submit to H.R.H. Until I have received H.R.H's instructions I will not further allude to it than to remark that your assertion as to Game Damage is effectually contradicted by a letter which I hold, <u>addressed by Mrs Cresswell to you*</u>; and by facts which I shall have no difficulty in proving. I regret extremely, and especially for Mrs Cresswell's sake, that she seems determined to force HRH to act upon his undoubted legal rights, instead of responding to the wish he has so markedly and repeatedly shown to treat her case with every possible kindness and consideration. The responsibility must rest with Mrs Cresswell and with those who advise her.
>
> Yours faithfully
Arnold W. White[101]
>
> *[*this phrase was underlined by Mr White in the original. Unfortunately, the letter he mentions, from Louise to Groom, is not apparent in the archive]*

While awaiting his London-bound train on Lynn station the previous Saturday, Mr White had run into Somerville Gurney, who had given him to understand that he [Gurney] was planning to revoke all liability for the Appleton rent as from next Michaelmas. And so the royal solicitor penned yet another letter, requesting Gurney to confirm his intentions formally in writing, to avoid any misunderstandings. He adds: 'I may remark that the Rent not having been paid at the audit on Friday, there are now two half years in arrear, and a third half year becomes due on the 11th of next month. This state of things cannot be allowed to

---

[101] Royal Archive LAW/SHM/12/10/67

continue and I earnestly wish that some definite proposition was made on behalf of yourself and your Co-tenant, Mrs Cresswell. Mr Groom did not come near us on the audit day, and, as it seems Mrs Cresswell's determination to force us to have recourse to our legal rights, it seems to me only fair to you to remind you of your legal position in the matter. You know what efforts we have made to befriend Mrs Cresswell: but the limits of forbearance are nearly exhausted.'[102]

Rising tensions had strained the relationship between Louise Cresswell and Somerville Gurney to breaking point. Her husband's will had appointed Gurney as her co-executor to the farm in young Gerard's name, and she herself had arranged that, in the event of her death, this same Somerville Gurney should become her boy's guardian. Now, it seemed, Gurney was throwing away all the trust she and her husband had placed in him. He was reneging on his duties as co-executor.[103] When Louise received his letter she wrote immediately to John Groom:

My very kind Friend,

I do not see that you can do anything more for me.

I do not doubt the Prince's kind intentions but they are not likely to be obeyed. On the contrary I am treated with every possible harshness and subjected in addition to gross misrepresentation. As to legal threats, I do not care now <u>what</u> they do. I can but be ruined and hounded out.

I have been on this estate for nearly 18 years, for nearly 15 alone, and have acted loyally and faithfully to the Prince during this whole time. If this is to be the end of it all <u>let it be</u>. As I began my letter so will I end. I have <u>nothing</u> more to say.

Yours ever gratefully, L M Cresswell.

Mr Archer* has <u>nothing</u> to do with my affairs – beyond some trivial matters he is not my legal adviser and I decline to communicate with him on this subject.

*[*her local solicitor – she had evidently fallen out with him, too!]*

---

[102] Royal Archive LAW/SHM/12/10/68
[103] Groom family records

Meanwhile Somerville Gurney, complying with official requests, sent Mr White a formal notice advising that as from Michaelmas next he would 'cease to act as co-Executor with Mrs Gerard Cresswell'.[104] In his covering letter he asks that, in any reply, will the solicitor please 'not allude to any former letters or interviews on this subject... [Please will you] write to Mr Groom informing him that you have received this letter and saying that as Mrs Gerard Cresswell has left herself entirely in the Prince of Wales' hands, and as she is quite unable to pay her rent, there is no course open to her but to leave her farm...' But, he adds warningly, the royal advisers will have to *serve* notice on Louise 'as it is quite impossible to get Mrs Cresswell to give notice'.[105]

This is borne out by a note from Louise to Groom, dated 25 March,[106] admonishing him: 'You are quite welcome to say as proposed "that upon whatever day I have notice sent to leave the place I shall be gone"...' However, on the reverse of this formal note she adds a typically petulant coda: 'I suppose there is no occasion to take any notice of the promised liberality? If so, all I have to say on that point is that up to the present time all the liberality has come from me and [I] have been ruined in return.

'PS I think S Gurney told you my private income was £600. I don't know that I shall have nearly as much as half.'

Across this page, in one corner (saving paper), she further adds: 'If any questions asked about it from Sandringham don't tell on any account.'

Once again John Groom did as he was told, penning a pathetic little note to the Crown solicitor: 'I am instructed by Mrs Cresswell to state that as soon as you, through HRH, give notice to leave, she will be gone. Of course I can only write as instructed.'[107] Poor old Groom!

Aware that Louise had gone to ground and must be forcibly dug out, Somerville Gurney had been spending sleepless nights trying to find an answer. He writes on 27 March to Mr White,

---

[104] Royal Archive LAW/SHM/12/10/73

[105] Royal Archive LAW/SHM/12/10/72

[106] Groom family records

[107] Royal Archive LAW/SHM/12/10/74

saying that he has discovered that, as one of the Executors of Gerard Oswin Cresswell, he has legal power to give notice on behalf of *all* the Executors. Thus, wasting no time, he encloses a legal notice confirming that the lessees will quit the farm from 11 October next: 'I do this as I wish to take advantage of the great kindness and liberality of the Prince of Wales named in the letter that you wrote to Mr Groom…'[108]

On the same day, he wrote to inform Louise of his decision. This letter is particularly interesting, written in a hasty, ragged hand which indicates the writer's agitation, and hinting at heated encounters. Also, Louise's reactions are clearly recorded, for between the lines she has jotted, in heavy pencil, her own acid comments, rendered here in different font:

Dear Louisa,

Of course I never have or should mention your private affairs to HRH or the Princess. I am very sorry to find that you decline to inform the Prince that you intend leaving Appleton at Michs next – you asked me to write a letter to Mr White saying that you can-not pay your rent and that you leave yourself entirely in the hands of HRH the Prince of Wales. *(Wholly untrue, LMC)*

Mr White on behalf of the Prince now writes to Mr Groom a letter which is in every way kind, considerate and liberal (*not considering I have been ruined by game*) but at the same time saying that there was no alternative but that you must leave the farm at Michs next.

Mr Groom informs me that he has written to Mr White saying that as soon as you receive notice you will go. This I maintain is not leaving yourself in the Prince's hands.

Mr Groom was appointed (and very kind it was of him to undertake it) to act for you and for me and for the creditors, in the best way he possibly could in his own judgement respecting the Appleton Farm but instead of acting on his own responsibility and judgement he only acts up to what you tell him. *(Untrue)*

I also find that in all probability I shall be personally liable for any deficit there may be in winding up the farm. *(I hope you will)* Therefore, I have quite…[109]

---

[108] Royal Archive LAW/SHM/12/10/75 and 76
[109] Groom family records

Although the rest of this letter is missing, we may surmise that he goes on to advise her that, as co-executor to the farm, he has made up his mind to give notice to quit.

News of this breakthrough spread rapidly within royal circles. Three days after Gurney's notice to quit was sent, Sir Dighton Probyn apprised Mr White: 'this is all most satisfactory. Gurney has behaved well. Beck must now look out for a [new] tenant.'[110] His large, sprawling handwriting reveals his relief and pleasure – and his utter self-confidence.

Realizing that she had been outmanoeuvred – yet again by that snake Somerville Gurney! – Louise shared her thoughts with Groom in two rushed notes, which read in part: 'I have written to ask S Gurney to resign all my <u>private</u> affairs, the guardianship in case of my death, etc. I wish to have <u>nothing</u> more to do with him or the Cresswells… Does this mean that he has given notice to quit for <u>me</u> and himself <u>too</u>? If so, can he legally do it…? What a fool I have been from a sense of honour giving him back the receipt for private money lent to Farm. However we can make Miss Hogge [Fanny Hogge, her eldest sister] claim her £1000 which I had also intended to take upon myself. <u>Now</u> S Gurney may go shares in that and other debts…'[111]

In her heart she knew she had no choice, but if she was to go it would be at the behest of the Prince of Wales, not because Somerville Gurney had gone behind her back!

Still hopping mad, she dashed off a furious formal notice to the Prince's legal adviser:

April 8th 1880

Mrs Gerard Cresswell repudiates the authority of Mr Gurney to give notice to quit the Appleton Farm without her sanction and she will not in any way adopt such notice.

On the 18th of March last she received through Mr Groom and Mr White the commands of HRH Prince of Wales K.G. to give up the Appleton farm on the 11th of October next which will be obeyed.[112]

[110] Royal Archive LAW/SHM/12/10/77

[111] Groom family records

[112] Royal Archive LAW/SHM/12/10/83

Revealingly, at the bottom of this declaration, scribbled in another hand, is the addendum: 'with Mr Groom's compliments and approval'. She needed some male endorsement and who was left except her faithful and compliant Farmer Groom? It appears, also, that it was he who suggested she should add the second, tempering, paragraph, for her original draft,[113] which remained in Mr Groom's keeping, contains only that first furious sentence.

An amusing snippet of gossip, retold among the Groom family to this day, recounts how, at some point at the height of this furore, John Groom was summoned to London for a private interview with the Prince of Wales. The farmer took his wife Celia along with him and they booked into the Grand Hotel. Next day, at Marlborough House, Groom met with the Prince for man-to-man discussions about Mrs Cresswell's problems. The Prince opened the conversation by remarking, 'They tell me, Groom, she is very handy with her pen...' (Evidently he was well aware of the Lady Farmer's penchant for firing off angry letters.) What they actually discussed is not recorded, but before they parted HRH advised the worthy farmer on the merits of 'not always taking one's wife along when spending the night away from home' (a subject on which the Prince could speak from much experience).

Groom's private audience with the Prince is confirmed by yet another revealing PS to a note which Louise sent to the farmer on 20 May 1880: 'We have often talked of your visit to HRH. I could not write [to Sir Dighton Probyn] of all your goodness to me but will take care that he and the Prince hear of it... The next time you are asked why we agree so well please say because you are not afraid to speak the truth to Royalty whether it offends or not... I don't think Mr White has been straight over this business, do you? Sir Dighton is the soul of honour and I wish you could have had a talk with him alone.'[114]

Fortunately for her, she was unaware of Sir Dighton's true opinion of her, as expressed in his letters to other people.

---

[113] Groom family records
[114] Groom family records

In view of Louise's overt and unrelenting hostility towards him, Edmund Beck found it increasingly difficult to show his face at Appleton, preferring to approach the more amenable Mr Groom instead. However, when Beck mooted the idea of prospective new tenants being allowed to look over the farm, Groom wanted nothing to do with it – don't send to me but let Mrs Cresswell know...[115] The two men were still arguing over money. Groom had submitted a final statement of account concerning sums expended by Mrs Cresswell on developing Appleton Farm, for which she expected to be recompensed in full. This amounted to a total of £1,566/17s/11d,[116] plus incalculable improvements to land etc, and – inevitably – untold losses on account of game damage. These claims struck Beck as ridiculous since, in his opinion, the sum involved was more in the region of five or six hundred pounds.

Through Mr Groom, the Lady Farmer now demanded to know what sum of money the Prince might see fit to offer her, as a 'present for her losses' if and when she left Appleton. As if this were not impertinent enough, in June Mr Groom enquired whether, in the event of no new tenant being found, Mrs Cresswell might be allowed to stay on.

Beck answered – an unequivocal NO![117]

The Ground Game Act, which came into force that summer, allowing land-holders, as well as landlords, the right to shoot hares and rabbits, arrived too late to save Louise. Across the country, other farmers had been agitating for this law and now at last they hoped for some relief. For Louise, however, matters had already moved beyond repair – she could not pay her rent, and she had been all too 'handy with her pen', and with her tongue, too ready with excuses, and tears as her last resort when all else failed. The Prince's representatives were losing patience.

But, even at this late stage, she was still appealing to her helpful MP, Mr Read, for help. She repeated her grievances

---

[115] Royal Archive LAW/SHM/12/10/84
[116] Royal Archive LAW/SHM/12/10/91
[117] Royal Archive LAW/SHM/12/10/85

about the Prince's hares in yet another letter which she sent off without seeking wiser counsel, and which, yet again, she instantly regretted. Jotting an everyday note to Mr Groom on 3 June 1880, she adds another telling PS: 'Before the Hares and Rabbits Bill came on in the House of Commons on Thursday, I wrote to request that the tale of my 1000s hares might not be named, otherwise I believe it might have been in every newspaper in the kingdom and on every breakfast table on Friday morning… Had no time to write and ask your approval or should have done so.'[118] Was she deluding herself about her own importance, or was the British press really agog to hear the latest news of the Lady Farmer's indiscretions?

Continuing debate of what monetary 'gift' the Prince might offer resulted in a reprimand to both Groom and Beck. As Sir Dighton Probyn informed Mr White on 5 July, while the Prince of Wales agreed and approved that the worthy farmer and the agent should endeavour to decide the legal liabilities of both sides regarding Appleton Farm, he stipulated that 'it must rest with him, and him alone, about the sum he may be pleased to give Mrs Cresswell over and above what he is legally bound to allow her'. Since this sum would be a personal gesture from HRH to Mrs Cresswell, in consideration of her losses, Groom and Beck would be taking too much on themselves were they to attempt to tell HRH exactly how much largesse he should offer.[119]

Stricken, Mr Beck denied any such intention – he kept trying to see Groom but the farmer kept making excuses. Finally he managed a meeting, at which Groom's main thrust was to ascertain what sum the Prince would be giving as his 'present', and to state that nothing short of £3,000 would be deemed satisfactory. Reporting this on 12 July, Mr Beck comments, 'I did not offer a single farthing or hint at what my views were…'[120]

---

[118] Groom family records
[119] Royal Archive LAW/SHM/12/10/88
[120] Royal Archive LAW/SHM/12/10/92A

A week later, solicitor White approached farmer Groom with an offer of a settlement in the sum of £600,[121] to which Groom replied in a forlorn little note: 'Dear Sir, Mrs Cresswell leaves everything to me. I will accept £600 and will leave the rest to HRH's liberality, Yours…'[122]

Goodbye to Appleton

Though Louise felt herself under attack from all quarters, still she was 'not wholly deserted', her farm workers being 'earnest in their condemnation of the measure being meted out to me. I am told they still speak of me with kindness and regret.' Her agricultural neighbours sympathized too, some of them confiding that they had also fallen foul of Edmund Beck, and one of them wondered why Louise should fret over 'an ould farm – why, yer'll be a London Lady!' As she says, there is always some comedy: 'One of my neighbours, as a piece of parting advice, entreated me, wherever I went… to boast of being ruined by Royalty. "Don't you forget now – rewined by Royalty, that'll help yer along, like."' Another neighbour told how she had given Mr Beck a piece of her mind, at which, 'He was angry and began to poke away at the fire. "No need for yew to poke away at the fire," says I, "it'll be poked hot enough for yew where yew'll go one day." Now, ma'am, that's what you ought to have said.'

Most of all, Louise recalls, her Royal Mistress did what she could, being 'so good as to say that she liked to have me at Sandringham, that I should not go, and what could be done… she was kindness itself when she came to wish me goodbye, driving down in the little pony-carriage with one of her ladies without a servant. I could not escort her to the door as usual and see her drive away for the last time, but she sent word back from the carriage, "Tell her I am so very sorry for her, so very sorry."'

Louise goes on, 'I do not call myself a religious woman; the goody-goody people turn up their eyes and think me past praying for, and I am glad they do, for I am painfully conscious of having "said a great many things that I regret, and done a great many

---

[121] Royal Archive LAW/SHM/12/10/90
[122] Royal Archive LAW/SHM/12/10/95

that I deplore." But I had tried to act for the best… How I lived through the next few months I hardly know; many have committed suicide for much less. I was so rooted to the place, it seemed as if the very fields would miss me… [It was] a real physical and mental torture… not only deprived of a home of such peculiar and endearing charm, but of my occupation and profession… Verily there are things far worse than murder…'

On 18 September 1880, the *Lynn Advertiser* carried notice of a sale to be held at Appleton Hall, Sandringham, on 1 October, of all the Live and Dead Farming Stock, comprising 24 horses, 88 head of cattle, 520 sheep and 120 pigs 'of Mrs Gerard Cresswell's improved Norfolk breed (as sold to the Royal farms of England, Denmark and Greece)'. These are detailed along with a steam plough and tackle, an 8hp traction engine, a 4hp portable engine, and a long list of other machinery and farm implements. 'Sale to commence at 10. Luncheon at 1 o'clock. Conveyances will run from Wolferton Station…'

Once again John Groom, acting as Louise's representative, took centre stage, though this particular task bothered him a good deal. He had written to Edmund Beck, wanting to make peace: with so many leading agriculturalists coming for the sale, Groom was anxious not to let it be said that Mrs Cresswell had not been treated fairly by the Prince. It being usual on such occasions to make speeches and drink loyal toasts, the farmer requested that, if he were called upon to propose a toast to HRH, he would be put in a position where he could say 'that HRH has been very kind and considerate to his Lady tenant under adverse circumstances'.[123]

Mr Beck replied, 'You are certainly in a position to speak of the justices and liberality… especially as you are so well aware of all the causes that prompt Mrs Cresswell to give up her farm… I should certainly like to have been present myself had I not been aware of the manner in which Mrs Cresswell speaks of me… my absence may therefore contribute to her comfort.'[124]

---

[123] Royal Archive LAW/SHM/12/10/96 A and B
[124] Royal Archive LAW/SHM/12/10/96 C

Groom had penned another letter, this one to Arnold White, asking the same question, and on 11 September the royal solicitor replied tersely that Groom could speak as he pleased.[125]

And so the sale of Appleton livestock and farm equipment went ahead, on a grey, windy Friday. Louise 'felt like some dull stupid machine whilst my favourites were being knocked down to the hammer... And I must confess it went a little against the grain to allow the Prince's health to be proposed at the luncheon; yet I liked to have the Princess and her children cheered, so could not in courtesy omit His Royal Highness.' Had she argued with Mr Groom over the proposing of loyal toasts?

She adds, 'When everyone had left... the deadly silence that reigned about the place with the empty stalls and stables was more overpowering and oppressive than what had gone before. The worst was not yet over. One more week and some of my household treasures must share the same fate and be scattered abroad...'

She had decided to wander the world, so could not take everything with her, nor would the rooms which had been lent to her in Lynn take all her belongings. On 8 October her household effects went up for auction – tables and chairs of varied description, a pianoforte in mahogany case, whatnots, carpets, mahogany four-post bed, feather beds... books, glass, china, culinary requisites; lawn mower, garden roller... It was another desolate day.

As the afternoon waned and sale-goers departed with their purchases, Louise and her house servants began 'the final dismantling process. The nurseries were the worst part, for everyone who has lost one child, and has only one left, knows how dear a relic becomes... The poor old nurse completely broke down over it...' Her sitting room furniture remained just as she and her husband had arranged it when they first moved into their new house sixteen years before, 'and when the huge packing cases were brought in, and a picture of herself that the Princess had given me was one of the first to be lowered into them, it

---

[125] Royal Archive LAW/SHM/12/10/96D

looked as if it was going into a grave.' (Her descendants in Texas still treasure this photograph and a companion one of the Prince.)

Louise was fifty years old; she had been at Appleton for eighteen years; she had had a hand in designing the house, had spent a small fortune on improving the roads and the land, planting orchards and flower gardens; she had tended the stock with her own hands, had known happiness and sorrow... Leaving her beloved home was almost too much to bear.

Around her the empty house echoed to every footfall; the packages she was taking with her stood drearily in the hall; the servants were to sleep in the village and only the former nurse, Lucy Sparrow, was to go with her employer. Outside, the conveyance waited, the horses restless and the driver growing impatient... 'One last look round the dear, dear rooms, a terrible wrench, and out into the darkness.'

In fact, she did not go quite as quietly and meekly as she would have us believe: writing in December, Mr Beck tells the royal solicitor that he has 'asked for the list of fixtures and fittings that had been valued by the arbitrators, as in consequence of Mrs Cresswell's behaviour on the valuation day I had been unable to learn what had been taken...'[126]

We can only imagine what kind of 'behaviour' prompted this observation. The arbitrators' list included such items as chimneypieces, door furniture, shelves, sinks and so forth, which, as part of the house, legally belonged to the Prince. Louise later claimed that when presented with the valuer's inventory, she had been 'forced to sign [it] by the clever London lawyer'.[127]

Beneath her outward composure she was deeply angry, deeply bitter. She needed time to consider a suitable riposte.

A new tenant for Appleton moved in the very day after Louise departed. Charles Horatio Day Blyth, a married man aged forty, with seven children, had already asked for £200 allowance for manure to 'put the farm into condition'. He wanted roads made and repaired; new yards and shedding; a pair of new cottages for

---

126 Royal Archive LAW/SHM/12/10/97
127 Royal Archive LAW/SHM/12/10/97

labourers, near to home premises; lands cleaned, drained and laid down to pasture by the landlord; roof heights raised… Louise despised the man as a crony of Edmund Beck: 'everything that had been refused to me, which would have enabled me to remain in my house, was granted to the newcomer…'

But nowhere in her book does she mention the small detail of her owing two full years' rent by the time she left.

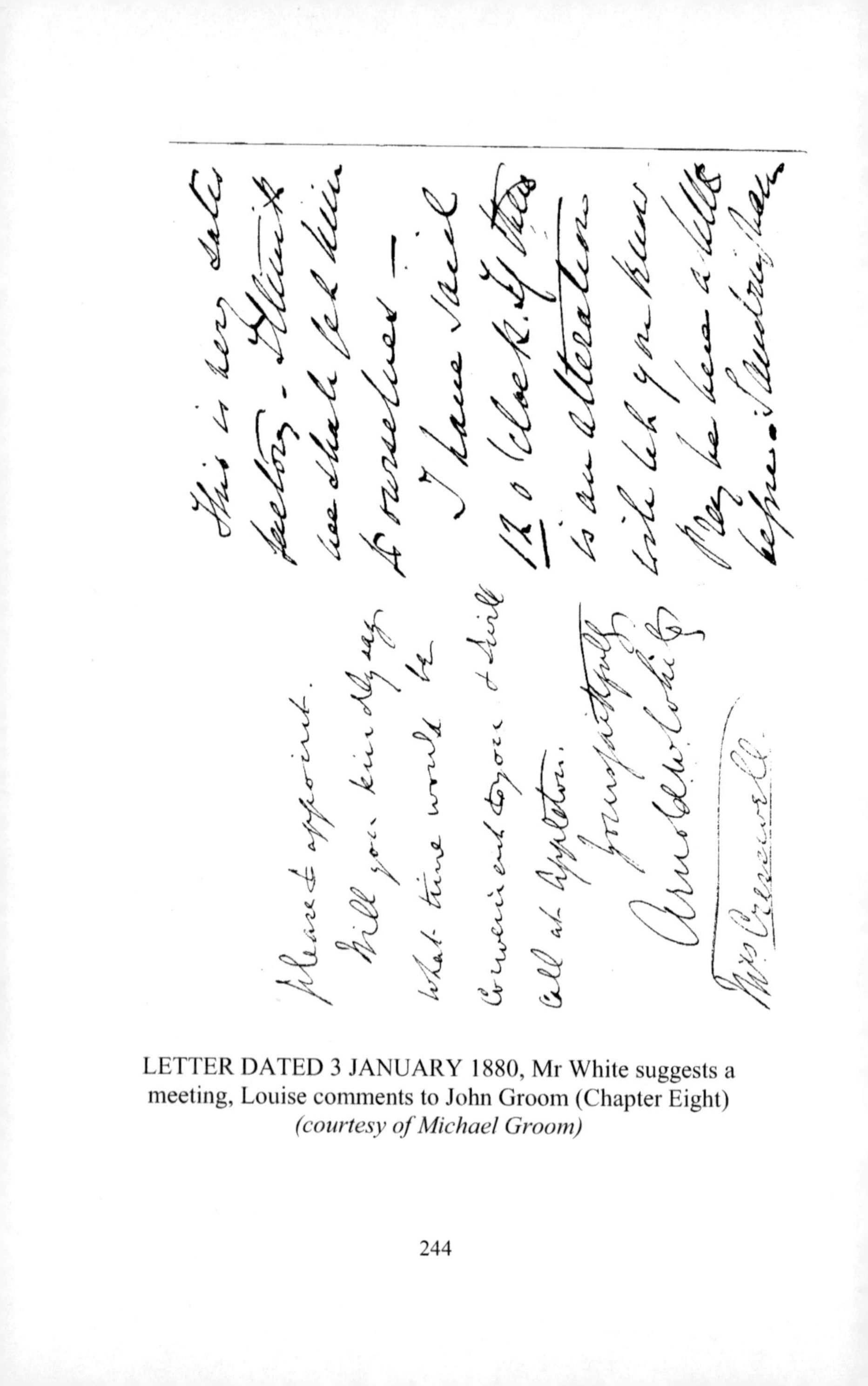

LETTER DATED 3 JANUARY 1880, Mr White suggests a
meeting, Louise comments to John Groom (Chapter Eight)
(courtesy of Michael Groom)

LETTER DATED 3 JUNE 1880, Louise to John Groom
(Chapter Eight)
(courtesy of Michael Groom)

LIVERY STABLE, ABILENE, TEXAS, 1880s

APPLETON HOUSE, 1900s
(Author's collection)

CRESSWELL FAMILY MEMORIAL, NORTH RUNCTON
CHURCHYARD
(Chris Mackie, 2007)

CHAPTER NINE

Lady in waiting

Though the farm business had failed, taking all her hopes with it, Louise did have her private income to live on. She also had a deep grievance to nurse. She could hardly believe what had happened. She, who all her life had prided herself on her self-sufficiency, come to this! Driven to bankruptcy and exile, pitied by her friends, mocked by her enemies... She was numb with shock, hardly able to think, hardly even quite sane. All she knew was that she *would not* allow it to end like this. Every bone in her body cried out for retribution.

She and her housekeeper Mrs Sparrow moved on together, staying for a time in Hunstanton St Edmund with a parlour maid to help out. They rented Brenda Lodge, at the end of Le Strange Terrace, where a sweep of fine dwellings (including brother Frederick's Cliff End House) turned the corner facing the Green, all with open views of the sea. Here Frank Cresswell and his family had often stayed, and here the Magniacs had lodged when they came to visit Helen and Edith at Thornham.

Brenda Lodge belonged to the Revd Thomas Beckett, vicar of Ingoldisthorpe and an old friend of the Onslows. Indeed, Agnes Onslow sometimes came to stay with Louise, their friendship continuing, but the lodge was bitterly cold and draughty that winter as north-easterly gales whistled in across the Wash, and in January six inches of snow fell.

Louise felt herself to be in mourning, waiting, as she had waited after her husband died, for time to do its work and heal her wounds. This was another cruel bereavement – the loss of her home, her daily employment, her pride... She had also lost most of her friends and fallen out with her husband's relatives, both Cresswells and Gurneys, not to mention the bitter quarrel with her own brother Frederick. Mists of uncertainty clouded her whole future. What was she to do with the years that remained?

Thank God she had her son, her fine young Gerard, now turned sixteen and dreaming dreams of his own. Bless the boy, he and his friends talked eagerly of emigrating to America and becoming cowboys!

Still battling...

Although Louise left Appleton Farm in early October 1880, she continued to fight, with her usual preferred weapons, paper and ink, through November and into December.

The Groom family archive contains several handwritten formal documents penned in that familiar sloping hand, in thick black ink, including a 'Statement' as to how, back in 1874, she was 'induced by Mr Beck to sign away the Agricultural Holdings Act...' (this Act laid down terms between landlord and tenant). The document includes a detailed statement of account for expenses on the farm during 1879-80, amounting to over £2,500 for which 'Mr Beck has only allowed £158'.

There is also a Valuation made by one James Barclay, MP for Forfarshire, 'whom Mr Read considers a shrewder and better man of business than himself'. In a note to Mr Groom upon this, Louise adds, 'I only sent this one item, the cake, corn and manure bills to Mr Barclay as, being a stranger to me, I did not know how he would act, but as he has taken so much trouble in the matter I have no doubt if I sent him the whole account of what I have spent in improvements he would value them also for us. We might then send it on to Mr Read and ask his opinion too... After Mr Barclay's claim for this one item I think I am bound to see if the law can do anything for me. You see, I lose £2,580 upon one item only.'

Another 'Memorandum' goes on about petty injustices over labourers' cottages, and the fourth formal document refers back to the time when Gerard Cresswell was offered the Appleton lease 'accompanied by a private agreement that we <u>should never be injured by ground game.</u> The farm being over-run shortly afterwards, and an <u>immense</u> amount of injury done, my husband refused to sign it. I refused to do so for some years but was at last <u>made</u> to do so but under <u>protest</u>. However, I secured a <u>written</u> promise for <u>hares to be kept down</u>...' There follows more in the same vein, concluding bitterly, 'the word "promise" by the Sandringham agent seems to have a totally different meaning to that which I have always been accustomed to'.

Her feelings towards Edmund Beck are further displayed in an acid little addendum intended only for the eyes of John Groom: 'With seizing covenants etc they have now had every shilling of rent. The next time Beck sneers at you in public, ask him if he has been allowed to receive the Sacrament again or has still to walk out of church.' Ouch!

Affairs wound with excruciating slowness towards a conclusion. Not until Christmas Eve did Louise's advisers, John Groom and Somerville Gurney, learn from Mr Beck the exact amount of money which the Prince had decided would be appropriate as a parting gift to the Lady Farmer. It turned out to be the noticeably unround figure of £525.

Loyal Mr Groom tried one final time to induce the Prince's camp to be more generous. He wrote to Edmund Beck saying that the amount offered as compensation was 'so thoroughly inadequate that if myself only were concerned I should refuse it at once. I was led to expect that 2 years rents would be given and a bonus of £600 and consider that any sum under that would be wholly insufficient.'[128]

His last throw of the dice is a brave statement of belief, of which only the rough draft remains: 'I, John Groom, consider that the Appleton farm as left by Mrs Cresswell on the 11th of October last, taking *[sic]* at a marketable value, to be worth £10,000 more than it was when first taken by the late Mr Cresswell owing to the fresh outlay in permanent improvement. I also consider it to be left in the highest and cleanest state of cultivation that I have seen this year in the County of Norfolk, showing an expenditure in labour and manure to an extent unusual in an outgoing Tenant. Am also of the opinion that if left in the state in which it was taken His Royal Highness would have been compelled to let it rent free for some years.'

---

[128] Groom family records

This draft is headed '(for approval)', so presumably he sent it to Louise and took her advice on the final form of this last desperate plea. Somerville Gurney may have been justified in his assertion that Mr Groom did not use his own judgement but only acted up to what Louise told him, although by his own lights the farmer was doing his best for the widow of his late apprentice. Gerard Cresswell had asked him, on his deathbed, to take care of Louise and her son. But by this time even the faithful Groom had run out of ideas.

As Louise remembers it, Farmer Groom 'declared he was "done" for the first time in his life. A few hundred were all he could get for me, and a few more added on and insultingly called a "present"... the entire hay and turnip crop was taken possession of to make up a balance of rental for the Prince, which was charged up to the "uttermost farthing"...' She repeats Groom's claim that she had raised the value of Appleton by 'at least £10,000', taking this as a fact, though this and other sums which she details appear arbitrary.

Her abuse is marvellous...
Writing to apprise the Prince's solicitor of the reaction to HRH's munificence Beck concludes, 'I also send her recent pamphlet, which will tell its own tale, her abuse of myself and everyone is marvellous. I don't care but it is very annoying... Keep the book, but perhaps she has sent you a copy as she has done to Sir Dighton Probyn...'[129]

The 'book' to which he refers was a long essay, entered into a competition for articles on the subject, 'How the Farming in Great Britain can be Made to Pay', for which a £5 prize had been offered. Louise's entry, titled *Farming with Profit*, was published in a series of 'Household Tracts for the People', in December 1880. It comprises twenty-four pages of text and ten pages of advertisements for such things as cattle cake, traction engines, and 'The Gift Book of the Day, *Black Beauty, The Autobiography of a Horse.* By A. Sewell'.

---

[129] Royal Archive LAW/SHM/12/10/97

Considering the traumas which were affecting Louise's life at the time she wrote this essay, it is a well-reasoned, articulate and intelligent attempt to answer the problems facing British agriculture. She advocates larger farms and mixed farming, and more use of labour-saving machinery, and she recommends that 'small land-owners' whose tenants have come to grief should take over their own farms and live in their own farm houses, 'and very comfortable, jolly abodes you will find them, minding no amount of drudgery, up early and down late, and toiling away as if you had emigrated with your family to the backwoods of America…' This need not be looked upon as losing caste: 'I have been grubbing on a West Norfolk farm for eighteen years, and on friendly gossiping terms with almost every dealer, drover and pig-jobber in the country side, without losing in the smallest degree the position of a gentlewoman'. She offers her services as an agricultural counsellor: 'In my own neighbourhood I should be very glad to give any assistance or advice that would be acceptable. I am looking out for a "place" and should rather enjoy setting up as a sort of itinerant and professional "help" to landlords in difficulties.'

Although she remains careful not to write anything that might be construed as an attack on the Prince of Wales, not when she was still haggling with him over money, her lecturing, moralistic side surfaces now and then. She berates the upwardly-mobile middle classes, especially farmers' wives and daughters trying to ape their betters, putting on airs and graces, hankering after 'gentility' and considering manual labour beneath them, so that father has to hire dairy maids and cooks rather than have his family lower themselves doing chores. If only these silly women would do more of the farm work for themselves, opines Louise, their menfolk might be better able to pay their rents.

She herself, of course, is of a more elevated class, occupying a very peculiar position – belonging in the echelon of the landlords by kinship [she doesn't say by birth] and to the farming community by goodwill and trade. She feels that many more Gentlemen might take up farming if only their status were to be recognized: 'you can hardly expect a gentleman of birth and education to be willing to look up to any one of whom he may happen to hire a farm as a superior being, or like to be spoken of as "one of my tenants", to do homage upon festive and feudal occasions, and to live on terms of intimacy and equality with all the farmers on the estate, whether they belong to the unpretentious homely sort, whom it is a pleasure to know, or the would-be swells, who are so truly objectionable…'

And as for land agents… Gentlemen tenants, Louise avers, soon find themselves isolated, caught between the suspicion and resentment of the ordinary farmer and the hubris of the agent who, 'exacting more deference than the landlord himself, looks with mortal jealousy upon any one above him in the social scale, or whose outspoken, straightforward ways are a standing reproach and contrast, and will probably contrive sooner or later to ruin and oust him from his holding, persuading the Squire by some cleverly devised misrepresentation (and it is marvellous the power these men so often acquire over their masters) that gentlemen and lady tenants are a grand mistake upon the property and the sooner they are got rid of the better, and after offering some wholly inadequate dole of compensation, may very likely end by securing his valuable improvements for people of his own class, who will be on visiting terms with himself, his wife and family, which is a very pleasant state of things for them all round, but has the opposite effect upon the unhappy victim.'

(In face of this libellous attack, Mr Beck's response of 'I don't care but it is very annoying' seems mild indeed!)

The pamphlet concludes, 'the happiest years of my life have been spent in a Norfolk farm house… and with a fair chance and fair play I might have held my own even through these disastrous times…' Instead, she is doomed to 'life-long exile and separation from nearly all that makes life worth having to me, although softened by the untiring kindness of friends, and the angelic goodness and sympathy of the gracious Princess…'

The bottom line
When all was settled and the sums added up, 'the Executors of G. O. Cresswell, Lessees of Appleton Farm' received the balance

of their account. Thanks to the Prince's gift of £525, it ended in the black, precisely £484/4s/3d.[130]

Incandescent with rage, Louise refused to sign the bank statement – doing so might imply that she was satisfied, which she most definitely was not. Somerville Gurney was willing to sign for both of them, but Mr White, unhappy about settling this last detail on only one signature, decided to make absolutely sure of his ground by submitting the case to arbitration. Which meant another delay. Counsel Charles Hall eventually returned his verdict on 4 April 1881, a hurried scribble on the bottom of the case sheet confirming that the matter could indeed be settled on the signature of only one of the Executors/Lessees.[131]

So, once again, Somerville Gurney pre-empted Louise and signed the final document on his own sole authority.

Betrayed for an unbelievable third time by the man whom her husband had chosen as her co-executor to his will and co-trustee to her son's inheritance, Louise grabbed a large sheet of brown paper, primed her pen with ink and, in a jagged, untidy hand, expressed her utter contempt for the lot of them in a statement which reads:

> London
> June 4th 1881
>
> Mr Somerville Arthur Gurney of Valley Field, Norfolk, Executor of the late Gerard Oswin Cresswell and co-lessee to the Appleton farm, Sandringham, Norfolk, having on the 26th April 1881 given to Mr Edmund Beck, acting as land agent to HRH the Prince of Wales, K.G., a receipt for a balance of £434 . 4 . 3 *[sic]*, the said receipt being signed by Mr Somerville Arthur Gurney in the name of the Executors and Lessees, and the said balance claiming to be an alleged settlement between HRH the Prince of Wales, K.G., and the said Executors and Lessees, and moreover the said account containing a statement to the effect that a sum of £600 was agreed upon by Mr Groom of Ashwicken Hall, Norfolk, as the valuation of the unexhausted improvements on the Appleton Farm, which statement the said Mr Groom wholly repudiates and denies, I, Louisa Mary Cresswell, Co-Executor to the late Gerard Oswin Cresswell, and Co-Lessee to the Appleton Farm, hereby wholly

---

[130] Royal Archive LAW/SHM/12/10/99
[131] Royal Archive LAW/SHM/12/10/100

and entirely repudiate the receipt given by Mr Somerville Arthur
Gurney for the balance of £484 – 4 - 3 *[sic]* and declare that it was
given without my knowledge and consent and that I will not be bound
by or abide by it.

Louisa Mary Cresswell
Co-Executor to the late Gerard Oswin Cresswell and
Co-Lessee to the Appleton Farm from the year 1865
to Oct 11th 1880[132]

This last act of defiance served no purpose, except to alleviate
her feelings of total frustration. The comment about Mr Groom
denying his agreement to the £600 valuation is, as we know,
untrue – his note confirming acceptance, however reluctantly, is
preserved in the archive *(see above, end of section 'Mr Groom's
last stand')*.

Convinced that she had been deceived, out-manoeuvred and
cheated of her due, Louise spent the next few years writing her
book about her years at Sandringham. She chose to end the main
narrative at the point when she left the farm, but, prior to
publication in 1887, she added a few final paragraphs in which
she alluded to one or two return visits to old friends in West
Norfolk, and she mentioned her 'exile and wanderings, extending
to wild frontier settlements and the prairies and ranches of the
Far West…'. That is all she revealed about her life beyond
Appleton.

It is, however, far from the end of her story.

After Appleton

Though she lodged in the new seaside town of Hunstanton St
Edmund for a few months, in June the following year Louise was
in London when she wrote her last defiant statement, quoted
above. After that she occupied herself in planning and writing
her book, waiting for her son to complete his education, and
visiting relatives and friends.

---

[132] Royal Archive LAW/SHM/12/10/101

Louise's close family in 1883

Mrs Eliza Beauford (72), husband Henry (70), with three unmarried
 daughters (43, 39 and 33), in Thrapston, Northants; two sons moved on
Miss Fanny Hogge (69), still single, living in Lynn
George Archdale (66), wife Mary, Bournemouth, Hants; no family
Mrs Harriet Lindsell (62), widow, in Hastings with unmarried
daughter Elizabeth (33)
Mrs Anna Douton (58), husband Revd Charles, vicar of Biggleswade,
Beds; two sons and a daughter, all in mid-twenties
Frederick Archdale (56), mainly in Baldock, Herts, third wife
Fanny (45); four sons and six daughters, infant to age 23
Charles Archdale (51), in Coltishall, Norfolk, with wife Emilia (47);
two sons and five daughters aged 5 to 18
Also widowed sister-in-law **Mrs William Samuel (Helen) Hogge** (55),
and her daughter, Mrs Edith Ames-Lyde (32), of Thornham

The last-mentioned in this list, Louise's niece, Edith Ames-Lyde,
lady of Thornham, lost her young husband (32) in February 1883
after ten years of marriage. Like her mother before her, Edith
was doomed to live as a widow for many years, though unlike
Helen she had not even one child to console her. After being
widowed, Edith resided mainly at Thornham, best remembered
for her enterprise in starting the Thornham Ironworks, which
made decorative pieces, some of which were purchased by the
Prince and Princess of Wales for use at Sandringham. (Most of
the ornate gates on the royal estate were made at Thornham, an
exception being the Norwich Gates).

Louise's closest confidante was her spinster sister, Fanny,
resident in King's Lynn. Some letters directed by Fanny to
brother Frederick in the 1880s[133] suggest that the forceful Louise
wielded great influence over her older sister, for, following
Louise's example, Fanny started to agitate about the security of
her inheritance: 'I have been thinking about the four thousand
pounds the interest of which is paid to me by Mr Hooper, and I
should like to have <u>good security</u> for it and also to know whether
it is in really <u>safe</u> mortgages and where it is. I should have done
this I know <u>long since</u>, but being so ill I put it off, but I do now

---

[133] Bedfordshire and Luton Record Office: HF/20/183/1

request he will send me all particulars at once as of course it is quite right that I should have them. I think in these times everyone ought to be careful where their money is placed. I hear Mrs Fitzroy* is with you. With love to all your family. Yours affectionately…' (*mother to Frederick's late second wife.)

A month later Fanny wrote again to say she had 'been expecting a letter by <u>every post</u>… Not hearing a word I write again to request that I may know without any longer delay where my £4000 is placed… I ought, I know, to have ascertained this long ago but I have [been] so ill… I hope this will be attended to as I do not want to keep writing, and waiting for an answer. I hope you are all well. Your affectionate sister… PS Would you ask them at the bank to send me another cheque book?' (Interesting that Fanny, again like Louise, uses the excuse of ill-health as both shield and weapon, though at least she signs off in a loving, sisterly fashion.)

Brother Frederick, wearied by this renewed harassment, sent the letters to his solicitor, Mr Hooper: 'Will you write to her or shall I do so? She is evidently very suspicious of the Trustees, I think the best thing will be to invest her money in the funds, it will serve her right to let her have three per cent instead of four and a quarter…'

Oh dear!

The other Cresswells

Some widows might have turned for support to their in-laws, but for Louise this was not so easy. Her quick temper, her rash behaviour, and her habit of expressing herself too freely on paper had inevitably served to distance her from the more circumspect Cresswells. As one of their descendants observed: 'Her husband's family found her a great trial; they tried to help her but she rejected their help…'[134] Louise had an unhappy knack of losing friends.

By the time she was obliged to leave Appleton, of her husband's immediate family only his elderly mother Rachel and his oldest brother Frank – and Frank's four adult children –

---

[134] Lady Wilhelmina Harrod, writing in the Eastern Daily Press, 23 Dec 1974

remained. Frank had worked at the bank in partnership with his great friend Somerville Gurney for many years, but he does not appear to have taken any major part in Louise's affairs. Being an easy-going type, perhaps he preferred to steer clear of unpleasant complications.

Despite the accident which had injured his side a few years before, Frank continued to enjoy his boating until, in June 1882, while handling ropes, he suffered further strain which triggered an abrupt decline in health. He died in the early morning of Tuesday, 19 September 1882, aged sixty. Three days later, eight pallbearers bore his coffin, which was shrouded with a military cloak, his sword and telescope lying on top. Seven carriages formed part of the cortège, with fifty fishermen walking behind and many citizens lining the route to pay respects to this well-known and well-liked local figure. He was buried alongside his wife, not far from all the other deceased members of his family, at North Runcton..

Mrs Rachel Cresswell (née Fry), dowager of the family, was almost eighty when her oldest and only remaining son died. Having outlived her husband and all of their seven children, she resided still at the Bank House, with faithful housekeeper Harriet Lancaster heading the staff, for another six years. She died on 4 December 1888, aged eighty-five.

Go West, young man!
At Easter 1883, Louise's son, young Gerard Francis Oswald Cresswell, left Harrow School, midway through his nineteenth year and inspired by dreams of becoming a cattleman on the rolling, virgin prairies of the West. America was the land of untold adventure and promise: public speakers extolled the rich prizes to be won there, while bookstalls sold lurid paperbacks telling tales of Indian wars, heroic cattle drives and bold pioneer settlers. Custer's last stand at Little Big Horn had taken place only seven years before and 'Buffalo Bill' Cody was soon to bring his Wild West Show to England, starring Sitting Bull and sharp-shooting Annie Oakley. Current best-sellers told tales of the outlaw Jesse James, shot to death in 1882. Many young

English, Scots, Irish and Welsh men found the lure of the American West irresistible.

Schoolmates of Gerard at Harrow included two of the seven Anson brothers, the Hon. Claud and the Hon. Francis (sons of Thomas, 2nd Earl of Lichfield). They had all lodged in Mr Watson's house at the school. Their boyish dreams may have crystallized when they encountered one Henry L. Bentley, a Columbia University-educated lawyer who came to England specifically to promote the attractions of West Texas and who later made his home there.

No sooner had they left school than Gerard and his friends the Anson brothers took heed of J. B. L. Soule's famous exhortation to 'Go West, young man…'

Abilene, Texas

Texas is a land of contrasts – long hot summers and bitter, snowy winters, with frosts from November to March; thick mud turning to choking dust; wild flowers carpeting the rolling plains with yellow, blue or red in springtime; and violent storms, including tornadoes. Since time untold it had been Comanche Territory. Few white settlers came there until after the Civil War ended in 1865, and the last fight with the Native Americans took place as recently as the 1870s. When young Gerard Cresswell arrived, Texas was still largely as untamed as Nature had made it.

The Texas and Pacific railroad reached milepost 407 in January 1881 and established a railhead way out on the empty, near-treeless prairie. Two months later, the first plots of land were sold for what was billed as the 'Future Great City of West Texas'; they named it Abilene in the hope that, like its Kansas namesake, it too might become a great cattle town. By 1882, the rapidly-growing settlement had a newspaper, a number of churches and a school, but it was still very much the Old West, wooden buildings with hitching rails, horses and wagons, livery stables and saloons, women in gingham and bonnets, and men in denim and leather, toting guns.

Abilene became capital of Taylor County, but it was to a corner of neighbouring Callahan County that Gerard Cresswell and his Old Harrovian friends gravitated. They bought adjoining ranchlands along the Jim Ned Creek, south and west of the future town of Oplin, and began raising cattle. Many other wealthy Englishmen engaged in the cattle business, but most of them did so from afar, investing only their money: Gerard Cresswell stayed, and put down roots, and prospered. Among the other inhabitants of West Texas he was noted as a genuine 'blue-blood' of ancient lineage, thanks to his Cresswell antecedents, who traced their line back through seven centuries to the time of bad King John.

G.F.O.Cresswell, cattleman

Two years after setting out on his great adventure, the younger Gerard Cresswell returned home to sign the necessary forms to secure his inheritance. On 9 October 1885, his twenty-first birthday, under trusts set up by his father and his three Cresswell uncles – Addison, S. Gurney and Oswald – he became a wealthy man, with capital in the region of £20,000. There would be a few more thousand to come from his grandfather Francis Cresswell's estate when grandmother Rachel died three years later.

The eligible young rancher and his mother Louise (now 55) set out for the return journey to the States almost before the ink had dried on the legal documents. They took ship from Liverpool, aboard the Cunard Company's first all-steel vessel, the SS *Servia*, fitted with twelve water-tight compartments and brightly lit by electricity, with the latest triple-expansion steam engine which allowed her to sail at more than seventeen knots. This magnificent, super-modern ship brought Louise Cresswell and her son safely in to New York on 26 October 1885.

At home in Texas, Gerard set his mind to work. His cattle business expanded. In time he introduced Aberdeen Angus cattle to Callahan County and ran the only registered herd in that area. His ranch eventually extended over 20,000 acres.

But, while her son relished the new life and the challenges it held, Louise remained restless, homesick for England. The town of Abilene was still raw and rough, the ranch-house out on the prairie primitive by her standards, little more than a shack in the first years. It was, however, soon fitted with one of the absolute necessities of that land – a lightning rod: this was 'Tornado Alley' and lightning rod salesmen had plenty of business. How different from sleepy Norfolk. Oh yes, Texas had horses and dogs – Louise had always loved animals – but herding cattle on miles of wide open, dusty plains was very different from driving them along leafy English lanes, to and from lush green marshes, or milking them in the shed and helping to birth their calves one by one.

Louise may have empathized with the hopeful farmers who began to arrive and plant crops, hoping to make the land greener, but, just as they began to establish themselves, the rains failed and the area's worst recorded droughts began, the severe winter of 1885 being followed by a seemingly-endless twenty-three months with no significant rainfall. Though this caused certain problems for the ranchers, for many of the new farmers it spelled disaster. Harvests failed for two consecutive years, bringing the inevitable hardship and foreclosures – all too horribly familiar and depressing.

Louise had often claimed that she would be happy to fend for herself and live a primitive backwoods existence, but reality proved less romantic. In England too much rain had been the problem: here in Texas the opposite was true. The heat, the storms, the dust were a trial for an ageing lady clad in stays and long petticoats. She was no longer young and resilient, able to work all hours while battling impossible foes. She had to accept that she had given the best years of her life to Appleton Farm. Little reward she had had for it. For such a proud woman the defeat was especially bitter, rankling away at her mind and soul as she dwelled on the injustice of it all.

She could not – would not! – let them get away with it.

Returning to England in 1886, to revisit some of her old friends and familiar places, she found her successor well settled in at Appleton, granted all the favours for which she had begged: 'the hares killed down in cart-loads, new cottages built… labourers who had offended him were refused employment at Sandringham… The Prince heaped numerous favours upon those who had contributed to my expulsion, whilst the "Royal thunderbolts" fell heavily upon some who assisted me…' Even so, it gave her some satisfaction to know that the Sandringham cohort were still wary of her: 'though they had the triumph and won all along the line, somehow I do not think they will ever feel quite safe and comfortable so long as I am above ground. I hear rumours of anxious enquiries as to whether I am writing a book…'

The anticipated book appeared in 1887, a contradictory tale which, while detailing many grievances and hinting at yet more dark secrets left unwritten, also gives a warm and vivid picture of country life in Victorian Norfolk, of some of its characters, and of the delights and pitfalls of living within the orbit of the Prince and Princess of Wales. Reading it, however, one must bear in mind Louise's purpose in creating the book – it was an act of vengeance, and she frequently allowed bitterness to cloud both her judgement and her memory.

Abusing Edmund Beck and his master the Prince of Wales in print was a reasonably safe ploy; she knew from experience that they would be reluctant to react in public, for fear of creating yet more scandal; but nowhere does her book allude to the other man she had come to hate, the man who had three times betrayed her – Somerville Arthur Gurney. Of course, if she had openly accused *him* of perfidy, Gurney might have sued her for defamation of character – unlike the royal camp, he did not have the press and public waiting to criticize his every move. However, Louise's true feelings towards him – and towards her in-laws – show through in a letter she wrote to John Groom, in which she stated that she wished 'to have nothing more to do with him [S. A. Gurney], or with the Cresswells'.[135] In later years the wealthy landowner and banker Somerville Gurney was a frequent guest at Sandringham and a familiar presence at shooting parties. And after the Prince became King a knighthood rewarded *Sir* Somerville Arthur Gurney for services rendered.

By publishing her story, Louise did cause a brief stir, but, as is the Royal Family's wont, the Prince allowed the ripples to run

---

[135] Lady Wilhelmina Harrod, writing in the Eastern Daily Press, 23 Dec 1974

their course, while he himself continued his life undaunted. The Lady Farmer had been a nuisance, but the thorn had been plucked, its prickles blunted.

(Historians writing about Sandringham often repeat a story that Edmund Beck bought up most copies of Louise's book and destroyed them. Indeed, some claim he burned them on the Prince's specific orders. None of the writers cite a source for this tale and, despite long enquiries, I have been unable to discover any evidence that it is true. There was, anyway, a second edition which appeared a short time later with only the most minor amendments. Even so, the fact remains that both editions of Louise's book are now very, very rare.)

In December 1887, following first publication of her book, the solitary Louise sailed again for the States, aboard the SS *Persian Monarch*, out of Hull and bound for Boston, Massachusetts. She travelled steerage, with nine items of luggage, in company with only two other passengers, a mother and young daughter heading for New York as immigrants. This was to become the pattern of her life – back and forth across the Atlantic, a year or so in Texas then home again to England. After Appleton, Louise lived a gypsy existence, with no settled home of her own. It was not a happy way to spend the remaining decades of her life.

However, some brighter moments remained to be enjoyed. One of these occurred on 7 September 1898, when, as described in the *Abilene Daily Reporter* for 9 September, Gerard Cresswell took the 'statuesque beauty' Miss Elsie May Buell, daughter of Major Allen Buell of the United States Volunteers, to be his wife. Gerard was a month short of thirty-four, his bride twenty-one. Attended by her sister Miss Genevieve, the bride wore a 'beautiful travelling gown of brown Marchesi cloth, Paris design, trimmed in velvet and cut steel buckles, a becoming sailor hat to match and white gloves with black stitching'. Her groom looked fine in 'a black Prince Albert [coat], white waistcoat and gray *[sic]* trousers'. The marriage was solemnized at the Church of the Heavenly Rest in Abilene by the Bishop of Dallas, and afterwards the pair set off for an extended honeymoon trip through the eastern states.

Gerard and Elsie's only son, Gerard Allen Cresswell, was born the following year, followed in time by four sisters named Dorothea, Elsie, Rachel and Sarah. They remained at the ranch until 1906, when Gerard (aged 42) brought his wife and children to live in the city of Abilene, in a spacious and attractive house which, a hundred years later, still holds the famous pipe organ of which gifted soprano Mrs Elsie May Cresswell was so proud – the only such organ in Abilene.

Sadly, but not surprisingly, considering her penchant for speaking her mind and upsetting people, Louise did not live with her son and his growing family; instead, she established herself in a suite of rooms in Abilene's Grace Hotel (a building which is now a museum).

Too many goodbyes
The aged Queen Victoria saw only three weeks of the twentieth century, dying on 22 January 1901, on which date her oldest son succeeded to the throne as King Edward VII. 'Bertie' was then fifty-nine, of portly figure, his fair beard turning grey, his hair thinning to baldness. He had waited a long time to take up his role as Monarch, but his coronation was further delayed when he fell ill with appendicitis which demanded immediate surgery.

During his reign, Louise continued to journey across the Atlantic, travelling to and from the Texas port of Galveston. She arrived back there in November 1903, and again in February 1907 accompanied by a paid nurse who was with her just for the voyage, and in December 1909 she journeyed with a lady's maid who was to go with her to Abilene but who had a husband waiting back in London. The proud and defiant Lady Farmer had become a lonely old woman, growing older and frailer and having to employ companions whenever she travelled. She was seventy-nine when she arrived at Galveston that December day in company with Susannah Odey, completing her penultimate transatlantic voyage.

She was fortunate to have the money to travel so frequently, thanks to her grandfather and her father, with various extra trusts and legacies which came to her at intervals. Following the death of Rachel Cresswell in 1888, Louise was at last paid the residue of her marriage settlement and her husband's share in his father (Francis Cresswell)'s estate, a total of £3,750, on which she had until then been receiving regular interest. Her son, too, benefited to the tune of £7,000.

Did she make up her quarrel with brother Frederick? After losing his third wife in 1890, the following year he sailed the Atlantic to New York, but sadly the records don't tell whether he went further. Like his siblings, Frederick was growing old, winding down. He moved to Southampton in 1895 and in 1898 sold up the family businesses in Biggleswade for £135,000. Three years later he inherited another considerable fortune from the Fitzroys when his mother-in-law died. Three-times married and three-times widowed, Frederick Archdale, aged seventy-six, died of a brain haemorrhage in 1903, a wealthy man, but, with ten children and a clutch of grandchildren to provide for, he left nothing for his troublesome sister Louise.

In 1901, brother George Archdale died, aged eighty-three. He too was a rich man, but childless; he left Louise a legacy of £2,000 and youngest brother Charles £6,000. A small bronze plaque in memory of the man who was for so many years a partner in the Setch brewery may be found on the wall of St Margaret's church in Lynn. He left his interests in the brewery to his nephew George Fitzroy Archdale, second son of Frederick.

A final boost for Louise's income came when her rogue cousin, the illegitimate but enterprising Fred Safford, natural son of Uncle Fred Hogg, left her £1,000. That was in 1914. That same year came news of the passing of her niece Edith Ames-Lyde, carried off by a heart attack while visiting Shanghai during an extended tour of the Far East. Edith had travelled far and wide seeking new ideas for the wrought-iron forges at Thornham. Was she also attracted to the Far East because of business interests left by her maternal grandfather, Hollingworth Magniac, who had traded out of Canton in his youth? Or was she visiting places remembered by her mother, Helen, born in Macao? Whichever it was, Edith died and was buried in China[136]. She left Thornham

---

[136] The Foreigners' Cemetery in Shanghai lies now under a factory

and her other properties to her cousins, children of her uncles Frederick and Charles Archdale (né Hogge).

Of the Biggleswade Hogges, only the two youngest remained – Louise and her brother Charles. Their four sisters Eliza, Fanny, Harriet and Anna, had all died in the last decade of the nineteenth century (Fanny was buried at Thornham on 31 January 1891). Sister-in-law Helen Hogge (née Magniac) also died in 1891.[137] Louise herself was ailing, descending into a twilight of confusion and physical debility. Did she even know of the war that broke out in Europe in August 1914 – the war that everyone said would be over by Christmas?

Taken into the care of Dr L.W. Hollis at the Hollis Sanitorium in Abilene, in March 1915, Louisa Mary Cresswell died there sixteen months later, at noon on Sunday, 2 July 1916, of what her death certificate names 'Senility, or Old Age'. Reporting her death, the *Abilene Daily Reporter* adds, 'She had spent the last twenty years in this country and in England, coming over for a visit of a year and then returning home. The Cresswell family is one of the oldest and best known in England. Funeral services will be held Tuesday at 6:00 o'clock p.m. at the residence of her son G. O. Cresswell… The body has been embalmed and will probably be sent to England at a later date for interment.' The undertaker bore the charming if unapt name, D. J. Laughter.

Back in Norfolk, in its Births, Marriages and Deaths column for 28 July, the *Lynn Advertiser* noted briefly: 'CRESSWELL – On 2nd July, Louisa Mary Cresswell, formerly of Appleton House, Sandringham, Norfolk.' Whoever paid for the insert did not waste money on unnecessary wordage. Those who had known her would note the fact of her death, though she had lived so long that few who had known her remained.

Her embalmed body lay in a temporary grave for three months, until arrangements could be made for its transfer to England. On 12 October, her son wrote a letter confirming: 'Our clergyman tells me that although he read the full burial service, except the committal part, that is all that would be necessary, but

---

[137] Several family memorials may be seen in Thornham church

he has no objection whatever to the whole service being again read if the English minister preferred to do so.'[138] A transit permit, issued in Jersey City on 31 October, gave permission for the remains to be removed from Abilene and taken for burial at King's Lynn; the form was then sent the few miles into New York City, where a five shilling postage stamp was attached on the reverse, over-stamped BRITISH CONSULATE GENERAL, NEW YORK, and dated 1 November 1916.

Wells Fargo and Company, the selected carrier and shipper, charged double the lowest first-class passenger fare for transportation of a deceased human body. Carrying coffins was a routine part of Wells Fargo freight business, 'Corpses' being listed alphabetically on their tariff after Cheese, Children, Chronometers, Cigar Boxes, Clams, and Colts (live stock)… and followed by Cows, Crabs and Crayon Portraits…

In Europe the Battle of the Somme ground on, destroying both Kitchener's army and the notion of war as a Boys' Own adventure: after the Somme, men knew that modern warfare was bestial, bitter and bootless – literally so for many of them. The United States remained neutral in the conflict – it would be April 1917 before President Wilson finally lost patience and declared war against Germany. But in 1916 the U-boats were less active, held in check by the Royal Navy; Louise's last voyage was uneventful. She came quietly home, sailing into the port of Liverpool and journeying on by train to King's Lynn, where her coffin was loaded onto a hearse and taken to wait overnight for the final leg to North Runcton.

The Becks
On the very day that Louise's body arrived back in Lynn, the local newspaper announced the appointment of a new agent at Sandringham. He was 'Mr Arthur Clement Beck, of Castle Rising, agent to His Majesty's Sandringham estate. He is the youngest son of the late Mr Edmund Beck, who was for 25 years King Edward's estate agent at Sandringham…'

---

[138] Norfolk Record Office PD 332/11

In the autumn of 1890, *en route* from West Newton to Babingley, Edmund Beck had been thrown violently from his horse, breaking four of his ribs. During the ensuing severe winter he developed pleurisy, but even so his death, on Saturday, 7 March 1891, at the age of sixty, came as a shock to all the neighbourhood. Reporting on the funeral, which took place on Wednesday, 11 March, the *Lynn Advertiser* said that he had, like many another good man, worked himself too hard: 'Those who knew him best speak of him as a courteous, genial and even-tempered man, who won the esteem of His Royal Highness and the many other landowners for whom he acted, and at the same time was looked up to as dealing fairly and honestly by tenants and labourers on the estates... His place will not be easily filled.' The paper has many other good things to say of Edmund Beck.

Was Louise entirely wrong about him? She did tend to let her emotions over-rule her reason at times of stress, and the land agent was the nearest, most obvious, target for her spleen. Agents of great country estates have an unenviable task, whipping boy in the middle, trying to please both landowner and tenant. Local gossip, passed down for over a century, suggests that Edmund Beck may have been a typical stern Victorian father – his daughters were not allowed out alone and only one ever married, so rumour says. But was he also an 'unpleasant man', as one resident put it? None of them actually knew him, after all.

Much of what is known and repeated about Edmund Beck has been borrowed from an earlier biography, *Whisper Louise*, written by David Duff and published by Muller of London in 1974.[139] This tells a romanticized tale, uncritically based on Louise's own version while adding the (entirely fictional) gloss that the Prince of Wales lusted after the 'sad and beautiful' widow. What is more, it portrays Edmund Beck as very much the villain of the piece, along with his royal master, while Louise is

---

[139] Devotees of *Whisper Louise* may have noted the newly-discovered portrait of the lady farmer, shown on the cover of this present book; she may have been a striking woman, she was hardly 'beautiful' and, besides, she was eleven years older than Bertie – not his type at all. Also, the photographs printed in the earlier book, 'thought to be' of Louise and Gerard Cresswell, obviously represent other people – Cresswells, perhaps, but not our pair.

the innocent, ill-used victim. This biased reporting may have unfairly damned the land agent in many minds.

In fact, Edmund Beck's death roused immense sympathy in Norfolk. His funeral was thick with flowers, wreaths and crosses by the dozen, and everyone went clad in deepest mourning, except for the bright splash of red from the cloaks of the local schoolgirls among the children who lined the path. Six hundred people – with Sir Dighton Probyn and his wife representing the Prince and Princess – filled every seat and standing place in the small church, latecomers obliged to stand in the porch or on the path outside. Mr T. G. Archer, once Louise's solicitor, was among them, as was E. C. Groom, one of John Groom's younger sons.

Edmund Beck now lies with his wife, not far from Revd Lake Onslow and his mother, in the quiet churchyard at Sandringham.

A week or so after the funeral, his third son, Frank Beck, was appointed land agent at Sandringham. Frank had been working on the royal estate since 1880, assisting with the management of the Royal Stud. In 1891 he was twenty-nine and had been married only a few months when he took up his new post. He remained in royal service for a quarter of a century, as had his father before him, and during the First World War he claimed his own special niche in history as commander of the Sandringham Company of the Norfolk Regiment.

The 'lost company'

The Sandringham company of volunteer militia was made up of local men, some of them servants in the big house, or grooms, carpenters and gamekeepers on the estate. When the Great War drew them in, Captain Frank Beck could have escaped the fighting had he chosen to do so – men over forty were not obliged to answer the call. But he refused to desert his men and led them on their posting out to Suvla Bay in Gallipoli, where, as legend tells, they 'vanished into a strange unearthly mist'. Recent research, while dispelling this mystic legend, nevertheless confirms that most of the Sandringham boys gallantly and tragically met their deaths at the hands of the Turks on 12 August 1915. Frank Beck died with them. He was fifty-four.[140]

Because of the confusion on the battlefield, months went by before the very few survivors returned home to tell what had happened, and for a while hope remained that others might still survive. Hence the long delay in appointing the new agent, Frank's youngest brother Arthur Clement Beck, in November 1916. He too remained in the post for many years, retiring in 1936.

The bodies of Captain Frank Beck and his comrades were not found until after the war had ended. They are remembered, with others who fell in both world wars, on a memorial which stands on the broad stretch of grass just outside the gates to the church and the park, opposite the visitor centre at Sandringham.

Home at last

In Flanders, on 18 November 1916, the slaughter on the Somme was ending in a mess of mud, blood and the first snows of a bitter winter. But in the churchyard of North Runcton, in the county of Norfolk, England, only the rooks disturbed the peace as the undertaker's men lowered Louisa Mary Cresswell to her final resting place.[141] The funeral service had been read five thousand miles away, with her son and his family dressed in sombre mourning. All that remained was for the local rector to intone the words of the committal: 'her body to the ground, in sure and certain hope…'

Few people witnessed the last act in Louise's drama. Of the living who had known her, few remained. Her only surviving sibling, Charles, himself an octogenarian, lived miles away on the other side of the county. Her nieces and nephews were widely scattered, some of the boys dead before her, killed in the Great War.[142] Sir Somerville Arthur Gurney, squire of North

---

[140] The disappearance of the Sandringham Regiment was the subject for a BBC film *All the King's Men,* first shown in 1999 and starring David Jason as Captain Frank Beck

[141] Burial certificate Norfolk Record Office PD 332/11

[142] Charles Archdale's only surviving son, Charles William Archdale (39), was killed at the Battle of Cambrai in 1917, leaving a wife, Evelyn, and two small children; his older brother George (34) had died unmarried in 1900, during the Boer War, when about to proceed to S Africa in command of his company of

Runcton Hall, must surely have been aware of the simple ceremony taking place at his own village church. But he too was over eighty and perhaps already ill – he died just six months later, on 17 May 1917. Would he have troubled himself to turn out on a cold November day to bid farewell to the woman who had made it clear that she hated him?

Her old friend John Groom had died in 1908, her old enemy Edmund Beck long before that. Even Louise's most illustrious adversary, the Prince who had waited so long to become King, had gone to his reward in 1910. Did his widow, the Dowager Queen Alexandra, now seventy-two, know that Louise Cresswell had returned to Norfolk? Did she even remember the woman with whose sorrows she had once so kindly sympathized?

But if few of the living remained to mourn Louise, of the familiar dead an ample number waited. She was laid to rest close beside her husband, Gerard, and their infant daughter, and his brothers, Addison and Frank, and Frank's wife, Charlotte. Close to the church, a tall monument bears details of all the other Cresswells buried there – Frances and Rachel, their other three sons Gurney, Bill and Ossie, and their only daughter Harriet.

On the Western Front the guns fell silent for a while. In the churchyard the winter night came early, accompanied by skeins of wild geese and the harsh cry of pheasants. Louise slept safely, home at last.

And afterwards...

Louise's successor, Charles Blyth, did not enjoy Appleton for long. After only a few years, he too moved on and the farmland was added to the acreage of one of the Home Farms on the main royal estate.

In 1892, when Prince Eddy died suddenly (creating more scandal and myth, one scurrilous rumour claiming he was Jack the Ripper), his brother George, the new heir to the throne, was made Duke of York and given a choice of homes – Appleton

---

Norfolk militia. Frank Cresswell's grandson, another Francis Joseph (31), was killed at Mons, leaving a wife and two small daughters, of whom Wilhelmina became Lady Harrod of Holt

House, or the Bachelors' Cottage, a house set within the park at Sandringham, only five minutes' walk from the big house. Prince George chose the latter, which was promptly updated and renamed York Cottage, becoming home to the young Duke and his Duchess (the former Princess May of Teck, who had once been engaged to Prince Eddy). They became King George V and Queen Mary in 1910, six years before Louise died.

But Louise's old home did not languish unloved and empty. In 1895, the Prince of Wales gave Appleton House to his favourite daughter, Maud, on the occasion of her engagement to Prince Charles of Norway (King Haakon from 1905). This ensured she would have a place not far from her doting papa. Her husband contributed many of the Norwegian spruce trees that still grow on the estate, and their son, later to be King Olaf, was born at Appleton in 1903.[143]

During the Second World War, when Sandringham House was closed for economy, King George VI and Queen Elizabeth stayed at Appleton to take a respite from the traumas of London and the Blitz.

Today at Appleton Farm, some of the attractive Victorian cottages still provide homes for farm workers, while a modern farmhouse stands back from the cattle yards and the huge tractor sheds and barns. But Louise's beloved house is gone, nothing left but a twisted fence, a tangle of trees and shrubs, and a few old flooring tiles half buried in the dirt. Across the lane still stands the ruined church that the Pastons knew and, on the hill behind the site, the elegant red-brick water-tower that was the cause of one of Louise's griefs now provides an unusual holiday home. The spot remains an oasis of peace and quiet, with birds singing in the overgrown trees, the harsh cry of pheasants in the undergrowth, and spectacular views across the beautiful Norfolk countryside.

Ten miles away, in the sleepy village of North Runcton, the old Hall where Daniel Gurney lived has been replaced by a knot of modern houses. But the gracious old church remains in its

---

[143] Duff, David: *Whisper Louise* (Muller, 1974) p151

quiet, bird-haunted, tree-shaded churchyard. If you visit the spot you may rouse one of the colourful pheasants that strut over Norfolk's fields and woods, still providing sport for royal shotguns every year as the shooting season comes around.

The Lady Farmer, who once managed nearly a thousand acres of Norfolk farmland, now inhabits only a few square feet. Her small plot of earth is marked by a square triple plinth which bears a plain square cross some four feet high. At first glance it looks stark and bare of inscription but, looking more closely, on one side under a layer of organic silver and green, seekers may just make out the words: *In Memory of Louisa Mary wife of Gerard Oswin CRESSWELL...* The rest is worn to illegibility.

APPENDIX A

Hoggs of King's Lynn (1697-1815)

George HOGG (I), b 1697, d 25 April 1767; Mariner, poss from
Paull, Yorks; Freeman of Lynn from 1727; on Common
Council Dec 1743-June 1762;
married (early 1720s), Mary *LORK?LARK?* (1687-1750)
one son>>>
> **George HOGG (II),** bap 3 June 1724, d 25 Jan 1772;
> Freeman of Lynn 1744-5, Mayor 1770
> married 2 April 1747 <u>first wife</u> Ann ALLEN (1727-68)

children>>>
> <u>George, Stephen, Mary and John</u> *(see below)*

After Ann died, **George Hogg (II)** *married,* June 1769, <u>second
wife</u> Mary SHARPIN (dates n/k)
sons>>>
> <u>Thomas</u>, b 21 July 1770 *died young?*
> <u>Edward</u>, b 9 March 1772 (posthumous), buried 18 May
> 1772

Oldest son of George Hogg (II), by first wife Ann>>>
> **George HOGG (III)** bap 3 February 1748, d 23 July 1811;
> Freeman 1792-3; Mayor 1806-7; married 23 Oct 1769
> Dorothy TAYLER*[sic]* (1751-1828)

Fourteen children>>> *(see Appendix B)*

Younger children of George Hogg II by Ann>>>
> **Stephen HOGG**, bap 21 May 1749 d 29 April 1785;
> Freeman 1784-5; m Alice Sophia, (1753-1838)

children>>>
> <u>Sophia,</u> b 29 April 1776
> <u>Stephen Allen HOGG,</u> b 9 Jan 1775, *at Camb Uni Trinity
> Hall from June 1793 (age 16);* Freeman 1795-6; wife

276

n/k but had son <u>Frederick Allen HOGGE,</u> bc1819 d in
China 12 Feb 1839, age 19

Mary, bap 29 June 1751, buried Narford 1 May 1780;
m 28 June 1769 <u>Brigg Price FOUNTAINE</u> of Narford
(1743-1825) (they wed only a few days before her father
George married second wife Mary Sharpin, and in the same
church, St Mgts, Lynn):
children>>>
<u>Andrew FOUNTAINE,</u> b 13 July 1770
<u>Mary Ann,</u> b 11 Aug 1772, buried 30 June 1775
<u>Elizabeth,</u> b 24 Nov 1773

John HOGG, bap 8 Dec 1752, d 1815 Aylsham (he made
the children of Geo Hogg III his main heirs)

APPENDIX B

Fourteen Hogg siblings
Children of George Hogg (III) (1748-1811) and Dorothy, née Tayler (1751-1828)

George (IV), bap 13 July 1772, d 3 Jan 1847; m 1818 to Margaret Ainslie (1789-1868); no children

Fountaine, b 12 Nov 1773, d 21 January 1843 (Lyndhurst, Hants); King's Royal Hussars from 1795; served in America during War of Independence; Egypt campaign 1801; Spain under Sir John Moore at Corrunna 1808/9, ended Lt Col; m 1808 to Harriett Carleton, ?in Ireland?; children:
>> Harriet (1813-30), mem'l in St Nicholas' Chapel, Lynn
>> Fountaine, bc1821, d1857, also a soldier, took name and arms of Allen (HOGGE-ALLEN) in 1857 when named heir to aunt Frances' husband Thomas Allen (q.v.), but died same year; unmarried

Dorothy, bap 8 Dec 1774, d 28 March 1798, aged 23 (the only one to die young)

Martin, b November 1777, d 24 May 1846 –vicar of South Acre & West Winch, Norfolk; m Elizabeth Swaine; eleven children, four died under two years old, others being:
>> George (1805-55), curate at Holme-next-the sea, later vicar of Beachamwell
>> Edward Martin, b1808, Lieut. RN, commander of coastguard at Hunstanton
>> Charles and Arthur (dates n/k)
>> Henry (1821-41), mem'l at South Acre, Norfolk
>> John Swaine (1824-63), Major in 5th Fusiliers, buried at Biggleswade, Beds
>> Emma Elizabeth (dates n/k), m Robert Henry LINDSELL of Biggleswade; children include Henry Martin, Arthur Knox and Robert James

Henry, b 31 Aug 1778, d circa 1842/3, son:
>> Henry (dates n/k)

Anna, b 18 Dec 1779, d 3 March 1856, unmarried; buried at
   Shouldham, Norfolk

Joseph, b 19 Jan 1781; lived at Saxthorpe Hall, Aylsham,
   Norfolk in 1830; d before 1861

Mary, b 31 Jan 1782, d 10 July 1849, unmarried (buried at
   Shouldham)

Frances, bap 9 Feb 1783, d after 1851; married Thomas ALLEN
   of Shouldham (1786-1844); no children. On death of heir
   apparent Fountaine Hogge yngr [qv above] the Allen estates
   passed to a distant relative

Edward, bap 9 Aug 1784, buried 26 June 1869; rector of
   Fornham St Martin, nr Bury St Edmunds, Suffolk;
   m Elizabeth of Sheerness, children:
   >> Edward (1840-69)
   >> Fanny Allen (Mrs Montagu BROWNING) bc1842

William, bap 25 Aug 1785, d 7 July 1862; m Elizabeth Wells of
   Biggleswade; nine surviving children (including <u>Louisa
   Mary</u>, *see full family list, p43*)

John, bap 31 Dec 1786 ; a Colonel in the army; married
   ?Fanny?; children:
   >> Maria Charlotte and Fanny Amelia, both b in 1820s, ?in
   Cork, Ireland?)

Frederick, b 9 June 1789, d 12 July 1878; businessman of
   Girtford, Sandy, Beds; unmarried; illegitimate son:
   >> Frederick SAFFORD (1841-1914), common-law wife
      Mrs Fanny Dixon, known as Fanny Safford); daughter
      Alice, b 1880s

Harriet, b 20 July 1794, d in Jersey, 28 May 1842; m John
   MINCHIN 1820, widowed; then m Dr Thomas INGLE 1838

*(Details taken from parish records, church memorials, family
wills and census records)*

APPENDIX C

Thornham Manor and the Archdale/Hogge connection

Thornham has two separate manors – the Bishop's Manor and the Priory Manor. According to Norfolk historian Blomefield, the Bishop's Manor has been owned by East Anglian Bishops from Saxon times, its first recorded lord being Ailmar [Agelmar] who was Bishop of the Saxon cathedral at Elmham, Norfolk, in the time of Edward the Confessor. Blomefield says that the BISHOP'S MANOR passed to one 'Arsdale, Esq.' [Archdale], and after him to his daughter's husband, named Wilson; the PRIORY MANOR belongs to the Dean and Chapter of Norwich.

The lease on the Bishop's Manor was purchased by the Archdales in 1699/1700 and passed down through the female line until it was bought by George Hogg III (1748-1811) in 1785; however, complications about establishing legal ownership of the manor caused a two-year delay and the purchase was not completed until 1787. In 1792 Hogg also acquired the leasehold on Thornham Priory manor, from Revd Briggs Cary. Thus Hogg held tenure of both manors and in time he purchased other plots of land in and around Thornham *(for full details, see below)*.

Note: The manor of Thornham Priory, owned by the Dean and Chapter of Norwich, is held by tenants on a renewing 21-year lease. The Bishop's Manor, containing Thornham Hall and Cottage, is held on a thousand-year copyhold lease from the Lord Bishop of Norwich. A lawyer who looked into the holding discovered that there is an anomaly – the current Term of Lease of 1000 years was created by one deed dated 1749, and by another dated 1750. *(In 2749 someone will have to sort it out!)*

The Archdales

The Archdales emerge from the mists of time on 22 June 1604, when *Richard Archdale*, a merchant vintner of Dowgate Street, London, purchased the manor of Loakes and Temple Wycombe, near Chipping Wycombe [now High Wycombe].

Richard's grandson John Archdale (1642-1717), was a Quaker, an Adventurer and early Governor of North Carolina. He first went out to New England in 1664, aged 22, as agent of his brother-in-law (his sister Mary's husband), Governor Ferdinando Gorges, of Maine. John returned to London for a while, and married there, but went out to America again and from 1687-9 was commissioner for Governor Gorges.

In 1695, aged 52, John Archdale became Governor of North Carolina, an office he held for two years. A peaceable, moderate man, he is credited with the introduction of rice cultivation, with quieting troubles between the colonists and the Crown, and with befriending the Indians. On his return to England, he was elected to the British Parliament as member for High Wycombe in 1698, but 'his conscientious scruples concerning the required oaths prevented his taking his seat' (his only son Thomas is cited as being 'vice' MP that year, ie 'acting as a substitute for'). The source adds that Thomas 'was the first member of the Society of Friends who ever sate *[sic]* in Parliament'.

In 1700, John Archdale sold his High Wycombe estates to Lord (later Earl) Shelborne. The manor house of Loakes (or Lokes), the seat of the Archdales, refurbished and largely rebuilt, is now a girls' school called Wycombe Abbey.

Proceeds from the Wycombe properties provided a marriage settlement for John's son and heir, *Thomas Archdale*, who married Jane Turner, daughter of Charles Turner of King's Lynn, in July 1699. The trustees of the settlement were instructed to purchase the manor of Thornham for Thomas and to provide annuities for Jane and for any children. By the time he died, Thomas had acquired several other properties in West Norfolk, based around the manor of Stanhoe.

Thomas Archdale died relatively young, in 1711. His daughters, *Anne and Mary*, were still minors, but he left to his wife, Jane, all his properties in Stanhoe, Barwick, North Creake and Docking – *his will fails to mention **Thornham***, possibly because he assumed that Thornham would revert to his father John, as specified under the terms of the marriage agreement. However, when John died six years later, in 1717, *he, too, forgot to mention the Thornham properties*. No-one appears to have noticed the omission and thus all of Thomas's holdings, including Thornham, passed to the possession of his wife.

The younger daughter, *Mary,* died (aged about 20) in 1726, leaving her sister, *Anne,* as the only descendant of Thomas Archdale. When Anne married *John Wilson,* the Archdale name died out in their branch of the family. Mrs Anne Wilson inherited all the Norfolk properties on the death of her mother in 1742 and by law they became the property of her husband.

The Wilsons had three children, a son (Archdale Wilson) and two daughters, *Jane and Ann.* The son dying early, after their mother's death in 1782 *Jane (Mrs Edmund Allen)* inherited the Stanhoe manors, while *Ann (Mrs Joseph Tayler [sic])* inherited Thornham.

By that time, Ann Tayler was a widow, with two sons and seven daughters. Needing ready cash, she decided to sell her Thornham estates to her wealthy son-in-law, *George Hogg III*, husband of her daughter Dorothy. However, in October 1785, solicitors dealing with the sale realized that Thornham had been left in something of a legal vacuum, neither Thomas nor John Archdale having specifically bequeathed the manor to anyone. Before Ann Tayler could sell the land, she had to prove that she was entitled to be copyholder; so lawyer Mr Fearnes was called in to arbitrate. In the course of his enquiries he uncovered the anomaly in the dates of the thousand-year lease, as noted above.

Fearnes eventually concluded that Ann Tayler did have legal title and so the sale of Bishop's Thornham finally went through, in January 1787, and the copyhold passed to Ann's son-in-law, *George Hogg.* He later also acquired the manor of Thornham Priory and other property in the area.

George Hogg, Squire of Thornham

George Hogg III (1748-1811) and his wife Dorothy (née Tayler) (1751-1828) had fourteen children and it was their oldest son, *George Hogge IV (1772-1847),* who next inherited Thornham. However, he and wife Margaret were childless and when he died he left the estate to his younger brother *William Hogge,* a brewer and banker based in Biggleswade, Bedfordshire.

William Hogge (1785-1862) had sired a large family and it was *his* eldest son, *William Samuel Hogge* (1812-1852), who became the next holder of Thornham, the manor being entrusted to him under a marriage settlement when, on 10 May 1849, he wed Helen Julia Magniac. Major William Samuel Hogge being only forty when he died, and leaving no will, after yet more legal wrangles his only daughter, Edith Eliza, born 30 September 1850, became Lady of the Manor of Thornham when she came of age. She married Captain Neville Ames-Lyde in 1873, but they had no children. She died of a heart attack, in Shanghai, on 23 March 1914, aged 63, leaving her estate to some of her cousins, children of Charles Wells Hogge/Archdale of Coltishall.

Three surviving brothers of William Samuel Hogge – George, Frederick and Charles – all changed their name to Archdale by deeds poll in March 1866, citing their female-line relationship to John and Thomas Archdale, as above.

(Information accumulated from Dictionaries of Biography, family wills, parish records and documents in Norfolk Record Office, Norwich)

APPENDIX D

Hollingworth Magniac and the opium trade

The Magniac family originated in Switzerland, but Hollingworth Magniac (c1785-1867) held British nationality. As young men, he and his brothers Charles and Daniel set up a trading company in Canton, where they occupied a riverside merchant house called the Creek Factory. They and others like them were free-traders, separate from the vast official enterprise known as the Honourable East India Company (HEIC), which, for most of the eighteenth and well into the nineteenth century, acted as a trading agent of the British Empire, in India and later in China. They dealt in tea, raw silk, spices, sugar, pearls, emeralds, and opium. (Francis Cresswell, Louise's future father-in-law, commanded one of the HEIC's great East Indiamen trading with China [q.v.])

The seeds and juice of the opium poppy have been used as effective pain-killers for at least two thousand years, but serious problems of addiction did not arise until the eighteenth century, when smoking of opium resin became rife, especially in China. Chinese authorities tried vainly to prevent both cultivation of the poppy and trade in its products, eventually placing a total ban on import of the drug. The directors of the East India Company (or 'John Company' as it was known in the East) encouraged the growing of the opium poppy in India, but, being much too respectable to deal openly in contraband, they stopped their merchantmen from carrying opium into China. However, smaller independent companies such as Magniac & Co. continued the illicit trade. Whatever the legal and moral arguments against it, China provided a huge, insatiable – and lucrative – market for opium (even the Emperor and his court partook of the soporific smoke), and the port of Canton was very far away from the centre of Chinese government in Pekin.

Many European merchants based in China disguised themselves under the diplomatic flag of some minor nation: the Magniacs, for instance, officially represented Prussia, with Charles as Consul, Hollingworth as Vice-Consul and Daniel as secretary. The business became Magniac, Jardine & Co. with the arrival of Dr William Jardine, a canny entrepreneur who had made a fortune while employed as a ship's surgeon with the HEIC. Jardine had fewer moral scruples about dealing in opium and continued the trade quite openly.

After Charles Magniac died in Paris, in the early 1820s brother Daniel resigned from the firm under a cloud (he had committed the unforgivable sin of actually marrying his Indian mistress); but Hollingworth remained, basing himself in Macao.

By 1832, Hollingworth Magniac had interests in a score or more of ocean-going clipper ships, plus hundreds of smaller vessels employed in coastal and river trading. However, being by then in his late forties, with an English wife and two small children living with him in Macao, he decided to retire back to respectability in England, leaving the firm continuing in the Far East under the name Matheson, Jardine & Co.

By the time he stepped into Louisa Mary Hogge's circle of acquaintance, when his daughter Helen married Major William Samuel Hogge, Hollingworth Magniac was well established as an English gentleman. His vast wealth had enabled him to buy the Colworth Park estate in Bedfordshire, to build up a fabulous art collection, and to earn the esteem of his neighbours, tenants and employees. He was also the father of eight children – Helen Julia and Charles, both born in Macao in the late 1820s, plus their three brothers and three sisters, all born at Colworth and baptized at the pretty church in Sharnbrook village.

In the census of 1861, Hollingworth Magniac described his profession as 'East Indian Agency'. He died in 1867, succeeded by his oldest son, Charles, who was MP for Bedford and first chairman of the County Council. However, by the time Charles died in 1891, thanks to the severe depression of the late nineteenth century, the family fortunes were dissipated and the estate heading for bankruptcy.

Colworth House is now the Headquarters of the vast Unilever corporation.

APPENDIX E

Cresswells of Northumberland, and the career of Captain Francis Cresswell

The Cresswell family originated in a small village, also named Cresswell, near the coast in Northumberland; they trace their lineage back eight hundred years, to the time of King John.

When John Cresswell inherited the family properties, in 1773, he was a widower with two five-year-old daughters. His wife Catherine (née Dyer) had died on 30 June 1768, aged 27, in or following childbirth. The daughters were named Catherine Grace (later Mrs Bernie Brown) and Frances Dorothea, born 11 June 1768 (the Cresswell papers[144] cite no separate birth date for Catherine Grace; so, since other documents say the girls were twins, perhaps this is true). Their father John appears not to have married again, so the male Cresswell line ended with him.

However, some time before 1788 (when their first child was born), Frances Dorothea Cresswell married one Francis Easterby, of Blackheath, near Lewisham in Kent; and he bought out his sister-in-law's moiety (share in the inheritance), changing his name to Cresswell, thus continuing the name and the bloodline.

He and Frances Dorothea had five sons, the oldest being Addison John, who retained the family lands and, through his wife, assumed the name and arms of Baker, thus becoming Baker Cresswell. He it was who built the mansion house at Cresswell, Northumberland; he had four sons and three daughters. His brothers were Francis, William, Cresswell and Oswald. Of these, William Cresswell, of Brighton, produced three sons and two daughters; (Sir) Cresswell Cresswell, a bachelor, was a judge presiding over the first divorce court; and Reverend Oswald Cresswell, in common with so many younger sons, earned his living with the Church of England, first as vicar of Seaham, County Durham and, from 1846, as rector of Hamworth, Middx

---

[144] NRO: ACC 2005/362 Cresswell Papers

(he performed the wedding ceremony when his nephew, Gerard Cresswell, married Louise Hogge).

The second son, Francis Cresswell, born on 20 October 1789, in Charlton, Kent, went to sea at an early age, working his way up through junior ranks until, at the age of twenty, he sailed as fourth mate aboard the *Earl Camden,* on 21 January 1810. The ship was fated to burn in Bombay harbour six months later, but Francis Cresswell survived and returned home to sail again, as third mate, on the 1200 ton schooner *Thames,* leaving Torbay on 4 January 1812, bound for St Helena, Bencool and China, and returning to Moorings on June 1813. Aged twenty-four, he made his third voyage with the HEIC, again aboard the *Thames,* this time promoted to first, or chief, mate for another hazardous, seventeen-month voyage to China and back.

Aged just twenty-six, he leaps from the records into vivid, swashbuckling life as Commander of the sailing ship *Astell,* a three-decked merchantman of 870 tons, 146ft 9ins [just under 45 metres] long and 36ft [11 metres] wide, one of the great fleet sailing under the red and white striped ensign of the Honourable East India Company (HEIC), which, throughout the eighteenth and into the nineteenth, acted as Britain's trading agent across India and later in China *(for more detail, see Appendix D).*

The East Indiamen were the largest merchant ships of their day, heavily armed to protect their valuable cargoes – *Astell* had twenty-six guns. Her Captain, wearing his elegant navy blue uniform and cocked hat, commanded five officers and a hundred seamen.

Most HEIC captains were gentlemen and some were titled aristocrats, but they had also to be proven professional seamen, with at least one long voyage completed, before the company would even sign them on. Before being awarded a command, they had to work their way up, starting as fourth mate, the most junior officer rank.

On 19 January 1816, three months after his twenty-sixth birthday, Francis Cresswell was sworn in as captain of the *Astell.* Three times he took her out to the Far East, each voyage lasting more than a year, bringing home raw silk, Nankeen cloth, woollens, musk, camphor, arrack, arsenic and other poisonous drugs, not to mention 'warlike stores', besides the pearls and spices and other exotic goods that comprised the wealth of the Orient.

Considering that a captain was allowed, for his personal profit, 56 tons of goods occupying 20ft of cargo space, or £3,000 in bullion with which to buy trade goods, Francis Cresswell must have won himself quite a fortune by the time he strode down the gangplank after his final voyage on 30 May 1821.

He married Rachel Fry and settled down as a bank director, raising his family in the Bank House, King's Lynn, Norfolk.

BIBLIOGRAPHY

Primary (unpublished) Sources

Sandringham Collection, Royal Archives, Windsor Castle (by
    gracious permission of Her Majesty Queen Elizabeth II)
The National Archive, Kew, Richmond, Surrey
The British Library, St Pancras, London
County Record Offices (Norfolk; Beds & Luton; Herts; Surrey;
    East Yorks; and Kent)
King's Lynn Borough Archives, Town Hall, Lynn
Parish register, Stradsett Hall, Stradsett, Norfolk
Correspondence with the late Lady Wilhelmina Harrod and her
    address to King's Lynn Civic Society, April 1986, which
    she kindly copied for my use
Correspondence with William Cresswell Cooper, Del Rio, Texas
    (Louise's great-grandson)
Correspondence with Mr & Mrs Eric Cresswell Lavelle, Abilene,
    Texas (Louise's great-grandson and his wife Shirley)
Correspondence with Major William Archdale (grandson of
    Charles W. Archdale né Hogge)
Conversation with Miss Pleasance M. A. Bett (granddaughter of
    Charles W. Archdale né Hogge)
Pratt, J.H.: *Recollections,* hand-written reminiscences, with press
    cuttings; (held at Lynn Library)
Turner, Karen A.: *Abilene at the Beginning of the Twentieth
    Century, An Analysis of the United States Census* (Thesis)

Main Secondary Sources

Berry, Veronica: *The Rolfe Papers* (1979)
Bidwell, W.H.: *Annals of an East Anglian Bank* (Agas H. Goose,
    Norwich, 1900)
Carter, Thomas (Ed): *Historical Record of the Twenty-Sixth or
    Cameronian Regiment* (1867)

Cresswell, Mrs Gerard (Louisa Mary): *Eighteen Years on Sandringham Estate*, by "The Lady Farmer" (The Temple Company, London, First edition 1887; Second, amended edition, date n/k)
Norfolk and the Squires, Clergy, Farmers, and Labourers, etc, by "A Lady Farmer" (Simpkin, Marshall and Co, London; Thew and Son, King's Lynn, 1875)
Farming with Profit, or How the Farms in Great Britain can be made to Pay (Jarrold and Sons, London, Dec 1880)

Duff, David: *Whisper Louise* (Fredk Muller Ltd, London ,1974)

Duff, Katharyn, with Seibt, Betty Kay: *Catclaw Country, An Informal History of Abilene in West Texas* (Eakin Press, Burnet, Texas, 1980)

Featherstone, Donald: *Victorian Colonial Warfare, AFRICA* (Blandford, London, 1992)

Fryer, Kath: *Henry's Children* (Hollinfare, 2004)

Fryer, Kath: *A Fine Strong Boy* (Hollinfare, 2000)

Gurney, Daniel: *The Record of the House of Gournay,* privately printed

Hansard, Vol 187, Col 908-910 (Debate on Game Laws [Scotland], 21 May 1867)

Hardy, Charles and Horatio C.A.: *Register of Ships of the Hon East India Company* (4th Edition and Supplement) (1835)

Harrod, Dominick: *War, Ice and Piracy* (Chatham Publishing, London, 2000)

Harrod, Lady Wilhelmina: *Review of 'Whisper Louise'* (Eastern Daily Press, Dec 1974)

Hepworth, Philip: *Royal Sandringham, The Royal Family in Norfolk since 1863* (Wensum Books, Norwich, 1978)

Hibbert, Christopher: *Edward VII: A Portrait* (Allen Lane, 1976)

Hillen, Henry James: *History of the Borough of King's Lynn* (EP Publishing Ltd, 1978)

Hope-Nicholson, Jaqueline (ed): *Life Amongst the Troubridges: Journals of a Young Victorian 1873-1884, by Laura Troubridge* (Tite Street Press, London, 1999)

Hope-Nicholson, Jaqueline (ed): *Letters of Engagement 1884-1888: Love Letters of Adrian Hope and Laura Troubridge* (Tite Street Press, London, 2002)

Jenkins, Stanley C.: *The Lynn and Hunstanton Railway and the West Norfolk Branch* (The Oakwood Press, 1987)

Jones, Mrs Herbert: *Sandringham, Past and Present* (London, 1883)

Lloyd's Register

Mackie, Charles (compiler): *Norfolk Annals Vol 2 (1850-1900) extracts from the files of the 'Norfolk Chronicle'* (Norfolk Chronicle, Market Place, Norwich, 1901)

'One of His Majesty's Servants': *The Private Life of the King* (Pearson, 1901)

Page, Ken: *The Story of Biggleswade Brewery* (Ken Page, Biggleswade, 1993)

Page, Ken: *Thirsty Old Town, The Story of Biggleswade Pubs* (Ken Page, Biggleswade, 1995)

Perrott, Vera: *Victoria's Lynn: Boom and Prosperity* (Vista Bks, E Sussex, 1995)

Perrott, Vera: *Life and Leisure in Victoria's Lynn* (Vista Bks, E Sussex, 1995)

Ransford, Oliver: *The Great Trek* (John Murray, London, 1972)

Rhodes, Mary: *The Hunstanton Story: The First Fifty Years, 1861-1911* (Mary Rhodes, Acle, 1990s)

Richards, Paul: *King's Lynn* (Phillimore, Chichester, 1990)

Rodliffe, Rosemary and Stan: *Glimpses of Fiddaman's Lynn* (Rodliffe Associates, Bristol, 2000)

Rose, June: *Elizabeth Fry* (Macmillan, London, 1980)

Rye, Walter: *History of Norfolk* (Elliot Stock, London, 1885)

Smithers, A.J.: *The Kaffir Wars 1779-1877* (Leo Cooper, London, 1973)

St Aubyn, Giles: *Edward VII, Prince and King* (Collins, London, 1979)

Thew, J. Dyker: *Personal recollections of a Lynn Septuagenarian* (Thew, King's Lynn, 1891)

Thompson, Col C. W.: *Seventh (Princess Royal's) Dragoon Guards, The Story of the Regiment (1688-1882)* (1913)

Turner, Hicks A. (ed): *I Remember Callahan, History of Callahan County Texas* (Taylor Publishing, 1986)

Watson, Alfred E.T.: *King Edward VII as a Sportsman* (Longmans, Green and Co, London, 1911)

Wylly, Col H.C.: *A Short History of the* Cameronians *(Scottish Rifles) 1689-1924* (1924)
Zachry, Juanita D.: *A Living History, Taylor County and the Big Country* (Quality Press, Abilene, 1999)
Also

Hunstanton, Lynn and Norwich Library collections
Newspaper archives: *Lynn Advertiser, Wisbech Constitutional Gazette and Norfolk and Cambridgeshire Herald; Lynn News & County Press; Eastern Daily Press; Bedfordshire Times; London Times; The Globe; Illustrated London News*